THE WORLD
OF
SLED DOGS

Prologue

You conquered the toughest country
Ever created on earth.
Where you led, man followed your footsteps,
And the North was given birth.

Brown-eyed, happy and gritty
You slaved, and your only pay
Was dry-fish, blubber, or muktuk
Thrown on the snow at your sleigh.

Without you, the Great North Country
Would yet be unknown to man.
There are insurmountable barriers
That only a dog can span.

Who went to the Pole with Peary?
Who carried the serum to Nome?
Who rescued our shipwrecked sailors,
From the ice pack, brought them home?

Who traveled the creeks to Dawson,
Hauled the mail and packed out the ore?
Left crimson tracks along the Bering,
Heard Aleutian sea lions roar?

Who struggled, helping his master
On traplines barren and dreary?
Fought polar bears from the caches
Stood guard over those held dear?

Descendant of wolf ancestors—
Tempered by hardship and pain,
Fighting a raw, tough country—
These bred the Husky Dog strain.

From a tribute to the sled dog,
written by CHARLES E. GILLHAM;
the Alaskan Dog Mushers'
Association Annual, 1965

THE WORLD
of
SLED DOGS

From Siberia to Sport Racing

by LORNA COPPINGER
with
THE INTERNATIONAL SLED DOG RACING ASSOCIATION

First Edition . . . Fifth Printing 1987

HOWELL BOOK HOUSE
230 Park Avenue   New York, N.Y. 10169

ROBIN THALER AND FRIEND in "Puppy Love."   *Courtesy Jack Thaler*

Coppinger, Lorna.
The world of sled dogs: from Siberia to sport racing/by Lorna Coppinger, with the International Sled Dog. Racing Association.—1st ed.—New York: Howell Book House, 1977.

304 p.: ill.; 27 cm.

Bibliography: p. 297-300.
Includes index.
ISBN 0-87605-671-0

1. Sled dogs.   2. Sled dog racing.   1. Title.

SF428.7.C66   798'.8   76-7131   MARC

About the Sponsor

THE INTERNATIONAL SLED DOG RACING ASSOCIATION was founded in 1966 to promote sled dog racing and standardize its rules and race management procedures. Both ISDRA and the sport have grown dramatically since. ISDRA now has over 600 individual members and over 50 member clubs located throughout Alaska, Canada, the United States and Europe. ISDRA sets standards for quality sled dog races through its sanctioning program. These sanctioned races annually attract hundreds of dog teams in exciting contests of skill and endurance with only seconds separating the winners in many races. ISDRA also publishes a quarterly magazine full of articles on sled dog feeding, care and training, and maintains a library of sled dog information, colorful slide shows and films for educational and promotional purposes.

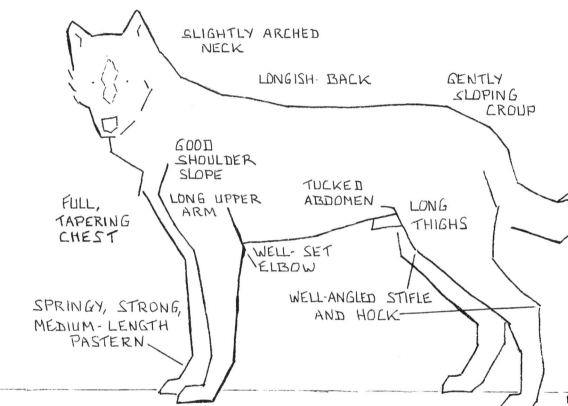

AN ALASKAN HUSKY'S ATTRIBUTES, lending him strength, speed and endurance. Drawn from a photograph of Brandy.   *L. Coppinger, Courtesy Norvik Kennels and Malcolm Wilder*

Contents

Prologue

Foreword *by Lowell Thomas, Jr.*   **9**

About the Author   **11**

Acknowledgments   **13**

Preface   **17**

1. The First Sled Dogs   **19**
The Cold Mists of Pre-history . . . Livelihood and Survival in the Arctic

2. The First Mushers   **31**
Europeans Discover the Native Art of Dog Driving . . . The Early Explorers Learn Sledging . . . Hunting and Trapping by Dog Train . . . The Mail Mushes Through . . . Dog-Punchers in the Gold Rush

3. The Twentieth-Century Sled Dog   **47**
Driving Dogs with the Mounties . . . Dog Teams in the Service of Science . . . The Great Race of Mercy to Nome . . . "Over There" with the Dog Teams . . . Old Jobs, New Jobs

4. Racing the Sled Dogs   **81**
The All-Alaska Sweepstakes and How They Grew . . . Sled-Dogging in the Lower Forty-eight . . . Racing Sled Dogs in the Great Lone Land

5. Gone with the Dogs   **109**
The Post-war Sled Dog Boom . . . Alaskans Rediscover Dog Sledding . . . A Sled Dog in Every State . . . From the Yukon to Labrador . . . Sleddogsport Comes to Europe . . . Back Across the Bering Strait . . . World Championships: The Pas, Laconia, Anchorage

6. Renowned Drivers and Their Dogs   **157**
The Dog Mushers' Hall of Fame . . . Leonhard Seppala and Togo . . . Scotty Allan and Baldy . . . Arthur Walden and

Chinook . . . Short Seeley and the Wonalancet Kennels . . .
Emile St. Godard and Toby . . . Roland Lombard and
Nellie . . . Charles Belford and Timmy . . . Jean Bryar
and Brandy . . . Dick Moulton and Attla . . . George Attla
and Tuffy . . . Dog-driving Dynasties in Alaska: Wright,
Redington, Norris

7. "They Are Only Dogs"   **205**
Siberian Husky . . . Alaskan Malamute . . . Samoyed . . .
Other Northern Breeds . . . Alaskan Husky and Village
Dog . . . Special Sled Dog Breeds . . . Other Racing Pure-
breds . . . Breeding Practices

8. Harnesses of Nylon, Sleds of Wood   **225**
The Dog Sled . . . Harnesses . . . Towlines and Hitches
. . . Hooks and Brakes . . . More Tools of the Trade . . .
Transportation for the Team . . . No-snow Rigs . . . Build
It or Buy It?

9. Think Sled Dogs   **243**
Selecting a Dog Team . . . In Training Together . . . Conditioning . . . What the Sled Dogs Eat . . . How to Make
the Winter Short

10. On the Runners   **261**
Before the Race . . . Race Day . . . Strategy for Winning
. . . The Lure of the Dog Team . . . The Family Sport . . .
Weight Pulls and Other Added Attractions

Postface
   I. *Rules Governing Races:* Nome Kennel Club Rules and Regula-
     tions, 1912   **288**
  II. *The Champion Dog Drivers:* All-Alaska Sweepstakes, 1908–17   **290**
     . . . North American Championships, 1964–75 . . . An-
     chorage World Championships, 1946–75 . . . Dual Cham-
     pions . . . Laconia World Championship, 1936–38, 1956–
     75 . . . Iditarod Trail, 1973–75 . . . ISDRA Point Cham-
     pionships, 1972–75
 III. *Sled Dog Clubs of the World*   **294**
    IV. *Sources of Equipment and Information*   **297**
   V. *Bibliography*   **298**

Index   **301**

Foreword

LORNA COPPINGER'S book about sled dogs will be of particular interest to Alaskans in these days of rapid change and industrial growth in our 49th state. How timely is its publication!

Dogs were an essential part of man's existence in early Alaska and, possibly, it would still be a territory without them. They hauled his wood from the forest, blocks of lake ice for drinking water; carried the sled-mounted hunter in pursuit of caribou and other game. But for sled dogs, missionaries would not have been able to make the rounds of their villages in winter as did Episcopal Bishop William Gordon for many years before taking to the air, mushing thousands of miles along the frigid Arctic Coast.

Sled dogs played an important part in my first visit to the far North, aiding a mountaineering expedition of which I was a member in moving supplies across the Brady Glacier and into the Fairweather Range of southeastern Alaska. That was in the summer of 1940. And dog teams have been used by many of the major Mt. McKinley expeditions.

In more recent times I've seen Alaskan Eskimos and Indians use their dogs as pack animals in the summer, carrying home birds and small game taken in the hunt.

Then came the advent of dog racing, which has yet to reach its zenith of participation and competitive excitement. All this is chronicled by Lorna Coppinger in this first comprehensive book on sled dogs.

LOWELL THOMAS, JR.
Lieutenant Governor, Juneau, Alaska

And just what makes you think these are show dogs?
Terry R. Vandertie

Sometimes I think Marland is a little too easy on his dogs!!
Terry R. Vandertie

About the Author

———————————————

LORNA COPPINGER comes uniquely equipped for authorship of *The World of Sled Dogs*. By her education, marriage, a successful career in research, professional writing and photography—and in her life style—she epitomizes the ideal commentator for the sled dog scene.

She attended *five* institutions of higher learning: the University of Vermont; Boston University, which awarded her the degree of A.B. *cum laude* in Slavic Studies; the University of Colorado; Middlebury College; and the University of Massachusetts, where she earned a Master of Science degree in Wildlife Biology.

Her writing and photographic credits, among others, include articles on ecology published in *Science*, "The Incredible Border Collie" in *Down East*, "Once a Girl Scout . . . ." in *Yankee*, and, with her husband, "Coyotes in New England" for *Massachusetts Wildlife*.

Mrs. Coppinger eminently qualified herself for the subject of this book by her articles "Sled Dog Racing Can Be Fun!" in *Mechanix Illustrated*, "Sled Dog Racing . . . an Amazing Sport" in the *Amherst Journal*, and "My Father Races Sled Dogs," by daughter Karyn Coppinger as told to her mother and accepted by the popular children's magazine *Jack and Jill*. In addition, Lorna has written features on what it is like to be a sled dog wife and mother, how to build a papoose board for your new baby, and how to build a dog sled.

The Coppingers are a sled dog family. Husband Ray won the New England Championship with his team in 1973, and their son and daughter are active in the sport.

Wielding her camera with the same proficiency applied to her typewriter, Lorna contributes many fine photographs to *Team and Trail—The Musher's Monthly News* and other publications. She is also an accomplished researcher, having served as chief writer and consultant on educational systems in the Caribbean islands and chief writer and photographer on ecology in St. Kitts, W.I., for the Behavioral Sciences Foundation in Boston.

She is a member of the National Society of Literature and the Arts and the Photographic Society of America.

When the Directors of the International Sled Dog Racing Association proposed Lorna Coppinger as author for this work, I was deeply impressed by her credentials, accomplishments and samples of her excellent writing skill. Now, having read the completed manuscript, I am overjoyed with the romance, excitement and fascination in her splendid presentation of the wonderful world of sled dogs and their followers.

It is with pleasure and the highest sense of honor that we publish this masterpiece. We commend it to sled doggers and to everyone else, everywhere, for the great reading and viewing adventure awaiting them in its pages.

ELSWORTH HOWELL
Publisher

Acknowledgments

THE EXCITING THING about writing this book on sled dogs is that the subject is only about a century old, and most of the people in the story are still alive or were known by people still alive. Modern mushers are proudly aware of the heritage passed to them by the sled-dogging heroes of early races, of the gold rush and arctic explorations. Dozens of these sled doggers contributed their favorite stories or photographs for this book, and it is to their credit that the scope and detail of the sled dog tale can now be portrayed.

Initial impetus came from Robert I. Levorsen, a quietly dynamic president of the International Sled Dog Racing Association. His continuing support, encouragement and talents as a writer and researcher (especially on the evolution of the dog sled!), and as a critic, form the backbone of the book. Bella Levorsen, his wife, also gave inspiration and information far beyond obligation. The Levorsens wrote extensively for chapters one, two and nine.

Mel Fishback, too, could be relied upon for a single fact or a string of paragraphs; much of the material on Samoyeds and equipment is hers. Beth Harris wrote about Malamutes. The drama of the serum race to Nome is due to the immediacy of Doris Lake's style. Ray Coppinger actually sat down long enough to write most of the section on breeding practices.

Without *Team and Trail* and the indefatigable spirit and willing aid of Cindy Molburg, a book like this would be unthinkable.

If Charlie Belford hadn't introduced my husband to the sport of sled dog racing, I could have spent the last three years on some other project. He is always available for advice and assistance, and I especially appreciate his additions to the manuscript.

Harris Dunlap, editor of ISDRA's quarterly, *Info,* has provided me with valuable communication to the members of ISDRA; he also conveyed his infectious devotion to the sport.

Ginger Dunlap drew the engaging illustrations in chapters one and two, filling a visual gap with her evocative, stylish images.

Besides the above, the following people from the world of sled dogs lent information, stories and photographs, or in some other way enhanced the book from their experiences:

W. Kent Allender, Thomas Althaus, Earl O. Anderson, Bill Arpino, Ethel Bacon, Diane Baruth, Mildred A. Beach, Penny Beard, Barbara Belford, Ivan Beliveau, Sue Binder, Guy Blankenship, Mick Booth, Rodger Booth, Leatha J. Braden, Jean Bryar, Jae Celusnick, George Chambers, Deane and Roma Cheadle, Sandy and Barbara Cheney, Art and Dorothy Christensen, Bruce Christman, Dick Cole, Ray Cote, Robert Crane, Gabbi Decker, Lorna Demidoff, Joe Dickinson, Jeffrey Dinsdale, Janice Dougherty, Richard and Judy Draeger, Howard Drown, Carol Dull, Barry Eton, Howard Farley, Jane Gaffin, Anne Gini, Elaine Gish, Ray Giteles, Peggy Grant, Frank Hall, Bob and Virginia Harrison, Mally Hilands, Dave Hobbs, Sue Holsclaw, A. Cecil Houghton, Leona Hutchings, Byron James, Annette Johnson, Oren Johnson, Burt Jones, Earl Kellett, Hans Keusen, Charles and Phyllis Kirkendall, Jr., Dak and Jeanette Klein, Reinhard L. Korgen, Duane Krause, Bob LeCour, Mrs. A.I. Levorsen, Judy Lewman, Gary and Joyce Lillie, Gary and Nancy Link, Dick Mackey (of Michigan), Pete MacManus, J. Malcolm McDougall, Scott McVay, Tom Makepeace, Esa Mäntysalo, John and Susann Martiniuk, Larry and Helen Masek, Tom and Gloria Mathias, Merle and Carolyn Mays, Jack and Judi Meakin, Roger Mendelsohn, Jim and Pat Mitchell, Dick Molburg, Dick Moulton, Lee Muller, Barbara Munford, Fred and Jackie Nall, Earl and Natalie Norris, Claire Ortalda, Betty L. Padgett, Buster R. Park, Alford S. Peckham, Lance Peithmann, Bernice B. Perry, Rick and Barbara Petura, Terry Quesnel, John Ramey, Joee Redington, Robert Reiber, Brian Riley, Jessica Roberts, Vern Roberts, Vic Rowell, Sandra Russick, John Ruud, Harvey Saltzer, Buster and Carol Samburgh, Gary Sanford, Sandy Saunderson, Stub and Stella

Saxton, Nancy Scarth, Anne Schaefer, D. Amelia Schamenek, Walt and Judy Schirber, Toni Schmidt, Bruce Schoenfeld, Abigail Shearer, William L. and Constance Shearer, Mary Shields, Paul and Miriam Slater, Lloyd Slocum, Joan Small, John Spreitzer, Roger Svoboda, Helmy V. Swanson, John D. Tanner, Jr., Jack Thaler, John Trotier, Bob and Nancy Trundle, Jim Uhl, Lisa Fallgren Uloth, Maxine Vehlow, Mary Lyman Walsh, Ralph Ward, Malcolm Wilder, Bill Wilson, Peter Winterble, Theresa Wog, Terry R. Vandertie and Faye Zipkowitz.

People within the following institutions also helped: Alaska Dog Mushers' Association, Alaskan Sled Dog and Racing Association, American Kennel Club, Canadian Department of Indian and Northern Affairs, Hampshire College Library, Hudson's Bay Company, Jones Library (Amherst, Massachusetts), Laconia (N.H.) *Evening Citizen,* Province of Manitoba, Minneapolis *Star Tribune,* National Archives, Nelson's Studio (Fairbanks), Northeastern University, Royal Canadian Mounted Police, Smirnoff and Associates (Anchorage), U.S. Army Office of Public Relations, U.S. Library of Congress, U.S. Olympic Committee, U.S. Post Office Department, University of Massachusetts Library and the Whitehorse *Star.*

A select and willing group of experts in the field read and criticized the manuscript with stunning ability: Charles Belford, Harris Dunlap, Mel Fishback, Bob and Bella Levorsen, Cindy Molburg, Earl and Natalie Norris, and Els van Leeuwen. Grammatical and stylistic refinements were contributed by my literary parents, Jean and Jerry Baxter, and my sagacious mother-in-law, Frances Littlehale.

A number of the staff and faculty at Hampshire College have contributed to this project, and the unflinching faith of the assemblage at Ragged Edge is wondrous indeed. Further advancement of this project, as well as of the dog teams, has come from all the people on Chestnut Hill. In particular, those who have helped to keep the dogs fed and running deserve more than acknowledgment: Bill Barnes, Emily Groves, Gary Hirshberg, and Dave and Denny Pinardi.

LORNA COPPINGER
Chestnut Hill
Montague, Massachusetts

15

Preface

No ONE HAS EVER UNDERTAKEN a comprehensive book on sled dogs before. In 1972, I suggested to the International Sled Dog Racing Association, of which I was president, that our organization should sponsor such a book. After all, ISDRA was dedicated to the promotion and improvement of the sport of sled dog racing and had enthusiastic members all over North America and Europe. These members could help write the book.

E.S. Howell, president of Howell Book House, had originated the idea of a "complete" work on sled dogs and racing in a letter to my wife, Bella, knowing of her work in the field. Bella, however, was too busy with other projects to take on this one. The time and effort which would be needed to research the historical aspects of sled dogging, and to compile the story of early and modern sled dog racing, were beyond our scope at that time.

In October of 1972, the ISDRA Board of Directors gave their formal agreement to the project; I was commissioned to locate an editor and handle contractual arrangements with Howell Book House. The following month, Lorna Coppinger, in Montague, Massachusetts, read about the proposed book in *Info,* ISDRA's quarterly publication, and wrote that she would be interested in editing it. She noted that she had "some time and a modicum of talent." Her husband, Ray, was a member of ISDRA

17

and he and their daughter, Karyn, ran sled dog teams, so I knew Lorna could tell the difference between a collar and a gangline, but could she write? A list of her writing accomplishments and some samples were so impressive that her offer was quickly accepted. Her competence as a photographer would also come in handy.

Now, three years later, with the help of ISDRA and its members, and of sled dog racers from all over, Lorna Coppinger has written the complete story of sled dogs and the growing sport of sled dog racing. It's a moving story, entertainingly and accurately written. It begins in Siberia, goes to both poles, and ends with today's thousands of mushers driving their friendly sled dogs across frozen lakes, down country trails and through silent forests.

You can watch these teams of man and dog this winter, wherever there is snow (and some places where there isn't!). Yet even if you don't get to see the sled dog teams in action, they will come to life for you in the pages of this book.

ROBERT I. LEVORSEN
Novato, California

1

The First Sled Dogs

Among the numerous animals which live in the Siberian North, the dog is without doubt the most useful. This Friend of Man, who like Man is capable of acclimatizing himself everywhere, who defends him and follows him on the hunt, who can nourish himself on bananas and other vegetation on South Sea islands, and who eats only fish in polar regions, fills here a use which elsewhere is foreign to his habits. Lacking horses, Man has made of the dog a draft animal. All the tribes of the Asiatic coasts, from the Ob to the Bering Strait, to Greenland and Kamchatka, harness dogs to their sleds, in order to make long journeys and to transport cumbersome burdens.

BARON VON WRANGELL, 1843

The Cold Mists of Pre-history

Who can say when man first hitched a dog to a sled? Lost in the long-ago mists is that cold image, and when or where it first happened can only be wondered. Man and dog have existed for thousands of years,

19

with similar requirements for food and shelter, and their pre-historic partnership was no doubt based on mutual assistance in searching for, capturing and consuming wild game. Perhaps they next shared companionship, and then shelter or at least the warmth of a fire. Even today, Aborigines in Australia measure cold by the number of dogs required to keep them warm, as the "one-dog night" of autumn soon becomes the "three-dog night" of winter. Man's intelligence, and dog's, too, must then have led to the training of the canines to hunt for man, and then to transport for him, possibly at first by dragging the capture home at the end of a line.

Recent research into the history of the sled dog suggests that the nomadic tribes north of Lake Baikal, in south central Siberia, were the first to hitch a dog to a sled, some four thousand years ago. In northern Asia, particularly in what is now called Siberia, some of the coldest and most brutal weather on earth results in almost frictionless snow and ice covering everything for most of the year. It would have been the most natural event for people living there to hitch up their dogs to help pull the game-laden sledges back to camp.

What these early men started, to give them an edge on surviving in Siberia, was to become a crucial tool for men in the North, and to figure importantly in a myriad of endeavors. Without sled dogs, many things would be different.

Over the centuries the art of driving sled dogs reached a high state with the Siberian peoples known as the Chukchi and the Samoyed. These tribes used their dogs as companions, guards, pets, hunters, reindeer herders and sled dogs. According to authorities, it was the Chukchi people who were the first to depend seriously on the ability of their dogs to pull loaded sleds. Dr. Robert Crane of Virginia, a Russian scholar and a Siberian Husky fancier, wrote that "climatic changes and displacement of the Chukchi people by a more powerful southern people combined to force the Chukchi to base their economy on sled dog transportation in order to survive."

Suffering from chronic scarcity of food, the Chukchis had to invent a means of travel not only sufficient to maintain access to the unreliable sources of food, but also one that was superior to that of other competing arctic peoples. They needed speedy and dependable transportation to journey long distances over the vast, irregular tundra and ice shelf. They developed the sled dog.

By 1800 B.C. there were Eskimos on the Alaskan shores of the Arctic Ocean. There is evidence that they used sled dogs to pull toboggans, harnessing three or four dogs in tandem, one behind the other. When the renowned Norwegian explorer, Fridtjof Nansen, observed North Ameri-

A THREE-DOG NIGHT. *Ginger Dunlap*

SIBERIAN HUNTERS HITCHED UP THEIR DOGS
to help pull game-laden sledges home. *Ginger Dunlap*

can Eskimos some 37 centuries later, what he saw must have been not too different from all that had gone before. In his two-volume history of arctic exploration, *In Northern Mists,* Nansen quotes from the fourteenth century Arabian chronicles of Ibn Batûta, a businessman trading near what is now Kazan in Russia. The Arabian dwelled with appreciation on the sight of sled dogs, noting that "the journey is only made in small cars drawn by dogs. For this desert has a frozen surface, upon which neither men nor horses can get foothold, but dogs can, as they have claws." The use of sled dogs was spreading across the globe.

History's first actual records on the use of sled dogs in the Siberian sub-arctic appear in Arabian literature of the tenth century; in writings of Marco Polo in the thirteenth century; and of Francesco da Kollo in the sixteenth. The records being written today about sled dogs contain more references to activities for fun than for survival, but the images of man and sled dog working together are similar, all the way from Siberia to sport racing.

Livelihood and Survival in the Arctic

The original sled dog was basically a hunter, descended perhaps from domestic dogs from southern latitudes, dogs which had accompanied their hunting masters north many, many generations earlier. The dogs that survived in the rigorous climate of Siberia were large, furry and wolf-like, the ancestors of today's "northern" breeds. Not only were their coats thick, but they developed undercoats for further protection against biting winds and bitter cold. Their ears were short, to minimize heat loss through such exposed appendages, and could be pricked upright, to maximize their efficiency. The ears were filled with soft, insulating hair. The pads on their feet were tough, to withstand the miles of tracking and hunting on frozen, jagged terrain.

As hunters, the northern dogs were instinctively efficient. The Tungus people of Siberia trained their dogs to bark when they sighted an elk. Other dogs would scent musk ox or polar bear, trail the animal, and attack—often while still attached to the sled. The coastal natives of pre-historic Siberia probably also used dogs, as they still do, to find seals out under the ocean ice. The technique for this was described for Eskimos on King William Land in the Canadian Arctic in 1938 by Gontran de Poncins in *Kabloona*. Each Eskimo walked with two trained dogs on long leashes out onto the snow-covered ice. The dogs sniffed along, questing for the breathing hole that the seal had made in the ice far below the surface of the snow. When the dogs began circling excitedly in one spot, they would be taken back and tied at a good distance away, down wind. The hunter, prodding with his harpoon, confirmed the existence of the hole and then man and dogs sat back to wait for the seal to return.

In the summer, early migratory peoples used their dogs as pack animals. Supplies would be put into two pouches, tied together, one on each side of the dog. Some pouches were enormous, almost dragging on the ground. At a walk, a dog could carry a pack equal to his own weight all day long.

It was in the long winters, though, that the sled dog contributed most to native survival. The increased mobility provided by dogs pulling sleds enabled the tribes to extend their hunting ranges. Some of the ancient Siberians were competent reindeer breeders and teams of reindeer were also used to pull sleds. It was the dog, however, more adaptable to adverse conditions and locations, that emerged as the favored sled puller.

Man and dog got on so well together, each providing the other with certain necessities, that they probably migrated together across the frozen Bering Strait to North America. In what is now Alaska, innumerable generations of descendants of the early Siberian peoples have depended on their dogs for transportation. Across the top of North America, in Greenland, Newfoundland and Labrador, travel for the greater part of the year is also on snow and ice. Sled dogs were, and still often are, the preferred method of travel.

The status of northern dogs among arctic peoples in eastern North America was described by J. Dewey Soper, an official in the Canadian Department of the Interior. His description, published in 1934, very likely reflects the life and times of the arctic dog from pre-historic right on up to modern decades.

Known throughout the arctic regions of the Western Hemisphere as the "husky," the original sled dog took its modern name from a slang word for "Eskimo," which in its turn is an Algonquin Indian word meaning "eater of raw flesh."

Soper described the typical, pure-blooded Eskimo dog as being of a whitish-grey color, but noted too that dogs in current use had markings and colors ranging from pure greyish-white to black, including some yellow dogs, grey or brown ones, and others bizarrely mottled.

"A sturdy animal," Soper wrote about the Eskimo dog, "of wolf-like appearance and characteristics, weighing from about 50 to 80 pounds . . . well-conditioned dogs may reach 90 to 100 pounds, or even more.

"The average height at the shoulder is between 20 and 25 inches. On the whole the Eskimo dog has a powerful physique, with heavy neck and chest,

KAZBEK, a modern descendant of the original sled dogs in the Kolyma region of Siberia. *A. Masover*

and short, strong legs. During the winter the body is thickly covered with straight hair three or four inches long, with a dense underfur which permits the animals to withstand the rigours of the long Arctic winter. There is a mane-like growth of somewhat longer hair over the neck and shoulders. The muzzle is pointed, rather short and broad; the thick ears are small and pointed, and the eyes are wide-spread. The tail is thick and bushy.

"During the season of winter travel the Eskimo dog lives principally on seal and walrus meat obtained by the native hunters. They will, however, eat meat of any kind, fresh or decomposed. The usual daily ration in winter travel consists of about 2 or 3 pounds of frozen seal or walrus meat per dog. Feeding time comes only in the evening. Under stress of circumstance, for relatively short journeys, half the above amount will suffice, or the animals may be fed a normal ration every other night. For continuous travelling, nightly feeding is usually the best. On the above diet Eskimo dogs maintain health and stamina in the coldest weather for trips of unremitting labor up to 1,000 miles or more. Periodical rest periods if not absolutely necessary are at least humane, and in the long run advisable.

"During the winter the Eskimos are very solicitous for the welfare of their dogs and feed them with as punctilious regularity as conditions will permit. Summer is radically different; unaccustomed heat, flies, mosquitoes, and the necessity of shifting for themselves make it in some respects the most trying time for Eskimo dogs. At this time no effort is made to feed them, though they secure small irregular quantities of offal and refuse about the settlements. The animals, therefore, singly or in bands, forage widely over the country in search of food on their own account. No doubt lemmings form a part of their diet at this time. But they more consistently follow the seacoast in search of shrimps, cast up animals, sculpins, and mussels, many of which are secured on the stony mud flats at low tide.

"In hard times they will gluttonously consume almost anything that is available. As a result they are good hygienic agents in cleaning up about the Eskimo dwelling places. When they are very hungry, as the expression goes, 'they will eat anything' . . . skin lines, harness, skin clothing, and kayaks must be carefully kept beyond reach at all times. Hungry dogs are notoriously greedy thieves; caches of meat must be well guarded with piles of stones that their most strenuous labors will fail to move.

"The endurance of Eskimo dogs is astounding and elicits the most unqualified admiration. In hardiness they surpass all other domestic animals, including the reindeer. They can endure the lowest temperatures and sleep out in the severest blizzards without shelter of any kind. In the lowest temperatures of mid-winter they contentedly curl up in the snow for the night in the most exposed positions with apparent indifference and enjoyment. Usually during the progress of blizzards, with high winds and fine, drifting snow, however, they endeavor to find shelter in the lee of igloos, discarded snow blocks, or other objects. They can withstand starvation while undergoing strenuous exertions to a marked extent, and cases have been recorded of dog teams that have worked hard under severe conditions with little or no feed for several weeks. It is a common experience, while travelling, for dogs to go for several days destitute of food with no visible diminution of strength or spirits. This, of course, is never required of them except under stress of unavoidable circumstances.

"In general disposition Eskimo dogs are reasonably affectionate. They reciprocate friendly attention, of which they appear to be somewhat jealous, in the usual canine fashion and do not often make any effort to bite a stranger, although with some dogs a lone stranger does run a risk, particularly if the dogs are hungry or if the stranger comes upon them suddenly. Cases have been reported of Eskimo dogs killing children, and in fact adults, but such occurrences are infrequent. Eskimo children may be seen daily playing amongst the swarms of dogs without any show of fear, but the parents do keep a rather close watch on the younger children. While they are puppies, dogs are made pets of, which probably accounts to some extent at least for the comparative safety with which the children move about. Under ordinary circumstances if dogs become attentive to a troublesome degree it is sufficient to pick up a few stones and hurl one or two with sound intentions.

"Amongst themselves the dogs are very quarrelsome and fighting ensues at the slightest provocation. Usually one dog in each group fights his way to the top and bosses and bullies the rest. If he is a good dog he can enforce discipline in such a way that he will be especially valuable to his owner. On the other hand, his love of fighting may make him a nuisance. No matter how good a fighter a dog may be, he stands a good chance of not surviving the period of introduction as a new member of a team because he will probably have to take on all the rest of the team at one time. If the owner wishes the new dog to become the 'boss' of the team he usually supervises the introduction. The 20- to 35-foot dog whip is not only useful in directing the team, but its liberal use helps in preventing them seriously injuring one another in their free-for-all fights . . .

"Dogs sometimes suffer a great deal from injuries to their feet in cold and hard travel, as particles of ice and snow collect under the nails and between the toes, resulting in cracks and sores. Under certain conditions of thaw, snow continually packs in little tubercles on the pads of the feet, which causes great temporary inconvenience and finally lameness; at such times the animals assiduously devote themselves on every halt to biting away the offending particles. They suffer most from feet trouble during spring travel. The snow is then soft in the day, but crusts with the colder temperatures of night; feet are softened with continual wetting and then scoured tender on the abrasive snow of morning and evening. During late spring, with continual daylight and marked fluctuations of temperature in the twenty-four hours, travel is largely conducted at night. This season is the hardest on the feet of the dogs; the 'candled' and sharply serrated surface of the sea ice, induced by the increasing warmth of the sun, causes cuts and bleeding of the tender soles. It is then necessary to provide some kind of footgear from skins, or pieces of canvas.

PATIENT HUSKIES AND PATIENT ESKIMO
can result in seal meat for all. *Ginger Dunlap*

VERSATILE SLED DOGS could track a quarry, help in
the attack, and then haul the meat by sledge. *Ginger Dunlap*

ALL IN A DAY'S WORK FOR PACK DOGS. *Ginger Dunlap*

SLED DOGS provided companionship and
warmth for Eskimo children. *Ginger Dunlap*

INDIGENOUS SIBERIAN HUSKIES, on the Kamchatka Peninsula in Siberia.
Northwest of the World

"The female dog usually gives birth to from six to eight young, and litters may appear at any season of the year. If the mother is left to her own resources at such a time, she generally retires to a wild, secluded place. She is then usually crabbed and suspicious, and resents the presence of male animals; some of whom are not averse to disposing of the defenseless puppies in the absence of the mother. When the event takes place in the winter the Eskimos are quite solicitous about the mother and her pups, building a little snow kennel and covering the floor with old sacks, moss or heather, to keep the youngsters dry and warm. Their growth is rapid, and before a year old they have taken their place in the dog team—to serve faithfully as draught animals, often taking quite a share of punishment, until accident, disease or old age marks the end of the long trail. Six or seven years is a good age for an Eskimo dog."

A tough life? Perhaps. Yet life in the Arctic is not known for its gentleness. With the great importance of the sled dog established for the arctic native, he would be endangering his life to abuse his dogs on the trail or in the village.

The sled dog, thus nourished, developed into a team dog and gained a sense of responsibility for the other dogs and the driver. The whole outfit shared everything, in times of plenty and in times of severe want. Yet the successful driver never asked more of his team than he asked of himself, and in return the sled dogs provided a loyalty and companionship that went far beyond the needs of the native for transportation or livelihood. That first pre-historic combination of a dog and a sled, to help that early hunter and his dog to survive, marked the beginning of a tradition which was also to have far-reaching importance as men from the Outside moved into the Arctic.

2

The First "Mushers"

In the performance of my own official duties I have travelled more than 1,000 miles during a winter along the frozen Yukon with my team of native dogs, my blankets, food, and the court's files and documents. He who gives time to the study of history of Alaska, learns that the dog, next to man, has been the most important factor in its past and present development.

JUDGE JAMES WICKERSHAM, 1938

Europeans Discover the Native Art of Dog-driving

"Ma-a-r-r-che!" shouted the French Canadian dog drivers to their teams during the opening up of the great northern wilderness. Translation: "march!" or "get going!" To the English adventurers also exploring and settling Canada, the word sounded like "mush!" A dog driver, then, became known as a "musher."

The first mushers were the explorers, hunters and trappers who moved into arctic latitudes and found that the best way to travel overland in winter was by the same method as the natives: by dog sled. From the

31

British Isles, the Scandinavian countries and central and eastern Europe, men came to the coldest parts of North America in search of adventure and wealth. The most successful explorers used dog teams; those who did not adopt native ways of life experienced great difficulties in the harsh environment. Many of them perished. Hunters and trappers established small settlements at far-flung places and communicated with the Outside by water routes in the summer, by dog team in the winter. A new breed of dog driver evolved, the "dog-puncher," who made his living by freighting goods, passengers and mail with his strong dog team. When gold was discovered in the Yukon and in Alaska, a good sled dog could sell for as much as one thousand dollars, and any big, nearby dog was fair game to be harnessed into the team.

The Early Explorers Learn Sledging

The first modern contact of white men with native dog teams no doubt occurred during the sixteenth century when explorers and traders from European Russia pushed east into Siberia and traded with Samoyed tribes. During the seventeenth and eighteenth centuries, Russian explorers came into less friendly contact with the Chukchi tribes in northeast Siberia, as the explorers tried to determine whether or not their continent was attached to North America. During the seventeenth and eighteenth centuries, also, the first explorers from Europe and Russia sailed into the far North, charting and observing, mostly from their ships. The British, especially, relied on their long and successful experience on the sea to guide them safely in the Arctic. Once on land, however, the seafarers had a lot to learn from the natives.

The Russian naval explorer, Ferdinand von Wrangell, began in 1820 a series of trips by dog team which finally proved to him that Asia and North America were separate. What was to become Alaska nearly lost its first governor, however, as Wrangell took a last sledging trip before returning to base. Seventy miles from shore, the solid ice Wrangell's group had been traveling on was ruptured by a gale, and ever-widening lanes of icy water separated them from land. There followed a frantic dash for shore, across the leads of water, and that he made it at all Wrangell attributed to the speed of his dogs and their ability to swim across the leads.

Well into the nineteenth century, however, ignorance of native survival techniques contributed to unbearable hardships suffered by many northern voyagers. The most famous of all is the disaster that befell the Franklin Expedition of 1845. Sir John Franklin, who in 1825 had sailed and mapped hundreds of miles of coastline in arctic America, was appointed by the British Admiralty to sail again, this time to search for the elusive Northwest Passage across the top of North America. Franklin's two ships, the *Erebus* and the *Terror,* were caught fast in the ice in the middle of September, 1845, 12 miles north of the desolate King William Land. After their third winter stuck in the ice, 105 of the original 129 men (the rest, including their commander, had perished) began their long, forlorn march to oblivion. Lady Jane Franklin sponsored voyage after voyage to the Arctic, at first to rescue her husband, then, despairingly, to learn of his fate.

Lady Franklin's continued pressure on the North to learn at least this secret resulted in many small triumphs, when American and British expeditions—some 41 of them during the 34 years following Franklin's disappearance—participated in a crash program on arctic travel and reconnaissance. The man who finally brought precise information about the death of Franklin and his crew was Leopold McClintock, in 1859. A careful observer of the Eskimo, McClintock is remembered as the master of arctic sledging, for he worked out detailed techniques which are still used by arctic explorers and scientists. These techniques included the meticulous weighing of every single piece of equipment and calculating as closely as possible the amounts of supplies that would be needed. In the autumn prior to a spring sledging trip McClintock would cache food and equipment along the planned route so that in the spring long distances could be covered with much lighter loads.

The list of arctic and antarctic explorers who depended on dog teams extends from eighteenth-century men like the Russian, Ivan Lyahov, to twentieth-century men like Wally Herbert, who trekked across the North Pole by dog team in 1968–69. In between are men whose names are synonymous with great explorations: Roald Amundsen, Richard E. Byrd, Peter Freuchen, Adolphus W. Greely, Charles Francis Hall, Isaac Israel Hayes, Elisha Kent Kane, Donald B. MacMillan, Fridtjof Nansen, George Nares, Robert E. Peary, Knud Rasmussen, Ernest Shackleton, Vilhjalmur Stefansson and Otto Sverdrup. All of these men wrote books about their experiences, and they all include glorious, gripping tales about life in the cold regions of the world, and the part the sled dogs played.

The major portion of an explorer's work is routine, however, an unglamorous collecting of data and charting of land and water. Only infrequently does a dramatic, long-sought-for goal catch the attention and imagination of the public as well as the explorers. Two such goals were, of course, the North and the South Poles.

The North Pole was assaulted for several centuries by ship and by men dragging sledges. Although John Franklin had used dogs and sledges in his early Canadian Arctic explorations of 1819–22, it was not until Kane, Hayes and Hall, in the 1850's, that dog teams were relied on to pull sleds on polar expeditions. Nares and Greely had dog teams in the late 1870's and early 1880's for their attempts to reach the Pole. In 1895 Nansen got the closest yet, with Eskimo dogs. A Lieutenant Cagni of the Italian Navy bettered Nansen's record by 22 miles in 1901, and then Robert E. Peary, in 1905, broke Cagni's record. It was not until a decade into the twentieth century that the North Pole was reached . . . by dog sled.

The existence of the continent of Antarctica, which surrounds the South Pole, was not even known until 1840. Norwegian whalers were the first to go ashore on the main land mass, in 1895, but concerted exploration and the race for the South Pole did not begin until 1902. It ended ten years later in two breath-taking tales, one of tragedy, one of triumph. In each story, sled dogs, or the lack of them, were a significant factor.

Hunting and Trapping by Dog Train

One of the major reasons for exploring the frozen latitudes of the earth, other than purely scientific, was to locate, gather and bring back to civilization the wealth of minerals, whale oil, furs, ivory and other valuable commodities. Rapidly on the heels of the early explorers came the hunters and trappers. Explorers in Canada had noted abundant wild game and the promise of riches in fur trading. In eastern Canada, around the French settlements of Quebec and Montreal, French-speaking traders and trappers became highly proficient in the use of sled dogs in winter as well as canoes in summer. Their services as "voyageurs" were indispensable for the opening up of the Great Lone Land, the Canadian sub-arctic wilderness.

Although the dogs worked long and loyally, making it possible for men to carry out their chosen tasks even in the heavy snows of winter, some of the sledging expeditions were more dastard than dutiful. Peaceful colonists in the young settlement of Deerfield, Massachusetts, relaxed a bit as the winter of 1703–04 provided over 200 miles of deep snow between them and the marauding Indians of the Canadian frontier. The snow, however, proved their undoing, as Indians and French soldiers traveled down the Connecticut River Valley by snowshoe and dog team. The resulting carnage is known as the "Deerfield Massacre."

Most of the westward expansion was through Indian territory, around the north side of the Great Lakes, across the Great Plains and to the north, down the Athabasca and the Mackenzie Rivers. Traders from the Hudson's Bay Company adopted native systems of travel in the 1840's, and

LONG BIRCH BARK TOBOGGANS AND BRIGHT-COLORED CARIOLES made up the dog trains of the North. At Norway House, Lower Ft. Garry, near Winnipeg, Manitoba, 1904. *R.C.M.P.*

ON AN ICE FLOE IN DISCOVERY HARBOR, Lt. Greely and Jens, during Lady Franklin Bay Expedition, 1881. *U.S. Signal Corps*

"NO COMBINATION MORE SPRIGHTLY" than the jingling bells and picturesque costumes of the Hudson's Bay Company dog teams.

Painting by C.F. Comfort for Hudson's Bay Company

built long birch-bark toboggans for the soft, deep snows of the forests. The birch-bark strips of the bed were held together by cross-bars, with a big upward curl in the front, about two feet high. When a hunter's load was more than four or five hundred pounds, additional sledges and dog teams were used, all traveling and camping together, one driver per team.

The teams, most commonly of four dogs, were called "dog trains" in those days, and more than one train was a "dog brigade." The lead dog was referred to as the "foregoer" and the dog hitched just in front of the sled was the "steer-dog." The steer-dog had to be the strongest on the team, as to him fell the job of holding the sled on a slanting trail or turning it with its heavy load between trees and around rocks. The driver walked on snowshoes most of the way, breaking trail for the rest.

Harnesses were made of moose skin, with a round collar slipped over the head of the dog and one line on the side buckled to it. These side lines, or traces, were also attached to wide leather bands called "tapis" which completely encircled the dog. This band was usually covered with little brass bells, with a few larger bells on the collar. Often the band was embroidered, and ribbons were sewn onto the collar.

With the driver bedecked in beaded moccasins, leggings and mittens, a colored sash about his waist, a caribou skin jacket and a brightly-colored knitted cap, a dog train of the 1880's was something to meet on the trail. It was a colorful spectacle, heralded in advance by the singing bells. As Caspar Whitney wrote in 1896: "Indeed, there is no combination more sprightly than a dog brigade, with its brilliant and many hued tapis, its nodding pompoms and streaming ribbons, and its picturesquely cos-tumed drivers. There is no sensation more exhilarating than running with the dogs on snowshoes and a good track, to the jingling of the bells; when storm obscures the pompoms, and the wind drowns the jingle, and there is nothing on the sledge to eat, the sensation is not so enlivening."

The Mail Mushes Through

The most popular drivers were the ones carrying mail packets for the Hudson's Bay Company. The "Northern Packet" left Fort Garry (now Winnipeg) around December 10th, for the 350-mile, eight-day trip to Norway House at the north end of Lake Winnipeg. Simultaneously, a mail packet came by dog train from York Factory on Hudson's Bay. After unloading and repacking, the Fort Garry and York dog trains returned to their original posts with mail and a new dog train headed west for Fort Carlton on the Saskatchewan River. This 650-mile trip took 22 days, more or less, depending on the weather.

READY FOR THE TRAIL IN 1903 ALASKA. The dogs, typical for those days, show their mixed breeding. The basket sled, sporting a "gee" pole at each end, carried (among other items) a big stove. *Nelson's Studio*

HAULING THE MAIL IN ALASKA, with businesslike dogs and a long basket sled. *U.S. Post Office Department*

The primary ambition of the mail drivers was always to get the mail in on time, weather notwithstanding. They invariably succeeded, and with such regularity that every 21 days during the winter, between two and three o'clock in the afternoon, the men who garrisoned the old Swan River barracks would be alert for a far-off sound or motion from the direction of the Snake Creek Valley. Bets would be passed at the noon meal as to what exact time Louis Laronde or Antoine Genoit would arrive with the mail. Sometimes the driver would be so early that his voice could be heard in the distance even before the bets were closed.

In Alaska, too, mail was one of the most important and certainly the most eagerly awaited shipment to come over the dog trails. From Seward to Knik to Iditarod, from Iditarod to Ruby to Nome, from Nome to Dillingham, from Nome to Ruby to Nenana, from Nome to Cape South Wales, the U.S. mail traveled by dog team. "All sled dog trails," it was said, "lead to Nome."

On those trails the mail driver was king. U.S. law required all others to give the right of way to the mail team, and so "the mail-driver was the single most important person on the trail, in the mail-station, or at the over-night roadhouse. He was given the best seat at the table, the first service of hotcakes for breakfast, and the best bunk at night. When the mail-driver pulled into a station or the roadhouse at the end of the day's run, he unhitched the team and turned all the dogs loose except the leader. His leader, his parka, gloves and whip were brought into the roadhouse. He put the leader under his bunk, hung his wet clothing on the best wires around the stovepipe . . . and woe to him who complained about the leader under his bed!"

The roadhouses were generally one day's travel apart, about 25–30 miles, although at times there were only unattended mail cabins for shelter and provisions. The mail teams varied in size, with eight to ten dogs being common, three to four not unheard of, and occasionally, after a bad snowstorm, bigger teams would be hooked up to try to keep the mail on schedule. The contract between the Postmaster General and the mail driver provided a yearly salary at the turn of the century of $2225 a year. It also stipulated that the mail be conveyed "with celerity, certainty and security."

In 1963 the U.S. Post Office Department honored the last mail driver, and a century of sled dog tradition passed into history. Chester Noongwook of Savoonga, on St. Lawrence Island in the Bering Sea, retired his dog team, because the postal service had found it more efficient to replace Spotty, Brownie, Mil-ko-lak and Donkey with an airplane. Even so, Noongwook was kept on a stand-by basis, for ultimately, in certain circumstances, the dog team can go when the plane cannot.

Dog-punchers in the Gold Rush

For mushers after bigger stakes, there was gold. Men either went after it themselves or they hauled supplies to the miners, their camps, the growing settlements. Gold was discovered in Sitka in 1880, the Klondike in 1896, Nome in 1898, Fairbanks in 1902 and Iditarod in 1906. The Gold Rush to the Klondike was as big as the one to California a half-century earlier. Instead of mules and oxen, however, overland travel to Alaska and the Yukon was by river boat in summer and dog team in winter. The quickest way to Dawson was through the ports of Skagway or Dyea, over the tortuous Chilkoot Pass, along the often treacherous Lakes Bennett, Marsh and Laberge, and down the Yukon River. From Dawson to the next gold rush town, Nome, the stampeders had to travel all the way west across central Alaska, down the Yukon, across to Unalakleet and around the Norton Sound coastline. Many a man, woman and child made it by dog team.

This was big, bold country, roadless and railroadless. The rivers were connected by trails, but from October to May the best traveling of all was done by dog team. Horses were brought to Alaska, but they were hard to feed and they bogged down in deep snow. It was the dog driver, packing his trail ahead of the team, feeding himself and his dogs from the abundant wild game, who mastered this great frozen land.

Hauling freight became a large, serious business, and good dogs to pull the freight were scarce. Prospectors and miners needed help in getting equipment to their claims, in packing the gold out if they were lucky and themselves out if they were not. The drivers were called "freighters" or "dog-punchers." They carried everything from mining equipment, building materials, tents, stoves and food to gold dust and sacks of nuggets. Hauling with as many as three "Yukon" sleds, the driver would hitch one sled right behind the other, with chains. The Yukon sled measured seven feet long and 16 inches wide, was braced and shod with iron and weighed as much as 80 pounds. For a good trail, a driver would load his three sleds with 600 pounds on the front sled, 400 on the middle one and 200 on the rear. The team: six or seven large dogs, strong and hardy.

On the right or "gee" side of the leading sled was the "gee pole," a six-foot sapling lashed to the sled at a 45-degree angle to the ground, extending forward from the runner to about a man's shoulder. The driver walked in front of the sled, the tow line between his feet and the gee pole in his right hand. He used the pole's leverage to steer the heavy sled, keep it upright on slanted trails and over bumps, swing wide around corners, break the sled loose when it was frozen in, and hold it back when going down small hills.

A NEWFOUNDLAND, SOME HUSKIES AND A BIG SPANIEL-TYPE DOG pulled this Yukon style basket sled. Note leather harness collars and tuglines.   *Nelson's Studio*

MOVING DAY AT FT. RESOLUTION, Great Slave Lake, N.W.T., in 1921.   *R.C.M.P.*

The dogs on these pioneering teams were of every kind and description. Many were bought or stolen outside of Alaska and brought north to sell at inflated prices. The canine hero of Jack London's *Call of the Wild* was drawn after these conscripts. The offspring of a St. Bernard and a Scotch shepherd dog, Buck's Klondike adventures began in California when his master's unscrupulous gardener sold him to an equally unprincipled "fence" for dogs going north. It was said that no dog larger than a spaniel was safe on the streets of Seattle, or San Francisco, or Los Angeles, during the northern Gold Rush.

Native dogs, however, withstood the climate much better and were in greater demand. From the Malamute Eskimo tribe near the mouth of the Yukon River came the dogs of that name. From the Siwash tribe of the Interior came Indian dogs, and from the far North came more Eskimo dogs, all bred for centuries to be trail or pack dogs, and all able to survive the rigorous winters while working hard for little food. Some of the best freighting dogs were the Mackenzie River Huskies (often called Porcupine River dogs), weighing up to 165 pounds and loving to pull. These dogs were a cross between native sled dogs and the large, imported domestic breeds.

Drivers also bred their sled dogs with wolves to obtain heavier, tougher animals. One of the most famous of these was a dog named "Hootchinoo," his mother half wolf, his father a wild wolf. He belonged to a dog-puncher named Arthur Walden, an adventurer who once supplied gold-hungry prospectors with his dog dishes, at $15 each, to use for panning gold. Walden later returned to his native New England to found the sled dog races which are still held there. In *A Dog-puncher on the Yukon,* Walden described his crossbred leader: ". . . light gray and white, and weighed almost a hundred and twenty pounds. His eyes were set obliquely in his head and there was very little drop to the forehead. His muzzle was fine, and even his teeth did not resemble those of a dog. He carried his tail low, wolf-fashion. He was absolutely tireless, and a remarkable trail-finder. After I got him broken in, he was the quickest dog to obey I have ever known . . . I could not catch him if he were loose unless I dragged out the harness. If I did that he would come and take his place at the lead . . . I never saw him show emotion of any kind, either in response to kindness or because of discipline. I never saw him wag his tail, but occasionally he would lead the whole band in howling to the wolves."

Walden mentioned the transportation system prevalent at that time. "First class passengers," he wrote, "we carry them and their baggage. Second class passengers, we carry their baggage. Third class passengers, they walk and carry their own baggage."

KLONDIKE MIKE MAHONEY carried a casket with the body of a judge from Fairbanks to Valdez, nearly 400 miles across the Alaska Range, by dog team.
Klondike Mike

SUNDAY AFTERNOON OUTING, early Alaska. *Nelson's Studio*

43

ALASKA

0   100
miles

Barrow
Wainwright
USSR
USA
Chukchi Pen.
Kotzebue
ARCTIC CIRCLE
Old Crow
Candle
Ft. Yukon
Huslia
Gambell
Savoonga
Council
Nome
Solomon
Golovin
Koyukuk
Tanana
Kokrines
Livengood
Nulato
Galena
Ruby
Hot Springs
Fairbanks
Shaktoolik
Kaltag
Long
Nenana
Unalakleet
BERING SEA
Dawson
Klondike
YUKON R.
McGrath
Tok
Iditarod
Willow
Knik
Bethel
Anchorage
Kenai
Soldotna
CANADA
Skagway
Juneau

SPRING PLOWING, ALASKA. Drawn from an old photograph.   *Ginger Dunlap*

These first mushers, the early professionals, set high standards for pioneering, exploring, loyalty and service to society, in partnership with their dog teams. No task was impossible, either for dog or man. Some of the tasks were simple but clever, such as the one set by Frank Lott for his lead dog: to make short trips with a hundred pounds of freight up the trail and back, all by himself.

Other jobs paved the way for a mechanized future, for example, the one described in an oft-repeated story about the trip made by "Klondike Mike" Mahoney when he pioneered a trail across the uncharted Alaska Range. His way led between Mt. McKinley (elevation 20,320 feet) and Mt. Sanford (16,208 feet). As if that were not enough, his sled carried a casket holding the frozen body of a Fairbanks judge who was formerly a mayor of Seattle. Mahoney drove his team south from Fairbanks up the Tanana River to the Big Delta, then up that wild river over the Alaska Range, down to the Gulkana and Copper Rivers and finally to the port of Valdez. He started with nine dogs: seven Mackenzie River Huskies, one Alaskan Husky and one mongrel. Wolves followed the team much of the lonely way and, according to the story, they managed to entice two of the dogs out of the protection of Mahoney's all-night fires. This part of the trip, according to Mahoney, was so exaggerated and played up by the press that he was forced to state, "Anyone that knows the first damn thing about the bush knows wolves won't attack a man so long as he has a fire. Staying awake to keep that fire going was the hardest part. I don't suppose the wolves ever came within forty feet of me."

The 400-mile trail he blazed was later used by hundreds of gold seekers traveling from Valdez to Fairbanks, a much shorter route than through Dawson. After the establishment of a packed trail and roadhouses, Mahoney made a return trip in 12 easy days, shaking his head wonderingly at the 28 back-breaking days and sleepless nights he had spent on his funeral trip. Mahoney's trail is still there. It is known as the Richardson Highway, renamed for the army officer who headed the Alaska Road Commission at the turn of the century.

The first mushers and their dogs, having proved their worth over and over in the opening up and settling of the arctic regions, were then ready for the next stage in their evolution: assimilation into the developing modern society.

LONG LEATHER TRACES were standard R.C.M.P. equipment. At
Herschel Island in the Beaufort Sea, where the R.C.M.P. had a dog
breeding station, about 1962.   *R.C.M.P.*

AN R.C.M.P. CONSTABLE VISITING A TRAPPER near Ft. Smith,
N.W.T., 1959.
                                                          R.C.M.P.

3

The Twentieth-Century Sled Dog

It is not possible to give to the wonderful dogs too much credit for any success on this journey. The day of April 17th, for instance, they were still hauling over two hundred pounds each. The snow was firm but rough, and the sled was continually going up and down over hard drifts . . . we made that day an average of nearly four miles an hour . . . An Arctic traveler's feeling of gratitude to the dogs can be scarcely less keen than to men.

VILHJALMUR STEFANSSON, 1925

It HAS BEEN SAID that the reason man and dog get on so well together is because the dog is smart enough to understand what man wants him to do and dumb enough to do it. The relationship, as any dog-lover knows, is much deeper than that. In what must be an under-

47

statement of appreciation, Inspector C.E. Rivett-Carnac of the Royal Canadian Mounted Police commented on his dogs: "On a long patrol when one is dependent on one's canine friends to a very large extent, it is impossible not to regard them with a certain degree of affection when they are straining their utmost to do what is required of them."

By the beginning of the twentieth century what was then the Royal Northwest Mounted Police had used dog teams for more than 25 years to assist in patrolling the vast, snow-covered distances of their territory. In the far reaches of the North, geographers, geologists and other scientists were accomplishing great researches by dog team. The system of mail cabins and roadhouses in Alaska was in daily use and was ready for the most gripping, suspenseful tale of life-saving yet to come out of sled dog legend. Adventurous Europeans and Americans who joined the Gold Rush as miners or dog-punchers were learning the immense value of a dog team's mobility in otherwise impassable snow drifts. This knowledge would be of military value in the coming World Wars. The tradition of the working sled dog was maintained, often in the face of more mechanized methods of travel, and it was enlarged upon and adopted for education and for sport.

Driving Dogs with the Mounties

Inspector Rivett-Carnac, a real-life colleague of the fictional but no less legendary Sergeant Preston of the Yukon, took most of the high romance out of mushing with the Mounties in an article he wrote for the *RCMP Quarterly* in 1938.

"I remember very well, some years ago, seeing a somewhat dramatic film about the North, in which the hero, riding on a sleigh, set off across the Barren Lands towards the Arctic Ocean, where he gallantly rescued a damsel in distress who was held captive by certain villainous characters. Every time they appeared on the screen, the hero and his dogs were seen to be skimming over the snow at full gallop. Despite the fact that the journey was one of some hundreds of miles, it apparently needed only a crack of the driver's whip, as he rested picturesquely on his sleigh, to maintain a speed of from 12 to 15 miles an hour over the whole distance. Furthermore, as far as the eye could see, the sled carried no food for man or dog. One could only assume that the driver in this instance was so confident of his dogs that he considered a few sandwiches in his hip pocket would be sufficient to sustain life until his objective was reached!

"Dog driving," the Inspector goes on, "is not as easy as that."

"On the contrary, as those who have traveled considerable distance by

AN R.C.M.P. "FLOATING" DETACHMENT traveled through the North from 1928 to 1950, frequently wintering in the Arctic and making sledge patrols to Eskimo villages. At Tree River, N.W.T., in 1931. *R.C.M.P.*

THE R.C.M.P.'s "ST. ROCH" AT TREE RIVER, 1931. The huskies curl comfortably on the ice except in severe weather. *R.C.M.P.*

means of dogs and sleigh know very well, it is an undertaking possibly as rough and as difficult as anything imaginable. While it is being performed little romance is evident.

"The Mackenzie River, before the advent of the aeroplane, was very sparsely settled and it was no uncommon experience for dog travellers to camp, night after night, in the snow at temperatures ranging to 60 degrees below zero, after a long day on snowshoes, during the course of which 30 or 40 miles had been covered. In those days, too, due to the absence of trappers' cabins, it was necessary to carry provisions for the entire journey. Now the custom is to make summer caches of food for men and dogs at various advantageous locations, preparatory to the winter months.

"Travelling conditions on the Mackenzie River are the worst that I encountered during periods of service in that territory, the Yukon, and the Western Arctic. The force of the current underneath the ice, as the river freezes in the fall, breaks the ice and forces huge blocks into every conceivable position. The chaotic mass freezes solid and effectually precludes any possibility of travel on any part of the river except in close proximity to each bank, where the water forced up by the pressure of the ice has frozen to form narrow, level strips. These convenient travel routes do not remain, however, as later in the winter the ice shrinks over the whole expanse of the river, canting the 'over-flow' ice, which is now deeply covered in snow, at an exceedingly steep angle. Since the rough ice remains an insuperable bar to travel on the river itself, it was necessary to continue to use the over-flow ice despite the angle it had assumed. Moving along the upper edge of the slanting place, with dogs hauling three or four hundred pounds of provisions, it was necessary to hold the toboggan in position by means of a line to prevent it from plunging down the slope, carrying the dogs with it into the rough ice. Proceeding in this way, strain in two separate directions was exerted on the toboggan, viz., the forward movement of the dogs and the sideways pull of the driver. Progress, as may be readily imagined, made in this manner, was necessarily slow and extremely arduous.

"After 30 miles of such travel, falling down concealed cracks in the ice at intervals and wrestling with the toboggan at the bottom of the slope on the frequent occasions when it slipped down, both the dogs and ourselves were always glad when darkness precluded the possibility of further travel at the end of the day.

"Camps had to be made at a suitable place where both green and dry timber were present to provide fuel and shelter from the wind. Having found a site, the work of making camp was apportioned among the members of the patrol. One would clear away the snow and cut spruce bows to make a bed, while the other would take his axe and bring dry timber for the open fire. On the spruce bows finally being laid in the excavation in the snow, the fire blazing strongly, the eiderdown sleeping robes spread out, and the requirements of the dogs having been attended to, one was ready to relax and cook supper. This generally consisted of beans, bannock, bacon (or other meat), black tea, butter and jam; a repast which comfortably satisfied the desires of a hungry traveller. After supper, when one's pipe was lighted and the fire, showering sparks into the frost-spangled air, cast a cheerful glow on the surrounding snow, it was possible to review the events of the day in restful contentment. This period compensated to a very great degree for the strain experienced during the day's journey. In the event of one's feet having been cut or chafed by the snowshoe strings, however, this enjoyment might possibly be allayed to some extent by a rueful contemplation of one's blood-stained moccasins and anticipation of the next day's travel. Once snugly ensconced in one's eiderdown robe, and providing that heavy snow did not fall during the night or the temperature sink much under 30 degrees below zero, one remained in comparative comfort until morning."

This description provides the essence of winter patrol by Canada's famous Mounties. Beyond every brutal stretch of trail there would surely be a more pleasant one, with time to watch the smoothly-running team, time for the driver to yield to the fascination that still inspires dog drivers today: "A team of dogs which has been carefully trained and to which proper care has been given, driven by a competent driver in whom the dogs have confidence, provides a sight as fine as may be seen. With their bushy tails curling over the backs, their ears cocked, and their eyes alertly bent on the trail before them, they make the miles flow under them in speedy succession."

Ending this article in praise of the sled dog, Rivett-Carnac noted astutely that "Modern methods of transportation have penetrated the northern regions of late years, and aeroplanes, tractors and mechanically propelled sleighs have been used. It is unlikely that the dog team as a means of transportation over the northern snows will ever become entirely obsolete, because, although it is a slow means of locomotion, it is one which will get the traveller to his destination—provided that his own powers are equal to those of his dogs."

Thirty years later, however, the Ottawa (Ontario) *Journal* contained a short news article headlined, "Mounties Forsake Dogs." From a peak of some 470 dogs owned by the force in 1930 and some 59,000 miles covered by dog team in 1955, the year 1967 showed only 13 RCMP detachments with dogs, and patrol mileage down to 22,000. By snowmobiles that year the force covered 42,000 miles. The last 78 official sled dogs at four outposts were replaced by machines in 1969 and the last patrol of any distance was made that year.

The first dog team patrol, almost a century earlier in 1873, had sought out whiskey traders operating among Indians on the west shore of Lake Michigan. Excitement and danger prevailed, with six men arrested and a quantity of liquor seized—an adventure worthy of romantic exploitation.

51

The last patrol was quietly routine, as Constable W.W. Townsend and Special Constable Peter Benjamin traveled for four weeks with two dog teams, 21 dogs, the five hundred miles from Old Crow to Fort McPherson, and back.

Nevertheless, not all Mounties have forsaken their faithful sled dogs. Dovetailing with the demise of dog teams as a method of transportation was the rise of Mountie interest in dog teams as a method of community participation and fun. Constable R.L. Julyan drove an RCMP dog team to fifth place in the 1965 Whitehorse Yukon Sourdough Rendezvous Sled Dog Racing Championship and donated the $50 prize money to a local charity. Special Constable Peter Benjamin drove the last official RCMP dog team to fourth place in the 1969 race. The 15 miles a day of packed race course must have seemed like a short pleasure jaunt to the human and canine veterans of the trail.

Even though official RCMP teams no longer race, the dog-driving tradition still lingers with the scarlet-coated policemen. In the force are men who drive their own dogs in local races as a hobby. When a twenty-year veteran such as Sergeant Sandy Saunderson retired, in the 1970's, what did he do? He moved from Ontario with its "milder" winters to Fort St. John, British Columbia, for big snows, cold blows, and a chance to train and race in the big western Canada sled dog races.

Dog Teams in the Service of Science

While the Mounties were policing the "populated" areas of the North, scientific explorers were slowly penetrating the last unknown regions of the Arctic. The great sea voyages of the eighteenth and nineteenth centuries had resulted in new maps and scientific knowledge of great areas of the Arctic and Antarctic. Explorers now knew the environment of the North and South Poles, but how to attain those remotest of goals?

The severely limiting problems of arctic travel which had plagued earlier explorers, problems such as scurvy, food storage, overland locomotion, or unmapped territories, were largely solved or at least lessened by the time the twentieth century began. It was at this point that civilized man approached closest in spirit to the native arctic dweller, in terms of living in the Eskimo's harsh land with a minimum of disruption and a maximum of accomplishment. For quite soon explorers and scientists would intrude with mechanized exploration, which to some is an aesthetic and psychological affront. "Exploration," wrote Robert Marshall, author of *Arctic Village*, becomes "chiefly a matter of getting machinery to run a

SPECIAL CONSTABLE PETER BENJAMIN (Loucheux Indian) breaks trail for R.C.M.P. patrol en route to Ft. McPherson from Old Crow in March, 1969. This was the "last official R.C.M.P. sled dog patrol," a 500-mile round trip. *R.C.M.P.*

little further than normal from the factory."

Just before airplanes and motorized toboggans made it to the Poles, however, there were a few brief decades of outstanding expeditions. They were the culmination of centuries of preparatory work. The first polar voyages were organized as a means, not an end, since the English, especially, were eager to find a trade route to the East not barred by Spain or Portugal. Polar adventures began with Robert Thorne in 1527, Hugh Willoughby in 1553, Willem Barents in 1596, and Henry Hudson in 1607. Not until 1773 did expeditions again sail for the North Pole, when Constantine Phipps searched for the elusive passage to the East. In 1806 William Scoresby, in 1818 David Buchan, and in 1827 Edward Parry, tried for the goal. Parry proposed a new technique for arctic exploration, that of traveling with sledge-boats from the ship. His sledges were pulled by men, and although they set the farthest-north record, the drifting ice nullified the greater part of their efforts.

Next came Kane, Hayes, Hall, Nares, Greely, Karl Koldeway of the German North Polar Expeditions, and Nansen, who in 1896 showed that the North Pole would have to be simply a spot on the shifting sea ice. The Duke of the Abruzzi led an Italian North Polar Expedition as the nineteenth century came to a close.

The new century brought a new method of attack on the North Pole. The great wooden ships were sailed to a northern land base, from which explorers headed out by dog sled. Robert E. Peary, single-minded now about reaching the Pole, had adopted Eskimo techniques of travel, shelter and clothing; Eskimos were his drivers and igloo-builders. They laid a trail and cached the food, according to the prescribed methods of McClintock, and the whole overland expedition traveled with the help of over two hundred sled dogs. Peary's group broke the Italian record in 1905, but severe ice conditions slowed their trek and forced an early return.

Peary was ready again in 1908 for his third attempt. The expedition, with 22 members, 49 Eskimos from Etah on Greenland's northwest coast, and 246 Eskimo dogs, made a land base at Cape Columbia on Ellesmere Island. From there, 24 men, 19 sleds and 133 dogs started out across the ice in February, 1909. In the final assault party were Peary, his black companion Matthew Henson, and four Eskimos. With their dog teams they covered the last 133 miles in five forced marches, arriving at that magic spot where there is no North, East or West on April 6, 1909. Their 485-mile trip back to base camp was made in a record time of 16 days.

Although books have been written disputing Peary's claim that he reached the Pole, some instigated by the claims of Frederick Cook that he got there a year before Peary, most of the arguments are based on the high rate of travel claimed for the return journey. Nevertheless, as aptly stated by William H. Hobbs in "Peary, the Ace Among Dog-Sledgers," from *Explorers Club Tales,* "Experienced dog-sledgers are pretty well agreed that over a marked trail and going homeward the rates of speed in sledging are almost doubled."

Meanwhile, in the Antarctic, another polar race was underway. Robert F. Scott, a British explorer who believed that using sled dogs on polar expeditions was unsporting, penetrated into Antarctica perhaps one-third of the way to the Pole in 1902. "No journey made with dogs," Captain Scott wrote, "can approach the height of that fine conception which is realized when a party of men go forth to face hardships, dangers, and difficulties by their own unaided efforts." Eight years later this bold romanticism was to cost Scott his life. Although Scott did use both dogs and ponies, he apparently was unable to take advantage of their greatest capabilities. Ernest Shackleton introduced sled dogs from Manitoba and ponies from Manchuria to antarctic exploration, and in 1908 he discovered a route across the Beardmore Glacier, reaching to within 112 miles of the South Pole.

The most exciting, the most tragic polar race took place in 1911–12, when Roald Amundsen and his dog teams beat Robert Scott and his ponies to the Pole by a month. A member of the first supporting party of Scott's last expedition, Apsley Cherry-Garrard, described the differences in adaptability between the ponies and the dogs. "The animals suffer most, and during this first blizzard all our ponies were weakened, and two of them became practically useless . . . Nothing was left undone for them which we could manage, but necessarily the Antarctic is a grim place for ponies. I think Scott felt the sufferings of the ponies more than the animals themselves. It was different with the dogs. These fairly warm blizzards were only a rest for them. Snugly curled up in a hole in the snow they allowed themselves to be drifted over. Bieleglas and Vaida, two half-brothers who pulled side by side, always insisted upon sharing one hole, and for greater warmth one would lie on top of the other. At intervals of two hours or so they fraternally changed places."

When Scott's final assault group reached the South Pole on January 17, 1912, after a strength-sapping march of 78 days, they saw paw prints in the snow and the Norwegian flag flapping in the wind. To have achieved so much and to have come in second was a bitter disappointment. Their journey back was no more than a crawl, as men succumbed to the terrible surroundings. A blizzard pinned them down, their food and fuel ran out. They set up a tent, only 11 miles from their One Ton Camp, and waited . . . "For God's sake," the heroic Scott wrote in his diary, "look after our people."

When Richard E. Byrd explored the Antarctic for the U.S. Navy, he had no reservations about using dog teams to their fullest to aid in the success of his work. In *Discovery* he wrote, "Planes and tractors are superb instruments, but there is no getting away from dogs. The Eskimo husky . . . can overcome terrain which a tractor can't penetrate and a plane can't land on."

Byrd's dogs came from all over. There were Eskimo dogs from the St. Lawrence, Labrador, Manitoba and indirectly from Alaska. He also had an Alaskan Husky-Siberian Husky-wolf cross, bred especially for his second expedition. These dogs were short, chunky and well-formed, with good shoulders and paws, fast like a Siberian, weighing about 65 pounds. The St. Lawrence and Labrador dogs were "motley in coat and blood history with a distant wolf strain, stocky dogs with wide foot pads and strong legs, averaging between 70 and 75 pounds." The thirty Manitoba dogs were descended from dogs of Shackleton's second expedition, big-boned, deep-chested, heavy-shouldered, strong-legged. They weighed from 80 to 100 pounds.

Byrd used tractors as well as sled dogs to help haul supplies from the ship to base camp, for moving equipment and stores to satellite camps, and for exploratory and scientific trips from base camp. He was impressed with the transporting abilities of both tractor and sled dog. Most striking to Byrd was the contrast presented "between tractors and dog teams, between the new and the old, between steel and the finely strung, highly emotional content of heart and sinew that is the Eskimo husky. The issue between dogs and tractors as to which was superior on barrier surface had at last been joined; and in the first telling test, on the same sort of rolling surface on which he had reigned from the beginning of time, the dog came out second best. In the decisive matters of speed and pay load the tractor, pending the more rigorous eliminations of the spring journeys, was well out in front. It was tireless, needing only a steady hand to guide it when it was running right . . ."

The tedium for a tractor driver of mile after mile of just holding the wheels on course, in the long run gave an edge to the dog teams. So did abrupt, unscheduled interruptions to the tractor trips in the form of breakdowns.

"The tempo of the tractor driver was set, not by the sun as in March sledging, but by the moods and stamina of the drivers. Not for them the rhythmic routine of the dog drivers, the morning and evening camps, the luncheon stops, the fifteen-minute resting spells for men and dogs, regulated by the limits of physical endurance and the food reserves either on the sledges or in the depots. Hindered by the constant cropping up of small

A "RETIRED" MOUNTIE, SANDY SAUNDERSON, still mushing—to a second-place finish in 1975's Yukon Sourdough
Rendezvous at Whitehorse.   *Jim Beebe, Whitehorse* Star

SLEDGING SUPPLIES from ship to base camp during Byrd's First Antarctic
Expedition, 1929.   *U.S. Information Agency*

mechanical troubles and irked by the necessity of heating the engines every time they were stopped, the tractor drivers' philosophy of *keeping her* rolling was animated by the simple necessity of cramming in all possible mileage so long as things held together. However, since the cars traveled in convoy, these mechanical faults could be counted upon to occur at frequent enough intervals, as the dog drivers helpfully observed, to keep the drivers from meanwhile starving to death for lack of time to eat."

John O'Brien, on Byrd's first Antarctic expedition in 1928–30, wrote of his experiences in *By Dog Sled for Byrd*. His appreciation for the huskies shows through his various descriptions:

"A husky's idea of a drink is a few bites of snow."

"Inside of two minutes they had run over me, saved a sledge, and started one of the prettiest little dog fights we had on the whole trip."

"On another occasion, on a downhill slope, with the team running at full speed, a bridged crevasse was reached and a team started over. The weight of the first three dogs broke through the bridge and they were left hanging in midair over the edge of a seemingly bottomless crevasse. Fortunately, the rest of the team stopped and pulled back with an almost miraculous promptness, drawing their unfortunate companions with them, until all of the dogs were on a firm surface again."

O'Brien's story of Norman Vaughan's lead dog, Dinty, brings out the depth of the involvement experienced by the sled dogs, whose feelings for being an important part of the team are often so transparent. Dinty had begun to sulk in harness, to slack off. Making sure he was not sick or injured, Vaughan then demoted the leader to a rear position in the team. The new leader, a ten-month-old pup, lorded it over everybody, and Dinty, in abject shame, merely walked through the motions of being a sled dog. After several days of this, towards the end of their trip, Vaughan decided that Dinty had probably learned his lesson.

"So when Vaughan began bringing out his dogs, he harnessed those next to the sledge first, then the next pair, and so on. Dinty, lying with his head on his paws and pretending indifference, was secretly watching the proceedings. When all the others had been put in harness and Vaughan went back to lead Dinty out to head the line and restore him to the lead for that last pull home, the big dog was fairly trembling with excitement.

"Who says a dog doesn't think, doesn't understand, has no pride of position? They would have had their opinion reversed in short order if they could have seen Mr. Dinty step off on that journey. Head erect and sensitive ears pointing, his eyes fairly sparkling and that great black plume of a tail waving wildly erect, Dinty was again a lead dog to stir a driver's pride. His mouth open as he panted with excitement, the dog seemed fairly to smile at all the world.

"And when Vaughan gave the signal to the animals, already tugging to be off, Dinty led the way as if he were not at the end of two and a half months' grueling work, but just out for a short run. So he brought the sledge back to camp, as he had led it out, as glorious a lead dog as ever guided his mates over snow bridges or swerved them expertly from a freshly opened crevasse which has suddenly yawned at their feet."

Sled dogs, in spite of the conveniences of airplanes, tractors and snow-mobiles, are still the transportation method of choice for arctic explorers in many situations. A Finnish physicist, Esa Mäntysalo, uses a dog team to carry supplies and equipment out onto pack ice for his investigations. Sociologists traveling and living among the Eskimos depend on dog teams for mobility. Fred Bruemmer, a writer-photographer who specializes in recording the changing lives of arctic natives, reported on a trip he took to study Greenland's Polar Eskimos. Near Thule Air Force Base he was picked up by an old, dark Eskimo with a dog team for the trip to the main settlement. The Eskimo turned out to be Anaqaq Henson, son of Matthew Henson, chief assistant of Peary.

In Canada, the people on the 1957–58 International Geophysical Year project on mountainous Ellesmere Island found dog teams invaluable. During the melting season dogs could cross river ice where tractors would have broken through.

The Juneau (Alaska) Icefield Summer Institute, an arctic and mountain environment study and student training program, tried out a sled dog team on an experimental basis in 1970 to see if dogs indeed were still superior to modern vehicles or manpower. The team proved so successful that an Alaskan teacher-dog driver, Terry McMullin, was hired to select dogs and drive the team for the Institute. He brought Alaskan freight dogs, mostly males, weighing from 100 to 150 pounds. The particular value of the dogs over machines showed itself in two main ways. The first was their instinct in detecting crevasses in the ice field and finding crossings with solid bases. A light dog team can often cross a snow bridge where a heavy vehicle would break through. During storms, the sensitive noses of the sled dogs enabled them to find their way along a buried trail. The second major advantage of the dog teams involved broken-down or foundered vehicles. Even a staunch defender of machines had to be delighted at the sight of a dog team bringing a spare part some distance from base camp . . . and more than one vehicle was towed out of a "bottomless" drift by dogs.

Dog teams in the service of science have one other immeasurable value, particularly for extended operations: they are alive. The dogs provide a great morale-boosting quality in that they require daily attention and consideration by the men. They respond positively to the care, which quickly establishes a warm, vital relationship between dogs and men. Sled dogs will work hard and loyally, all the while maintaining their independent spirit. They are businesslike in harness, but capable of humor. A sled dog will grab a mitten for a game of "keep away" or sit unconcernedly on a piece of needed equipment, eyes alight with mischief. It is these qualities, in addition to their uncanny talents for keeping on a drifted trail or sensing danger, that would prompt most arctic explorers to agree with Richard Byrd: "The Eskimo husky still is, as he always has been, the one absolutely reliable means of polar advance."

The Great Race of Mercy to Nome

That sort of reliability and life-saving instinct with which the sled dog is endowed received world-wide acclaim in 1925 during the most celebrated of all sled dog missions. Most of the gold was gone from Nome in 1925, and most of the miners, prospectors and adventurers had moved on. The population of the city of Nome was 2,000 people, mostly natives, and it was their lives that were at stake in this mission. Also involved were some twenty Eskimo, Indian and white dog mushers and mail drivers who laid their own lives and the lives of their dogs on the line for the isolated, diphtheria-stricken city.

It took one week, from January 27 to February 2, 1925, and it was the biggest race in the history of dog driving. Starting at the "end of the steel," at the railhead at Nenana, 225 miles north of Anchorage, the drivers and their dogs relay-raced a twenty-pound package of diphtheria antitoxin over a trail that ordinarily took 25 days but had been run in 15 days. The Nenana to Nome trail featured over 674 miles of the roughest, most desolate country in the world. In the middle of winter the temperature ranged somewhere between 19 and 64 degrees below zero and it was pitch dark most of the time.

For this race there was no prize money, and the competing team was driven by Death.

Gunnar Kasson and Leonhard Seppala got the credit and the glory for the big race against a potential diphtheria epidemic and secured their places in history. Kasson's was the final team in the relay, and Seppala traveled the greatest distance. The Eskimos, the Indians and the mail drivers who ran most of the trail, in the worst storms and the severest cold, were not glorified in contemporary accounts of the event. Those men, among the bravest the North has ever known, were officially

ON A WARM DAY IN THE ANTARCTIC, Dorsey and Healy pause with a dog sled loaded for a trail trip, 1941. *Public Buildings Service*

DOG TEAMS AT WORK at Point Barrow, Alaska, in 1934. *U.S. Signal Corps*

thanked with a medal and a certificate signed by President Coolidge, but they were largely overlooked by newspapers and radio accounts. Few remember that it was mostly native drivers who contributed so unselfishly. The government had offered fifty cents a mile for the special trip, but the drivers took to their sleds without thinking about pay. The need in Nome was all the justification they asked.

The story began on a day in mid-January when Dr. Curtis Welch, the only doctor in Nome, discovered a case of diphtheria. He immediately sent out a desperate wire for help. His supply of antitoxin was woefully small, and Nome was the medical center for a vast district of some 11,000 natives who were dangerously vulnerable to what they called the "Black Death." Antitoxin was located in Anchorage, but how to get it quickly and safely to Nome? There were two open-cockpit biplanes in Alaska at that time and naturally the pilots wanted to try to fly with the serum. Alternatives were agonizingly debated, until Governor Scott Bone made the decision that the risks of flying were too great. It would be a superhuman feat and probably beyond the technical capabilities of those early airplanes. The cold was brutal, the weather the worst, and the daylight lasted only two or three hours. If the plane crashed, the only serum in Alaska would be lost.

Dog teams were the only answer, so the word flashed by wire out across the tundra from Nenana to Nome. Relays of dog teams and drivers were posted at way stations along the route.

The Alaska Railroad sent a special train out of Anchorage, north to the end of the line in Nenana, with the small package of serum aboard. Waiting at Nenana was William "Wild Bill" Shannon, the U.S. mail driver for the Northern Commercial Company. He set out late on the 27th of January for Tolovana, 52 miles to the northwest, with a team of nine Malamutes, a big working team for those days. The thermometer at the station read −50°. The serum was wrapped in blankets to keep it from the damaging cold.

At noon on the 28th Shannon turned the serum over to Dan Green at Tolovana. Green raced his eight dogs the 31 miles to Manley Hot Springs in weather featuring temperatures of −30° and a wind of some twenty miles an hour: a chill factor of −70° for Green and his dogs.

At Manley Hot Springs, the Athabascan Indian Johnny Folger took over and ran 28 miles to Fish Lake with a team of eight dogs and the temperature still standing at thirty degrees below zero.

From Fish Lake to Tanana, Sam Joseph carried the serum 26 miles at an amazing average of nine miles an hour. The temperature was dropping.

From Tanana to Kallands, 34 miles away, Titus Nicholi mushed his seven dogs through weather at forty below. There, Dave Corning took over in $-42°$ temperatures; he averaged eight miles an hour for the 24 miles from Kallands to the Nine Mile mail cabin.

He was met by Edgar Kalland who raced his seven dogs to Kokrines, thirty miles away, with the temperature now at $-44°$.

From Kokrines to Ruby, another thirty miles, Harry Pitka fought his way through a white-out at 47 degrees below zero. He somehow managed an incredible nine miles an hour. At Ruby, Bill McCartney took the package and raced with his seven dogs the 28 miles to Whiskey Creek in slightly warming weather: $-43°$ now.

At Whiskey Creek, seven o'clock at night, Edgar Nollner continued on at $-40°$ for the 24 miles to Galena, with seven dogs.

Edgar's brother, George Nollner, carried the serum 18 miles from Galena to Bishop Mountain with the same seven dogs, and the temperature began to plunge. The dogs trotted the whole 42 miles for the Nollner brothers; it was too dark to lope.

At Bishop Mountain, the 22-year-old Athabascan Charlie Evans began with a team of nine dogs the run to Nulato, thirty miles away. The temperature dived to 64 degrees below zero and the trip was a nightmare for Evans. He had no rabbit skins to protect the vulnerable groin area of his dogs, and two of them began to freeze, even as they ran. Loading the crippled huskies onto his sled, Evans continued on. He ran in front of the sled, pulling on the traces, trying to help his seven remaining dogs. Five hours after leaving Bishop Mountain he reached Nulato. It was four o'clock in the morning and all he could manage was to carry his sick dogs into the cabin and collapse beside the stove. Recalling the event some fifty years later, Charlie Evans said, "It was real cold."

Tommy Patsy loaded the serum from Evans' sled onto his own and sped off into the darkness toward Kaltag, 36 miles distant. Urging his team on at 58 degrees below zero, it took him three and a half hours to cover the distance. He got there Friday noon, January 30th. In less than three days, 13 dog teams had covered 377 miles. They were a little over halfway to Nome.

At Kaltag, the trail left the Yukon River and headed over the mountains to the coast. In the mountains, the weather grew worse. The Athabascan river pilot Jackscrew took the serum at Kaltag and cursed his way through a blinding snowstorm at fifty below zero to Old Woman shelter cabin, forty miles away. There he was met by the Eskimo Victor Anagick who took off in blowing, drifting snow toward Unalakleet, 34 miles away on Norton Sound.

At Unalakleet, another Eskimo, Myles Gonangnan, was waiting, and set off in his turn with the serum for Shaktoolik. He had to break trail for his eight-dog team through waist-high drifts for the entire forty miles. They were traveling in one of the worst snowstorms in memory. He made it in just under 12 hours and fell exhausted and frostbitten, but with the serum safe for the next sled.

Harry Ivanoff then started for Golovin. Half a mile along the trail the team picked up the scent of reindeer, and bedlam broke loose. Fighting to straighten out his dogs, Ivanoff looked up to see Leonhard Seppala and his team of racing Siberians, the only such dogs in the relay, hustling down the trail.

Apparently the blizzard had interfered with communications and Nome thought there was no relay team available at Shaktoolik. So Seppala had driven his team a good 150 miles, from Nome, to meet the precious package. Ivanoff gave him the serum, and Seppala, turning back, chose the straight route across Norton Sound, a route traditionally avoided by dog drivers. The high winds were pushing sea water up over the ice, which promised to break up at any moment and drift out into the Bering Sea, Seppala, serum and all. But Seppala's confidence in his proven fast dogs and his successful crossing of the creaking ice once that day stimulated his belief that he had a reasonable chance, with luck, to make it back across to Golovin and save hours, perhaps days.

In warming temperatures which made the ice more dangerous, Seppala sped off for Golovin, 91 miles west by the route across the Sound. The little Norwegian and his lead dog, Togo, made 84 miles that day. Twenty of those miles were across the heaving, sloshing, breaking sea ice. But Togo, the hero of many a sport sled dog race and veteran of many a trail, knew the dangers. He also had the uncanny ability to begin carrying out Seppala's wishes even before Seppala gave a command. Togo led the fragile train of dogs, sled and driver as quickly as he could across the massive array of jagged, groaning ice floes. They reached Isaacs Point, on the other side, late Saturday night. There Seppala stopped to feed his team and tend their raw, cut feet. Continuing on next morning in the blizzard, he met Charlie Olson at Golovin in mid-afternoon. There were eighty miles left to go.

At three o'clock Charlie Olson left Golovin for the 25-mile run to Bluff. He fought his way through a blizzard with a gale wind of fifty miles an hour throwing him and his team of seven dogs from the trail time and time again. The thermometer read thirty below zero, Olson's hands froze, his dogs froze and stumbled, but they all fought on through the night. His vision obscured by the raging blizzard, Olson had to trust his lead dog to stay on the trail. At 7:30 P.M., only four hours and fifteen minutes after leaving Golovin, he reached Bluff and passed the serum over to Gunnar Kasson.

THE SNOWMOBILE GAVE UP—but the dogs did not. In New Hampshire, 1970.   *R. Coppinger*

TEN YEARS AFTER this photograph was taken, descendants of these dogs ran in the serum race to Nome. Leonhard Seppala and his first All-Alaska Sweepstakes victory team, 1915.   *The Great Dog Races of Nome*

65

IN CENTRAL PARK, NEW YORK CITY, THE STATUE OF BALTO KEEPS THE COURAGEOUS IMAGE OF THE SLED DOG ALIVE. The inscription reads: "Dedicated to the indomitable spirit of the sled dogs that relayed antitoxin six hundred miles over rough ice, across treacherous waters, through arctic blizzards from Nenana to the relief of stricken Nome in the winter of 1925. Endurance. Fidelity. Intelligence." *R. Coppinger*

Kasson ran the last 55 miles to Nome, to honor and fame, with 13 dogs in harness. Somewhere along the trail he bypassed the next relay driver, Ed Rohn, who was waiting at Safety to take the serum on the final lap into Nome. "Intentionally bypassed," chuckled the old-timers many years later.

But, for Kasson, leaving Bluff at 10 o'clock in total darkness and an eighty-mile-an-hour wind-driven snowstorm, no landmark was familiar and he could easily have missed the roadhouse. Dressed in seal mukluks that reached to his hips, sealskin pants, a reindeer parka and hood with a windbreaker over that, Kasson could still feel the sting of the wind. Two of his dogs, long-haired veteran trail huskies, began to succumb to the weather and Kasson had to stop and buckle on their rabbit skins. The sled kept tipping over in the soft snow; he couldn't see; he didn't really know where he was.

The only way for Kasson to survive, the only way he could even attempt to get the serum through the storm, was to give the direction of the team to the leader, Balto. Balto, one of Seppala's Siberians, was a powerful, experienced leader, but Seppala had not taken him for this run because the six-year-old dog's speed was not as fast as it had been. Kasson needed the leadership, however, and borrowed Balto from Seppala's kennel. Given his head in the worst of the weather, Balto put his nose down and sniffed and felt his way along the buried, invisible trail. All Kasson could do was trust the dog's instincts and experience. The efforts of over one hundred and fifty other sled dogs and nineteen other drivers depended solely now on Balto. The lives of dozens, perhaps hundreds, of Alaskans depended on the doughty little sled dog and his team.

In the tradition of the great lead dogs, Balto, ears flattened against his head to keep out the storm, nose working to pick out the trail, guided the team and the serum directly to Nome.

When they got there, at 5:30 in the morning on February 2, the half-frozen Kasson collapsed beside his battered, depleted dog team and began pulling ice from Balto's feet.

"Balto," he was heard to mumble . . . "Damn fine dog!"

"Over There" with the Dog Teams

Not as instantly dramatic as the Nome serum run, perhaps, but no less heroic to the people whose lives and fates were involved, was the use of dog teams during both World Wars.

At the start of World War I two residents of Nome, René Haas and a man named Mufflet, left to join the French Army. Several months later Nome's most famous dog driver, Scotty Allan, received a message from

Lieutenant Haas, asking him to secretly gather a hundred good sled dogs and all their equipment for use in the snow-choked mountains in France. Men, horses and mules were helplessly bogged down along the Vosges Mountains, and Captain Mufflet and Haas had convinced their superiors that in Alaska the sled dog kept the roads open in winter. They were sure they could serve the same purpose in France.

Scotty Allan began casually buying up the best dogs he could find in the surrounding Eskimo villages, so that by the time Haas arrived Allan had assembled 106 dogs, plus sleds and harnesses and two tons of dried salmon for dog food. Twenty-eight of those dogs were sons or grandsons of Allan's famous racing lead dog, Baldy.

To transfer the 106 dogs from Allan's kennel to the *S.S. Senator* Allan hitched up the longest towline ever used. Over three hundred feet of heavy rope, with iron rings for the dogs' harnesses every six feet along its length, was hitched to a big truck. French tri-color cockades decorated each dog's collar, and all the residents of Nome, including the school children, lined the streets to watch the longest dog team in the world. America's first unit in World War I had started on its journey.

After the boat trip, they crossed Canada by rail. On orders from France, Allan picked up over 300 more sled dogs from eastern Canada, dogs used for winter hauling in the north woods. With well over 400 dogs, Scotty Allan's "Foreign Legion" debarked from Quebec on an ancient sea tramp named, incongruously, the *Pomeranian*.

Arriving at Le Havre, Allan learned with dismay that the outfit his dogs were to work with, the Alpine Chasseurs, had no experience at all in handling dogs. Nevertheless, the fifty young "Blue Devils" were a self-controlled, confident, well-trained unit. With Lieutenant Haas as interpreter and assistant, Allan divided his "K9 Corps" into sixty different teams, reserving some dogs for packing, sentry or Red Cross duty. They marked each dog's collar and harness with brass identification tags: name, number, position and team. They taught the Chasseurs how to harness and hitch up the dogs and to use the commands "gee," "haw," "whoa," and, ironically, "mush."

On the battlefront in the Vosges Mountains, the sled dogs immediately proved their value. A battery high in the wilderness had been cut off and was out of ammunition. For two long, agonizing weeks rescue attempts had been made and had failed, horses and mules just not being adapted for mobility in deep snow. The dog teams, sleds loaded with ninety tons of bullets and shells, reached the isolated French unit within four days.

Communication with another separated detachment was re-established in one night by the Chasseurs, who with the swiftness provided by their dog teams, were able to string over twenty miles of telephone wire right

HEADING FOR EUROPE DURING WORLD WAR II. Members of the Arctic Search and Rescue unit's sled dog section.

Courtesy New England Sled Dog Club

ON THE FIFTIETH ANNIVERSARY OF THE NOME SERUM RUN, a packet of commemorative envelopes was relayed over the same route by relatives and friends of the original drivers.
L. Coppinger

UNCLE SAM'S SLED DOGS. The U.S. Army maintains dog teams in Alaska for rescue and reclamation. *Courtesy Joe Redington, Jr.*

ANOTHER WAY for sled dogs to earn their keep. Boston, Massachusetts, 1934. *Courtesy Lorna Demidoff*

under the Germans' noses. Supplies and ammunitions moved rapidly by dog team to far-flung units unreachable by any other means.

Wounded men, too, were speedily evacuated and sledged to field hospitals where prompt attention saved lives.

The sled dogs were heroes, acclaimed in newspapers on both sides of the Atlantic. Three of the dogs were decorated with the illustrious Croix de Guerre for valor in battle, a fine tribute to the Scotsman, the Frenchmen, the Eskimos and Alaskans who contributed to their success.

Further military use of sled dogs was made by the Russians, who used them in both World Wars for evacuating wounded and ferrying supplies. The Russians also set up sled dog breeding, training and research stations during the 1930's, and by 1946 had published a 250-page book covering sled dog nutrition, work ability and genetics. Both the Russians and the Finns used sled dogs during World War II, counter-attacking and harassing, then disappearing silently into the snowy wastes.

Also during World War II, the Danes and the Americans set up a weather station on the east coast of Greenland. Manned by Scandinavians who formed an unofficial "Greenland Army," the station's meteorological observations were of prime importance to military maneuvering in the North Atlantic. Dog-sledding was the only method of travel, and provided a hasty means of retreat when a German reconnaissance group also decided that eastern Greenland would be a good place for a weather station. David Howarth's striking account of this mission, *The Sledge Patrol,* also includes some delightful insights into beginning dog driving.

Over in Alaska, Japanese spies had mapped coastal details, especially along the Aleutian Islands, during the 1930's. Alaskans anticipated their strategy and made contingent plans under the direction of Colonel Marvin R. "Muktuk" Marston, who traveled thousands of miles by dog team, organizing the natives into a "tundra army," the Alaskan Territorial Guard.

The United States Army also developed sled dog units for World War II. Dogs and drivers were assigned for training and use in arctic rescues, the three main camps being in Alaska, Montana and Maine. The drivers used the War Department Field Manual, *Dog Team Transportation,* a manual resulting from the Army's many years with working dog teams in Alaska.

In February of 1943, Norman Vaughan, whose arctic experience included Byrd's first antarctic expedition in 1928–30, was assigned the task of organizing the Arctic Search and Rescue Section of the North Atlantic Division of the Air Transport Command. Vaughan, a dog driver since the age of nine when he had hitched the family's German Shepherd to a sled, began recruiting drivers and sled dogs. The dogs came mainly from New

England kennels, especially from the famed Chinook Kennels run by Milton and Eva Seeley, where the special husky crossbreds for Byrd's second expedition had originated. Some two dozen expert dog drivers joined Vaughan's "Arctic Rangers." Their experiences with sled dogs had been gained mushing in Alaska, with the Byrd expeditions, as northwoods trappers, or as sport sled dog racers. The new unit carried out training missions from 1943 to 1945, staging search and rescue maneuvers in the White Mountains of New Hampshire.

One mission, undertaken alone by Colonel Vaughan, involved a hazardous journey by dog sled on the Greenland icecap to find eight crash-landed airplanes. Working his way slowly over the ice from one plane to the next, Vaughan removed the bombsights and other valuable equipment and supplies to prevent their being salvaged by the enemy.

In March of 1945 the call came to Presque Isle, Maine, where the Rangers were headquartered, from the snow-covered battlefields of Lieutenant General Omar Bradley's Twelfth Army Group in Belgium. Stretcher bearers were floundering through the snow at a rate of just over one mile an hour. Dog teams should be able to travel four times as fast. So Colonel Vaughan assembled his 25 sled dog drivers, over 200 huskies, two dozen sleds and toboggans, and they headed for the western front. By the time Captain Bill Shearer, with the dogs and drivers, got to Belgium, the Battle of the Bulge had been won and a spring thaw had melted all the snow.

Nevertheless, by the end of the war Colonel Vaughan could speak of dozens of rescues and scores of servicemen and civilians aided in the northern regions, thanks to the brave, willing huskies and their drivers.

The end of the war did not mean the end of rescue work for the dogs. Newspapers a year later carried a photograph of nine huskies pulling a rescue sled down the slope of Elk Mountain in Wyoming, where an airliner had crashed on January 31, 1946. From Truckee, California, a dedicated sled dog driver, Lloyd Van Sickle, time and again made his team available for otherwise impossible mountain rescues. In 1954 Norman Vaughan was back at it: an airliner had crashed on Mt. Kearsarge in New Hampshire and he took his dog team to join the search.

Sled dogs and dog sleds: the number of times they have made it through difficult terrain where men on foot or machines could not succeed are prodigious.

"Sledge dogs," dryly reports the U.S. War Department Field Manual, "have generally proved most reliable because of their ability to surmount the obstacles of uncertain weather, treacherous crevasses, and rough and hilly terrain."

Near the end of the twentieth century, in spite of the RCMP retiring their dog teams in favor of snowmobiles, and the U.S. Post Office Department retiring their dog teams in favor of airplanes, sled dogs are still of great economic value in many parts of the world and in many walks of life. Scientists on polar expeditions still rely on sled dogs, and visitors in places like Alaska or Greenland can hire a dog team for sight-seeing tours. In Churchill, Manitoba, Jane's Dog Taxi is available for short rides or trips across the ice to Fort Prince of Wales.

What is most interesting is that in northern Asia, where the sled dog and hence the dog sled were "invented," natives still rely on dog teams to help them earn their livelihood. A Swiss member of the International Sled Dog Racing Association, Toni Schmidt, received some information in 1970 from the Department of Nature Preservation of the Ministry of Agriculture in the USSR about contemporary use of sled dogs in Russia.

Along the coast and on the islands of Russia's northern polar seas sled dogs are still consequential to society. On the Yenisei and the Ob Rivers, the thick-furred dogs with the short, pricked ears, the obliquely-set eyes and the heavy-duty builds, work daily at various tasks. Local families keep six to eight dogs each; hunters and trappers also keep a good number of dogs. The state farms, collective farms and the fisheries maintain dog teams, keeping sometimes as many as 500 to 600 dogs. In winter the dogs pull sleds for hunters and trappers; in summer they pull loaded boats upstream. Hunting and transportation are the main jobs for sled dogs in the forested areas of Siberia.

The best working dogs, according to the writer from the Ministry, are on the Chukchi Peninsula and the lower parts of the big inland Rivers Kolyma, Indigirka, Yana and Lena. The people of these areas live primarily from fishing, hauling great loads of fish by dog team. They are experienced dog breeders, their dependence on big, strong dogs extending back before recorded history.

Far above the Arctic Circle in north central Alaska, the Nunamiut Eskimos, great caribou hunters, are said to have traded for dogs from Siberia. A dog is a distinct economic asset to these nomadic people, and a man is judged by the number, power, endurance and size of his dogs. Not until a Nunamiut boy reaches his middle or late teens does he get to use or care for his parents' dogs. When he marries and leaves home, some of these dogs go with him. The dog team, it is said, reflects the owner's personality. It also holds the Brooks Range people together, enabling them to pursue their encampment style of life.

Even farther above the Arctic Circle, right on the northwesternmost coast of Alaska, on the Arctic Ocean, a Wainwright Eskimo family keeps up to 16 dogs, putting nine to 11 of them together for a good-sized team. Sixty years ago their average team had four to five dogs. They are more affluent now, can afford more dog food and hence more dogs. Again, dogs are a status symbol for these natives, lending them prestige as well as increased mobility. Recently they have taken advantage of this mobility to run their teams in local sled dog races (they can race thirty miles in two and a half hours) or to drive the hundred miles to Barrow (in 24 hours).

Outside of Dawson, in Canada's Yukon Territory, lives Roger Mendelsohn, who still runs his trap line with a dog team. He also commutes to town once in a while during the winter to shake off some "cabin fever." A few Indians in the area keep dogs and have small teams, but the snowmobile seems to be more popular around Dawson. Mendelsohn keeps twenty purebred Siberian Huskies, which he likes because although they are not as big, they are faster than Malamutes, the traditional freighting dogs.

According to Mendelsohn: "When I check trap lines 10 to 15 miles on the river I take the dogs, but back in the heavy bush I walk or may take one dog with a light toboggan. I use them to haul firewood from the drift piles out on the river and I go to town which is about 32 miles down the river. Takes three hours, fifty minutes with seven or nine dogs, hitched in pairs with a single leader. Usually we are breaking trail in three to four inches of snow with a big 110-pound freight sled. Instead of yelling at them to get along I sometimes sing. They look at me kind of funny and twitch their ears, but they don't mind it so much. Anyway they seem to have a favorite, a rock and roll type song, *The Train Called the City of New Orleans.*"

Reinhard Korgen accompanied explorer Donald B. MacMillan on his 1954 Summer Expedition to the Arctic, and reported that "as a vessel approaches any coastal Eskimo village on the shores of Labrador, Greenland or the northern islands, the Eskimo dogs rend the air with a raucous music fit to herald Götterdämmerung."

Since then Labrador has experienced a "twilight of the dogs," for the traditional transportation for doctors, nurses, missionaries, trappers or explorers has largely been replaced by the snowmobile. Reluctant to let the legend of the stalwart sled dog dissipate in a cloud of blue smoke, citizens have formed the Kemutsik Association in Nain. Incentive for building up good dog teams to run in the annual Easter races from Davis Inlet to Nain is being provided in the form of cash awards for the top teams in the race.

A major limiting factor on how many sled dogs a man or a village or a

NORTH OF ETAH, Greenland, an Eskimo girl and her huskies greeted MacMillan's
1954 expedition. *Reinhard L. Korgen*

tribe can keep has always been food. Being omnivores, dogs are in direct competition with man for food. This common need may have brought them together in ancient times and may still work where the food supply is plentiful, but in some modern situations it can also keep them apart.

In much of the Arctic, according to Fred Bruemmer, "motor toboggans" are replacing the "faithful but voracious husky." On Southampton Island in Hudson Bay the 400 sled dogs at Coral Harbor eat 115,000 pounds of meat and 36,000 pounds of fat every year. Walrus and white whales have been readily available to the Eskimos there, so feeding the dogs has not been a great problem. Increasingly, however, in more densely populated areas where large bulk-food animals are now rare and where petroleum supplies from the south are easily obtained, it is not at all unusual to see one or two snowmobiles parked beside a native dwelling.

Farther north in Greenland, Bruemmer found that the sled dog still could support its master, and vice versa. The main settlement of the Polar Eskimo is at Kânak, across an arm of Greenland's awesome icecap. The Eskimos moved there in 1953, two years after the United States built its billion-dollar, noisy air base right across from their sod-house village. The district has 1,200 sled dogs, requiring 400,000 pounds of meat and 100,000 pounds of fat each year. The hunters have been able, so far, to provide plenty of meat and blubber for their people and enough for the dogs. There is extra food, too, for the extra dogs kept by the younger hunters who like to add to the optimum eight- to twelve-dog hitch and to drive a showy, super-team of sometimes twenty dogs.

The dog teams contribute to their keep in traditional ways. Cash for dog team work is also possible, for the Greenland government has worked out a schedule of charter rates for dog sled travel. Professionals working for the government, such as doctors and dentists, rely on dog teams to transport them to the isolated villages. For Bruemmer's four-day trip from Thule to Kânak (including Anaqaq Henson's return trip), his charges were tallied on an adding machine by an efficient young lady in the government office: ". . . so much per day per dog, so much for the sled, so much for crossing the ice cap . . . that will be $160."

The extra dogs for showy teams or sport racing indicate that day-to-day living is not as tight in these places as it once was. These dogs represent "disposable income"; they are not absolutely required for economic purposes. They can be assimilated into man's leisure time or used to enhance other aspects of his life.

There are probably as many sled dogs today in the great leisure activity of sport racing as there are used for a regular day's work. An outgrowth of this increasing interest in sled dogs as a form of recreation has led to the enhancement of another aspect of modern, high-quality life: that of education.

A good teacher understands that the best way to educate his students in broad concepts is with a series of specific activities to which the students can relate in a personal way. If, for example, a teacher of fifth and sixth grades is in a small rural school 25 miles from Fairbanks, Alaska, and the students go "sled dog crazy" during the racing season, what better way to teach social studies, mathematics, physics, biology, nutrition, English or physical education than with sled dogs?

"If a dog team in the Iditarod Trail Race can cover an average of fifty miles a day, how many days will it take to go the thousand miles from Anchorage to Nome?"

"How does the metabolism of both driver and dogs change with the extended exertion and exposure to intense cold, wind and sunlight? What kind of foods are best for such a trip?"

"Create an original play using a sled dog race or similar background for the dramatic interest."

This is the way Guy Blankenship approaches elementary education at the Two Rivers Elementary School. Another way he sparks interest in learning is by offering rides on his dog sled to students with perfect papers in spelling or math. During the 1973–74 school year, every one of the 54 students earned at least one ride. The enthusiasm of the children for sled dog racing is overwhelming. Their knowledge of dogs, equipment and racers is not unlike the expertise of youngsters in the lower 48 states in football or baseball. A bubble gum manufacturer might do quite well in Alaska with sled dog cards featuring the canine grins of Balto, Togo or Hotfoot.

Closer to Fairbanks, Mary Shields taught a sled dog course during the winter of 1974. Students received an hour of classroom instruction and three trail sessions. These latter were supposed to be one-hour outdoor laboratories, but always developed into all-day affairs, ending with coffee at the instructor's cabin. University of Alaska students could also sign up for a three-week course taught by Shields. This course ended with an overnight ski and dog sled trip.

Meanwhile, in the lower 48, where interest in sled dogs and racing can be just as high as in Alaska, twenty students at the University of Wisconsin at Three Rivers were learning sled dog racing for credit. Physical Education 107, "Outdoor Recreation for Wisconsin Winters," was taught by physical education instructor and wrestling coach Byron James during the winter quarter of 1972–73. Wisconsin winters are not quite so severe as Alaskan ones, but below-zero temperatures and an average snowfall of almost four feet makes winter a serious business there. Yet northerners

ON HIS FIRST BIRTHDAY, King Husky of Northeastern University received a huge post card from Boston University, a mat to lie on from Northeastern's Class of 1923, and, of all things, a meat pie.

Northeastern University

COMMUTING TO WORK, Alaskan-style. Teacher Guy Blankenship would rather mush than motor to the Two Rivers Elementary School north of Fairbanks.　*Guy Blankenship*

respond to the long, cold, dark winter by getting outside in the good weather and taking advantage of the snow and the cold. Training students to supervise outdoor winter recreation requires thoughtful attention, and courses about sled dogs are not easy-credit, cinch courses. James's course, stemming from his own interest in sled dog racing, covered in a practical and comprehensive way all aspects of the sport. In addition to learning how to select, train and care for sled dogs, and how to make and care for equipment, the students studied the history of sled dogs, the kinds of breeds used and the evolution of sled dog equipment. They were also taught how to prepare both themselves and the team for actual driving, and learned the rules and etiquette of driving in a race.

A sensitive student quite often found that he could learn more from an experienced team than from the professor, for veteran dogs can make dog driving look easy.

Also for college credit, but with a slightly different slant than Wisconsin's course, was a January term course at Hampshire College in Massachusetts. Called "Going with the Dogs," the course caused raised eyebrows among professors from the nearby, more traditional Amherst and Smith Colleges, who saw pictures in local newspapers of students building dog sleds. But Ray Coppinger, another avid sled dog racer, stressed comparative anatomy and behavior of the canine family (which includes wolves, coyotes and foxes). Students spent days in the field tracking New England's "mystery dog," a wild canine. Each student also drove a five-dog team in an organized race. One student was so enthralled by the entire experience that she kept hounding the professor after the course was over, drove in several more races, trained a team of her own, and finished in an impressive tenth place in the World Championship at Laconia, New Hampshire, in 1975.

Three other universities focus on the sled dog in a less academic way. The University of Connecticut, Boston's Northeastern University and the University of Washington in Seattle have all kept huskies as team mascots, calling their sport teams the "Huskies." Northeastern's first husky had quite a history.

King Husky I was born on St. Patrick's day, 1926, in Nome, the offspring of two of Leonhard Seppala's famous racing huskies. When Seppala came to New England in 1927 to race in Maine, he met Dr. Carl S. Ell, then vice president of the University, and presented him with the puppy.

It's a fairly soft life for husky mascots. They are kept as pets by a member of the school and the closest they come to wearing a harness is when they dress up in a dog blanket with the school's colors on it for a game. Connecticut's pure white husky used to go to the sled dog races in

New England, and if he was not thinking about the romance and adventure of the northern trail, his master must have been.

There are lots of other jobs for the sled dog in modern society. In Idaho, Robert Black drove a 21-dog team, stretched out some seventy feet, and had to devise a battery-powered radio system so the lead dog could hear his commands as they "marched" in local parades. This team of Samoyeds contributed to their keep by hauling passengers from the Sun Valley parking lot to skiing areas some distance away. Mrs. Black found another economic use for the dogs, one that was probably known by the Samoyed women of long ago, but nevertheless a novelty in twentieth-century America. Each spring Mrs. Black combed out the pure white Samoyeds, gathered the fine hair, washed and spun it. The resulting "Sammy wool" was an odorless, angora-like wool that could be crocheted or knit. The most popular item in the Black's pet shop was baby booties—soft, white and steeped in hundreds of years of arctic tradition.

Stuart Mace is a veteran dog driver who received nationwide television exposure in 1973 on *Bill Moyers' Journal*. He maintains a kennel of Malamutes and Siberian Huskies at his lodge near Aspen, Colorado. His statement about keeping the dogs and driving them through the humbling wilderness, about the sense of community the dogs bring and about man's need to mature in his relationship with natural things, evokes a philosophy to which many dog drivers would readily subscribe. Mace was a member of the Arctic Search and Rescue Unit during World War II and after the war helped to train and drive a dog team for a 1953 Hollywood production, *Those Redheads from Seattle*.

Other sled dogs and drivers have found a brief burst of fame in making films. Trapper Roger Mendelsohn's team has been filmed by British and French television crews and by Hollywood cameramen. An Italian version of Jack London's *White Fang* features dogs and drivers from The Pas, Manitoba. Several of 1975's best drivers and their teams appear in a feature film called *Hotfoot*. The story calls upon the special talents of men like George Attla, Harris Dunlap, Merv Hilpipre, Carl Huntington, Roland Lombard, Earl Norris and Joee Redington, as they search for the ultimate sled dog, the quintessential leader, companion, athlete—the wonder dog of the contemporary racing scene.

Many people keep sled dogs for almost purely aesthetic reasons. They like sled dogs, like working with them, enjoy the satisfaction of putting a team together, and appreciate the two-way responsibility that they share with the dogs. The primary reason for keeping sled dogs has little to do with economics and much to do with aesthetics and modern man's ability to cope with life's pressures. If a certain utility can be worked in with the pleasure, so much the better for both man and dog.

4

Racing the Sled Dogs

Long ago I ceased to wonder why so many of the teams I met along the main "dogways" of Alaska were either going to old Nome, or were outward bound from that famous iceport. Bleakly situated as it was, huddling along the narrow strip of auriferous sand from which it sprung almost overnight 36 years ago, Nome is more closely associated with sled dogs than any other community in the land. Seventeen thousand miles of dog mushing, along the gale-ridden coast and through the deathly cold stillness of interior Alaska forests, has led me into full agreement with its paraphrase, "All dog trails lead to Nome," for it has long been a focal point for the pattering feet of hundreds of busy huskies.

FRANK DUFRESNE, 1953

The people of New England have had a taste of the finest winter sport that any man can find anywhere, and I am sure they will stay with it.

ARTHUR WALDEN, 1922

WHO CAN SAY when the very first sled dog race occurred? Long, long ago, back on those ancient ice fields in Siberia, surely there must have been quick challenges between dog drivers. Such impromptu races must also have been held on the scientific expeditions in the Arctic, between mail teams in Canada or Alaska, outside Royal Canadian Mounted Police barracks, at Hudson's Bay Company settlements, and at lumber camps throughout the north woods. Even though these pick-up contests are not part of recorded history, there can be little doubt that a certain competition between men who drove dogs would have resulted in some friendly—or maybe not so friendly—sport.

National sports often take their shape from the conditions of the countryside and the character of the people who live there. Frequently the sport has direct roots in the workaday world. It was gold that brought thousands of dogs north to Alaska at the turn of the century and it was dogs that gold seekers depended on for their livelihood and often for their lives.

When the first gold stampede camp grew up around Dawson in Canada's Yukon in 1897–98, sled dogs began to assume their pervasive economic importance among white men. Unsuccessful Klondike prospectors had tended to drift, panning for gold as they went, down the Yukon River into Alaska. Many wound up in Nome, where, in 1899, gold was discovered on the beach between low and high tide marks. By June of 1900 some 10,000 gold seekers were in Nome, with another 25,000 expected during the summer. Good dogs to take prospectors into the surrounding tundra were scarce, and once obtained and trained, a good dog was a highly personal item. Hopes and tensions ran high in gold-rush Nome, and arguments developed over whose dogs were the strongest and the fastest. The best way to settle these disputes, of course, was by a race.

Out of these small races came the first organized sled dog race, the All-Alaska Sweepstakes, held in Nome in 1908. From Nome the new sport spread across Alaska, into Canada, then south to Idaho and California, and jumped across the continent to New England. By 1932 sled dog racing was sophisticated enough to merit a two-day international demonstration race at the Third Winter Olympic Games at Lake Placid, New York. Ten years later World War II brought a temporary halt to the sport of sled dog racing, but after the war it was taken up again with even greater excitement and refinement.

The All-Alaska Sweepstakes and How They Grew

Nome was so civilized by 1908 that it boasted a kennel club, the express purpose of which was to put on a big sled dog race. The winter is long and

"THE" WAY TO GET AROUND NOME IN 1900 ALASKA.   *Compliments of a friend*

The Great Dog Races of Nome

Held under the Auspices of the Nome Kennel Club, Nome, Alaska

Official Souvenir History

by Esther Birdsall Darling (PRESIDENT, 1916)

THE AUTOGRAPH OF THE MUSHER who dominated the All-Alaska Sweepstakes graces this cover of sled dog racing's first history.
Courtesy William L. Shearer, III

83

dark this close to the Arctic Circle, and the prospects of constructive outdoor activities are bleak. The idea of an important sled dog race perked up the isolated citizens. Many of them contributed time, money and energy in helping to prepare for the First All-Alaska Sweepstakes, scheduled for April. By April in Nome the length of daylight has doubled from seven hours in mid-winter to over 14 hours. Winter's back is broken and it is time for some serious revelry.

The rules governing this first organized race were slowly hammered out by Nome Kennel Club officials, with plenty of input from local dog drivers. The final course was designated out of Nome along a telephone line to Candle, a small gold-rush town 204 miles to the northeast. On reaching Candle, the teams were to be inspected by officials, and only then could they resume the race back across the Seward Peninsula to Nome. This race was a "go-as-you-please" race, which meant that the drivers could stop whenever they liked to rest, feed or otherwise care for their dogs. Stops would mean loss of valuable time, however, since the winner would be whoever got back to Nome in the least amount of time. Therefore, any stops were carefully considered by the drivers so as to provide needed rest at the right times.

With thousands of dollars in prize money offered, excitement about the race was rampant, and drivers planning to enter were wise to begin training both themselves and their dogs months in advance. Physical exercise and special diets became major topics of conversation.

Most of the rules finally agreed upon for the All-Alaska Sweepstakes are still in use today, which attests to the knowledge and thought put into them. The number of dogs on a team was optional with the driver. Since a team can run only as fast as its slowest dog, a small team of fast dogs might seem advantageous. Over a trail as long as the Nome-Candle run, however, fewer dogs would have less endurance and therefore less total speed over the distance. On the other hand, too many dogs would increase the chances of trouble. Most Sweepstakes drivers harnessed between ten and twenty dogs. No matter how many dogs a driver started out with, he had to return with all the same ones: he could not drop or add any dogs along the trail. If a dog became exhausted or lame, he had to be carried on the sled for the rest of the race. This was standard practice for dog-punchers and a rule for maintaining the quality of sled dog races.

Cruelty was absolutely forbidden and a violator would not only be disqualified but would forfeit his dog team. Experienced mushers realized, of course, that in order to depend on their dogs over long trails they could not afford to be cruel or to debilitate any of them. With top team dogs commanding prices of hundreds of dollars, it would have been no less than foolhardy for a driver to punish or force his dogs.

"Gone to the Dogs" read the signs in Nome as schools and most businesses closed for the start of the All-Alaska Sweepstakes. People crowded into the narrow streets, many wearing the colors of their favorite team. "Inside information" and "straight tips" were eagerly sought and dispensed. Those with a little information or a little money backed certain teams with judiciously-placed bets. A Queen and her court, wrapped in furs, added to the glamour; they were driven in dog sleds, as ceremoniously as possible, to the judges' stand.

The noise of the dogs was deafening as they barked incessantly, reflecting the excitement around them, and more than ready for the trail. The drivers busied themselves nervously around their teams, checking again the harnesses, the lines, the long sleds. Food for men and dogs had been distributed at the relay stations along the route, so sleds were loaded with only those necessities for the trail: boots and covering skins for the dogs, a windbreaker and water boots for the driver, and perhaps a small packet of food in case of emergency.

When the Queen let fall the starting flag, the first team became suddenly silent and charged out of the starting chute. All business now, they raced down Front Street across from Barrack Square and headed out of town. The course skirted out along the ice fields of Norton Sound, following the coastline east to Safety and Dickson, where it headed inland. The trail featured the "best" of Alaska terrain: towering ice hummocks along Norton Sound; plains of unbroken, soft snow; steep slopes up Topkok Hill and down the other side; desolate, storm-swept, icy wastes; pleasant, protected, winding wooded trails; glacier-cold rivers and lakes.

The first driver out that early April morning in 1908 was Paul Kjegstad, owner of the team he drove. Nine other teams followed him at two-hour intervals. One of the most popular teams was that of Scotty Allan, noted Nome kennel operator, driving a team for Jacob Berger.

Five days later the first teams began arriving back in Nome, and although the thrilled townspeople had a pretty good idea of who was ahead, thanks to the telephone stations along the trail, not until all the teams were in was the official announcement made.

The winner of that first race: John Hegness, driving a team owned by the president of the Nome Kennel Club, Albert Fink. His elapsed time for the 408-mile trip: 119 hours, 15 minutes, 12 seconds. Scotty Allan with Berger's team placed second with an elapsed time only 52 minutes, 40 seconds behind Hegness. Considering the total time of the race, that was a close finish. Allan had run the race at an average speed, including rests, of 3.40 miles an hour, Hegness at 3.42.

The dog drivers were hooked on racing. So was Nome, the rest of Alaska, and a large segment of the Outside. As Scotty Allan and the other race organizers had planned, the All-Alaska Sweepstakes proved to be a valuable measurement of and an incentive for improvements in the care, breeding, training and racing of sled dogs. Lessons learned during the running of the first races provided information which clarified and enhanced the running of the next races. Later, the Nome Kennel Club rules became the basis of regulations for sled dog clubs around the world.

In 1909 the Second All-Alaska Sweepstakes race attracted 13 entries. Not only did Scotty Allan race to a record victory at an average speed of five miles an hour, but another extremely significant event occurred.

Nome's finest dog drivers, all set to race for the $10,000 first prize, were only slightly disturbed at the news that a team of "veritable wind-splitters," some huskies from Siberia, might show up to challenge the predominantly mongrel Alaskan teams. Ed Johnston, a Nome fur trader, had recently returned from a sojourn in eastern Siberia and told about a team of huskies which had averaged nine miles an hour for eleven straight hours across the Anadyr delta. When William Goosak, a Russian fur trader, arrived in Nome with some ten of these little sled dogs, the Alaskans were not too impressed. The new dogs were, to be sure, more beautiful than most Alaskan working dogs, but they were much smaller and lighter than the big, powerful freighting dogs of Alaska. "Fuzzy-wuzzy lap dogs," the Alaskans assured each other. The drivers doubted that the husky from Siberia could last the trail at any significant speed.

Goosak trained his dogs around Nome for several months prior to the Second All-Alaska Sweepstakes, and enlisted as driver a Norwegian immigrant, Louis Thrustrup, who knew Alaskan trail conditions.

At noon on Thursday, April 1, 1909, Percy Blatchford, third-place finisher the year before, drove his team of nine dogs out of the chute, down Front Street, off toward Candle. A 35-mile-an-hour snowstorm swirled around dogs, drivers and spectators, but at fifteen-minute intervals 12 other teams disappeared after Blatchford. The last team out was Goosak's Siberian team, a long shot to win.

By noon on April 2 the storm had let up and the Siberians were found to be some thirty minutes ahead of the other teams. On the outward trail to Candle they averaged close to 5½ miles an hour, with Thrustrup resting them only rarely. By the third day their pace had slowed to under four miles an hour, as Thrustrup finally stopped for a four-hour rest. During the fourth day he rode first one dog and then another on the sled in order to give each a reprieve.

·Scotty Allan, consistent and careful, took the race. Driving again for Berger, Allan improved his previous year's time by nearly two days, and won the first prize of $10,000 and a tall trophy. Blatchford mushed in only 16 minutes in elapsed time behind Allan. The Siberian team arrived

WINNERS OF THE FIRST MAJOR SLED DOG RACE, the All-Alaska Sweepstakes, in 1908. Albert Fink's team of freighting dogs was driven by John Hegness. *The Great Dog Races of Nome*

THE SECOND TEAM OF SIBERIAN HUSKIES TO RACE IN ALASKA. John Johnson mushed to victory in the Third Sweepstakes (1910) with Fox Maule Ramsay's imported, crisp-looking, dog team. *The Great Dog Races of Nome*

SCOTTY ALLAN'S WINNING TEAM IN THE FOURTH SWEEPSTAKES in 1911. The dogs were owned by the Allan and Darling Kennels and worked as a freighting team. On left point (third dog from the left) is the famous Baldy of Nome. *The Great Dog Races of Nome*

in third place, at nine o'clock on Monday morning, after 89 hours, 46 minutes, 15 seconds on the trail—only 7 hours, 44 minutes longer than Allan. The little dogs, still alert and excited, sought out friends among the spectators.

Goosak, however, was in trouble. He had been counting on first-prize money to get himself and his family back to the Anadyr district. With only $1,000 in winnings, he was short of funds. When Captain Charles Madsen of the schooner *Mary Sachs* offered to buy Goosak's wonder dogs, Goosak proposed instead that Madsen take the team, harnesses and sled in trade for transportation back home. Madsen accepted.

Thus the first Siberian sled dogs came to North America. But these were not the only ones. Later in 1909 the Honorable Fox Maule Ramsay, a nobleman from Scotland, engaged in mining in the Nome area, went to Markovo on the Anadyr River and bought perhaps sixty of the speedy huskies. In 1929 Olaf Swenson imported seven more Siberian dogs. None of these were purebreds in an American Kennel Club sense but rather they represented the fastest and hardiest of a natural breed of Siberian working dogs, a thick-coated, prick-eared, tough-footed, swift little foxy-looking dog. Several of these huskies are the ancestors of the original purebred Siberian Huskies that were developed in Alaska and New England, and are still influencing the sport of sled dog racing all over the world.

Fox Ramsay divided his Siberians into three teams for the 1910 All-Alaska Sweepstakes. Only Scotty Allan, driving his own crossbred freighting team, was able to prevent Ramsay's teams from sweeping the race. Allan took third, his record run of the year before having been shattered by Ramsay's "third" team, which consisted of Siberians that had not made the first two teams. Driving for Ramsay was John "Iron Man" Johnson, his own blue-eyed Siberian leader Kolyma out front. His time of 74 hours, 14 minutes, 37 seconds set a new record for the course, a record that has yet to be bettered.

In the Seventh All-Alaska Sweepstakes in 1914 another portentous event for sled dog racing occurred. Young Leonhard Seppala appeared on the racing scene. He finished last that year but enjoyed the race so much that he made the decision that was to have an influence on the rest of his life and on the lives of hundreds of others as well. He put together a team of Siberians, and his talents with these dogs led him to solid victories in the final three Sweepstakes races. This placed Seppala beside Scotty Allan as the only other triple winner of that first, classic series of sled dog races.

The entry of the United States into World War I in 1917 caused Nome citizens to focus on more pressing matters. The Tenth All-Alaska

Sweepstakes that year marked the end of the first decade of organized sled dog racing.

During the years of the great dog races of Nome there were several other races held nearby. The Fort Davis races were short, from Nome to the Fort Davis bridge and back, 6⅓ miles. These races were of frequent occurrence and offered much diversion due to the number and varied qualifications of those who entered. The course, through the crowded streets of Nome to the unobstructed trail to the bridge, demanded navigational skill of both dogs and drivers. The Nome Kennel Club also sponsored an Annual High School Race over the same course, and a Ladies' Race.

Two other significant races were the Boschen Cup Race and the "Joy Race." This latter was a celebration of the coming spring and the break-up of the ice. The course covered 75 miles from Nome to Council, via Solomon, and was known officially as the Kamoogen Handicap Burden Race. A prospective driver, experienced or not, used any team in Nome that he could legally acquire, and on his sled he carried a burden, the fair lady of his choice. Time was of little importance in this race; amusement provided most of the incentive. At Solomon and then at Council the drivers were welcomed as heroes, and they stopped over for as long as they could to imbibe in the joyful hospitality.

The Solomon Derby, second in importance only to the Sweepstakes, was held in February and served as a preparatory race for the Sweepstakes. The course was 65 miles, from Nome to Solomon and back. Being relatively short, this trail provided a good measure of the speeds of the racing teams. Charles Johnson, who had finished fourth with Ramsay's new Siberians in the Third Sweepstakes, raced a perfect trail in 1912 at the then-incredible speed of 11.2 miles an hour. Nome drivers waited four years until trail conditions were again ideal, and then Johnson's record was broken twice. Fred Ayer, with a team of so-called Alaskans (these were Foxhound and Malamute strains) averaged 11.7 miles an hour. His dogs were then dubbed the "Ayeroplanes." William Webb chased Johnson in at 11.3 miles an hour.

Far up the Yukon River, to the east of Nome, the enterprising town of Ruby had also developed a kennel club. They sent a cordial invitation to Nome in 1916 to enter a team in their annual Ruby Dog Derby. The invitation was accepted, to Nome's great pleasure, by Leonhard Seppala. In order to compete, Seppala had to drive his team the 450 miles to Ruby, traveling over much of the same trail that he and other mushers would drive almost ten years later with diphtheria antitoxin.

The course of the Ruby Derby was steep and rough, 58 miles from Ruby to Long City and back. Joe Jean's 1913 record was the pride of local

SCOTTY ALLAN INTRODUCED RESORT GUESTS to sled dogs
in Soda Springs, California, in the 1920's.   *From an old post card*

NOBODY WORKED OR WENT TO SCHOOL in Nome at the finish of the Sweepstakes races. Beneath an array of international flags, Norwegian Leonhard
Seppala brought his Siberian Huskies in first in the 1916 race.

The Great Dog Races of Nome

fans, and not many thought that Seppala could beat it. With four other teams the "Hardy Norseman" set out, and five hours, 26 minutes, 18 seconds later he was back. Over eight minutes had been subtracted from Jean's record as Seppala's Siberians ran the tough route at better than ten miles an hour. The people of Ruby gave the out-of-towner a tremendous ovation as he crossed the finish line.

By 1917, these early races had firmly established the sport in Alaska. During the next decade no big races were held, but the dramatic and highly publicized serum run by dog sled did a lot to call Alaska and the value of sled dogs to world attention. Drivers began working with the imported husky from Siberia, breeding for a hardy dog with even greater speed, but keeping a reasonable eye also on hair coat, color and conformation. From the early fun or grudge races a whole new sport had developed, a sport with high standards built in from years of experience with the working teams.

The high regard of Alaskans for sled dogs and dog racing in those early days was probably best expressed by a Nome judge, originally from Kentucky bluegrass country. He was presiding over the trial of a sled dog accused by an irate resident of killing a sheep. When the jury found the dog innocent, the judge was called upon to explain the verdict.

"In Nome," he stated solemnly, "sheep must look out for themselves. This aims to be dog country."

The next series of officially recorded sled dog races in Alaska began in 1927 in Fairbanks. This future "Sled Dog Racing Capital of the World" began three series of races in the late 1920's. These were the Signal Corps Trophy Race, the H. Wendell Endicott Trophy Race and the Fromm Trophy Race, this last one for women only.

The Signal Corps race, whose trophy was placed in competition in 1927 by the Washington-Alaska Military Cable and Telegraph System, required that a racer win three times before he could maintain permanent possession of the trophy. Great skill and endurance were needed to successfully complete the course, a 58-mile trail from Fairbanks to Summit and back which included a rise in altitude of over 1800 feet. The Endicott Race, by comparison, was a sprint race. Speed counted more than endurance for this 17¼-mile trail.

Three native dog drivers dominated these races from 1928 to 1930. Joe and Fred Stickman of Nulato were one of the great racing brother combinations in sled dog racing history. Joe's win in 1928 was accomplished with a completely stiff, broken knee. The racing exploits of the Stickmans and of Walter Nollner of Galena are still remembered, with great respect, by modern mushers.

A change in emphasis took place in sled dog racing during these years.

The men who had been working with Alaskan dogs and Siberian huskies were concentrating on small, fast dogs, making improvements in breeding and feeding programs and working out training procedures for teams of racing dogs. The well-known kennels of men like Judge Cecil H. Clegg, Thomas B. Wright and District Attorney Julian H. Hurley produced the best teams they could and hired drivers for the races. Races became shorter and faster, reflecting perhaps the pace of the post-war world. The strong growth of sled dog racing in the early thirties was largely due to the time, money and devotion spent by these kennel owners and the drivers, not only in Alaska but Outside.

The manifestation of the success of the breeders and racers was the change from marathon races—the long-distance affairs like the All-Alaska Sweepstakes—to shorter "heat" races, like the Signal Corps Race. The new concept included shorter courses run for two or three successive days, with the total time for each driver determining the winner. This system has been perfected over the years and is today standard in all but a few races. One attraction of this method is that trophies or prize money can be distributed to the winner or the top three finishers of each day's heat, thereby heightening the excitement of each daily race.

The new system lent itself well to the talents and team of young Bob Busby. The Endicott Race was shortened in 1931 to 16 miles and the Signal Corps Race was changed to two thirty-mile heats. In 1933 Busby made a clean sweep of both races. By 1935 he had won the Signal Corps trophy three times in a row, and the trophy was retired, after having been passed around during nine years of competition. The Endicott races ended in 1933, probably due to greater interest in the Signal Corps races.

Organized racing continued in Fairbanks, with a new three-day, ninety-mile Sweepstakes. From the lower Yukon River came an Indian named Johnny Allen. He had racing experience in the Ruby Derbies under his belt and had been crossbreeding Irish Setters with native dogs for a strain of fast, uniform racers. His success can be measured in terms of his record: he won the Fairbanks Sweepstakes in 1936, 1937 and 1938, another triple winner. In 1939 Bergman Kokrine ran all three thirty-mile heats, did not win any of them, but ran such a consistent race that his total elapsed time of 9 hours, 2 seconds, was less than anyone else's, and he won the race. Kokrine and his brother Andy were another brother combination, top contenders around Fairbanks in the 1930's.

In 1940 and 1941 the races took a nostalgic return to the marathon classics of Nome. A course was laid out over a mountainous route to Livengood, 80 miles north of Fairbanks. This Livengood Sweepstakes provided for a ten-hour stop at Livengood before the mushers were allowed to return to Fairbanks. Bergman Kokrine won the race in 1940,

Jake Butler in 1941. Today the old course is lined with a different kind of excitement: the Trans-Alaska Pipeline.

The third series of races begun in Fairbanks in the late twenties, the Fromm Trophy Ladies' Race, lasted through 1934. The course was the same as for the Endicott Race. A sister combination, Genevieve and Hortense Parker of Fairbanks, dominated the early years of the race with their Siberian Huskies. When Hortense won it the first time, it was her first race, and she was all of 14 years old. A mother and daughter competition in 1931 kept the town buzzing: Irene Coulombe won, racing over the finish line ahead of her mother, who came in third.

These women's races ended a year after the Endicott Races, in 1934, but Fairbanks was to be the scene, almost twenty years later, of the start of another series of women's sled dog races, the famed Women's North American Championship.

Down in Anchorage, the future World Championship Fur Rendezvous Sled Dog Race was starting out on wobbly puppy legs. What is now one of the largest and most prestigious of sled dog races began in 1936 with a one-dog race for the children.

Anchorage's commercial ventures of trade and tourism were melded with the native custom of "potlatch," or festivities, and by 1937 the Fur Rendezvous celebration in the middle of February was a major attraction. In addition to the popular public auctions of furs, buyers from all over the world were treated to three days of sports and spectacle. Competitions in skiing, hockey, skating, boxing and basketball were interwoven with visions of the Fur Rendezvous Queen, a high school band concert, a fur fashion show, a torchlight parade and fireworks.

In 1941 the U.S. Army's Fourth Infantry Band from the newly-constructed Fort Richardson led the "Rondy" parade, and then World War II brought sled dog racing skidding to a halt in Alaska. The mushers enlisted and the dogs stayed behind. Some drivers and teams were able to contribute to the war effort, training soldiers for arctic survival and training themselves for search and rescue operations. The Alaskan Territorial Guard and the Cold Weather Test Units also used dog teams to help get their jobs done. Racing was not forgotten, just postponed for the duration.

Sled dogging in the Lower Forty-eight

Nineteen-seventeen was the last year the All-Alaska Sweepstakes were held in Nome, but it was the first year of organized sled dog racing in the lower 48 states. Out West, in Ashton, Idaho, where a few people kept dog teams for winter transportation or for hauling the U.S. mail, a barbershop proprietor regaled his customers with compelling tales of Scotty Allan's racing exploits. Tud Kent and George Zarn listened to Jay Ball with increasing interest, and plans for the first sled dog race took shape. Gus Isenberg was drawn in, and the four men organized the first sled dog club in the lower United States, the American Dog Mushers' Association.

Sled dog racers always hope for good snow for their competitions, but in the case of this first lower 48 event, they were overwhelmed. On March 4, 1917, a blizzard accompanied the five hardy entrants in the American Dog Derby, and they had to break trail along the 55 miles from West Yellowstone, Montana, to Ashton. Tud Kent won that race at the underwhelming speed of 1.88 miles an hour.

The men of Ashton may have been cold and wet but they were not discouraged. The American Dog Derby was run annually until 1948, with the exception of the war years, and the year 1920, when there was absolutely no snow.

In 1921, there was plenty of snow, and thanks to someone's terrific promotional coup, 10,000 spectators were brought in by the Union Pacific Railroad to see the race. The young Fox and Pathé film companies were there to film six dog teams as they tore three times around an 8⅓-mile track. This use of a track for a sled dog race was a big departure from Alaskan practice, but the sponsors and spectators wanted to see the whole race. Sled dogs, bred for the open trail, have strong ideas about repeating a course they have already run once that day. That the Ashton races were run so successfully for so long on a circular race track, complete with bleachers for the spectators and a platform for officials and the press, indicates that the American Dog Derbies had an atmosphere and a philosophy unlike any other sled dog races before or since.

The secret of Ashton's success lies in the kinds of dogs being raced. Tud Kent, seven-time winner, drove a team of bird dogs. In 1919 he won with five English Setters, and by 1925 his team was made up of a Belgian Shepherd-Gordon Setter-Staghound cross, two Irish-Llewellyn Setter crosses, and four Targhee Hounds. A Targhee Hound, named for the Targhee Mountains near where they were bred, is a cross between an Irish Setter and a Staghound and has been popular in the West for years.

Even though Shorty Russick arrived in Ashton with a team of husky-hound hybrids in 1924, the "Dog" in American Dog Derby referred more to English, Irish, Gordon and Llewellyn Setters, Wolfhounds, Targhee Hounds, Belgian Police Dogs, Foxhounds and Labrador Retrievers than to any northern breed. The 1930 race featured a first prize of $1,000 and it was won by Earl Kimball and his seven Irish Setters, beating Delbert Groom's eight huskies by 48 seconds.

Huskies may have been down, but they were not completely out. Delbert Groom and Scotty Allan's son George drove huskies to second and seventh place finishes, respectively, in 1920. The success of the setters, hounds and retrievers was perhaps partly due to the length of the course. A mere 25 miles, and around a circular track to boot, might be construed as somewhat beneath the dignity of the trail-wise northern dog. Idaho mushers found that their sporting dogs were first-class sprinters, which gave them an advantage in the shorter races. By today's standards it does not seem very fast, but in 1935 Don Cordingly's seven lanky red setters wound around the 25 miles at better than 13 miles an hour. This was a record time for the American Dog Derby.

The early professional drivers from Ashton were joined by other newly-inspired dog mushers and the West had its first racing circuit. Friendly rivalries developed, and it was a proud day for Tud Kent at Soda Springs when he won over the man who had sparked his interest in sled dogs in the first place, Scotty Allan.

During those years Kent and the other drivers found outlets for their dog-driving addiction in races at McCall, Idaho; Red Lodge, Montana; Jackson, Wyoming; Ogden, Utah; and Truckee, California. The Truckee race course was arranged to be visible from many good vantage points, and a popular weekend activity for the people of San Francisco and Sacramento was to take the train up into the Sierra Nevada Mountains to Truckee to watch the sled dog races. Jack London even went up once. Truckee also had four moving picture companies filming there on permanent sets. Before the advent of sound, many a sled dog picture was made at Truckee. A team of dogs rented for $110 a day.

In the late 1930's and into the 1940's watching the mushers lost some of its fascination to schussing down a mountain, as skiing rapidly grew into the nation's favorite outdoor winter sport.

After World War II the American Dog Mushers' Association sponsored two more derbies in Ashton, in 1946 and 1948. The last race, around a ten-mile course shaped like an "E," earned Lloyd Van Sickle $1,000 for his first place finish—with a team of hounds.

If early dog driving in New England resembled dog-punching on the Yukon, there was good reason. The team of half-bred St. Bernards which appeared in New Hampshire around 1909 belonged to Arthur T. Walden, and team and driver had come straight from the gold fields of Alaska. Walden, a native of New Hampshire, had spent his late twenties and early thirties as a freight driver in Alaska, then went back east with his working team to become the sled dog's most enthusiastic promoter.

Walden also had a litter of pups born of a mongrel father and an Eskimo husky mother, a leader from Admiral Peary's polar expedition. These pups became the basis of Walden's own well-known breed of sled

SIX HUSKIES pulled Leonhard Seppala to victory in the 1929 Eastern International Dog-sled Derby in Quebec.   *Courtesy Cascadian Kennels*

LEONHARD SEPPALA IN NEW ENGLAND, 1926, with his earliest models of the now-classic Siberian Husky.   *Courtesy New England Sled Dog Club*

dog, the Chinook. These broad-headed, flop-eared yellow dogs appeared in exhibitions of what a dog team could do, capturing imaginations throughout the Northeast. The leader, named Chinook, was not only a willing canine ambassador for the world of sled dogs, but he led Walden's team in many of the early races in New England and Canada. He was also the subject of a children's textbook, used in many schools.

By Alaskan standards, New Hampshire's first official sled dog race may have been modest (in 1921, two three-dog teams raced six miles from Berlin to Gorham) but the second, in 1922, evoked Alaskan tradition in good style. W.R. Brown of the Brown Paper Corporation in Berlin, inspired by Arthur Walden, sponsored the first Eastern International Dog-Sled Derby. This race was also a "point-to-point" race, but the trail from Berlin to Colebrook, through Dixville Notch at an elevation of almost 2,000 feet, was a respectable 123 miles and it took three days to complete. Arthur Walden hitched nine dogs single file, with Chinook on lead, and won. Newspapers from Boston and New York covered the race, and Walden, Chinook and sled dog racing gained wide popularity.

People from all over the region were so captivated by these novel and romantic events that impetus grew for the formation of a sled dog club that would promote the sport and put on some races. Walden, backed by Boston businessman and gentleman sled-dogger Walter Channing, hosted a meeting of the most enthusiastic would-be mushers. The result was the New England Sled Dog Club, its original constitution and by-laws adopted on November 5, 1924, and now the oldest sled dog club in continuous existence. Walden was elected the first president, aided by six vice-presidents who represented each of the six New England states. Sixty charter members launched the New England club; by 1975 there were over 400 paid-up members.

"Green dogs and green drivers" were the entrants in the new club's first two races in 1925. Seven novice teams competed in Newport and in Meredith, New Hampshire, and this exotic sport was on its way.

Sled dog racing in New England received a tremendous boost when, in 1927, the already-legendary Leonhard Seppala arrived from Alaska with his famous serum-run team. He stayed at the Waldens' Wonalancet Farm Inn, where Walden had been driving dogs for the pleasure of his guests and teaching New Englanders the intricacies of the dog team. Walden was New England's champion, winner of the first Eastern International in 1922, the Poland Spring, Maine, race in 1926, and the first person to undertake the inevitable stunt of driving a dog team up treacherous Mt. Washington in the middle of winter. Seppala was just as eager as Walden and the rest of New England for a race between the two giants.

Walden had left Alaska just as the first Siberian huskies were being

97

imported, and was no doubt as amused as the Alaskans had been at the initial sight of the small, light, furry dogs. Seppala did little to dispel his amusement and even held his team back during training runs at Wonalancet. His eyes were fixed on the upcoming race at Poland Spring.

The two 25-mile heats were run on January 25 and 26, 1927, and they started badly for Seppala. "It seemed that this first race in New England was destined to be a series of hard luck incidents for me. At the word 'go,' my dogs, instead of taking off down the race course, bolted over a stone wall on the way. While I was getting the dogs in line again, I overheard remarks from the crowd to the effect that I didn't know how to handle dogs and that my little Siberians had no chance at all with the big local sled dogs."

About ten miles out on the trail Seppala passed the team of young Elizabeth Ricker, wife of the owner of the Poland Spring Hotel. She lost her team as they bolted after Seppala and her sled overturned. Quickly establishing priorities, Seppala stopped his dogs, caught the other team, and restored his future kennel partner to her sled. In spite of this diversion, Seppala finished the race seven minutes ahead of the disbelieving Arthur Walden.

Suddenly the wiry Norwegian and his "cute" Siberians were the subjects of unabashed awe and admiration. New Englanders wanted to drive these beautiful sled dogs, and Seppala was soon in the kennel business. Most of the forty-odd dogs that Seppala had brought to New England stayed with Elizabeth Ricker at the Poland Spring kennel. Other dogs went to the St. Jovite, Quebec, kennel of Harry Wheeler, and some individual animals were sold to new sport racers to found their teams.

Arthur Walden, 57 years old in 1928 but after adventure once more, sold a partnership in his Chinook Kennels to Milton and Eva Seeley and went to Antarctica as chief dog handler for Admiral Byrd. The Seeleys were instrumental in breeding a true Siberian Husky, recognized by the American Kennel Club. Their first bitch came from Seppala's stock. Even now, almost fifty years later, Siberian Husky dog teams all over the world can trace their lineage back to the Seppala dogs.

New England dog drivers quickly embraced Seppala's philosophy of improving the racing abilities of the Siberian as well as breeding for the striking physical appearance of the dog. Club races would measure their success and provide weekends of continuing discussions, theories and counter-theories, about how best to breed that ultimate sled dog. Throughout the late 1920's, 1930's and into the 1940's the New England Sled Dog Club's winter race schedules were full. Traditionally, the first race was held near New Year's Day at Tamworth, New Hampshire, beginning and ending on picturesque Lake Chocorua. A regular nucleus of

MRS. ELIZABETH RICKER (NOW MRS. ELIZABETH NANSEN OF OTTAWA) with her lead dog, in the late 1920's.

Courtesy William L. Shearer, III

serious sled dog drivers loaded their small teams (rarely over eight or ten dogs) into modified pick-up trucks, trailers, or even the family beach wagon, and every weekend drove to another race. They traveled to New Hampshire towns like Wonalancet, Tilton, Sandwich, Peterborough, Jaffrey, Newport, Meredith or Exeter, and sometimes to Chester, Vermont, for a Saturday and Sunday afternoon of racing their huskies. They were a close-knit group, putting on colorful races for sponsoring towns, enjoying the friendly competition.

Ruling over the management of the races, responsible for everything from the layout of the trail to announcing the finishing times, was New England's personification of the race manager, Kenneth "Stubby" Saxton of Greenfield, Massachusetts. From 1939 until well into the 1970's this jovial, authoritative gentleman set the style for race managers everywhere. His big voice, still booming at drivers and spectators during Laconia's World Championship, kept the early New England teams running on schedule.

With the exception of the "point-to-point" races of 1926 through 1928, no cash prizes were offered by the club until 1964. A "Treasure-Trail Race" in 1938 did tantalize nine teams with one-dollar tags tied at one-mile intervals along a trail, but the total purse for winner John Piscopo of Laconia was seven dollars.

Other diversionary events cooked up in New England included a 220-mile race from Berlin to Boston (1929) and another winter trip up Mt. Washington (1932). The Berlin to Boston run, as long as some of the Alaska races but requiring overnight stops in selected towns along the way, alternated from bare roads to a below-zero, biting snowstorm. Not all six teams finished, but one that did was the Eskimo dog team of Mrs. E.P. (Florence) Clark. Mrs. Clark also decided to be the first woman to drive a dog team up New Hampshire's 6,300-foot Mt. Washington. The weather for her journey was not officially designated as a blizzard, but the wind blew 100 miles an hour, nearly lifting her eight-dog team off their feet. Near the top, some confusion arose as to the right way to go. The leader, Clarkso, in fine lead dog tradition, won the ensuing debate by taking over and bringing them all out at the Summit House.

When Arthur Walden began promoting sled dog racing in New England in 1909, could he possibly have envisioned the scene in Laconia early in February of 1938? For Laconia, New Hampshire, confidently standing up to Alaska by calling itself "The Sled Dog Capital of the World," was overwhelmed by the number of dogs descending on the town for the third running of its World Championship Sled Dog Derby. According to a news release: "Laconia is literally in the dog house looking for housing accommodations for 500 sled dogs. Earl Stanyan, chairman of the dog housing committee for the international sled dog derby at Laconia on February 4–6, has issued a call for offers of comfortable barns, sheds or other shelters, declaring the tremendous increase in the number of dogs expected at the meet this year has created an acute dog housing shortage."

Laconia's World Championship continues to attract hundreds of dogs and thousands of spectators, but it was not always so. The first sled dog race there was held in 1922, just to see what it was like. Five years elapsed until the next race, but by 1928 the town was ready for its "third annual" race, sponsored by the New England Sled Dog Club. The course that year was formidable, covering 57 miles the first day, 34 the second and 43 the third. The victor: Leonhard Seppala.

The 1929 race bears noting more for the third-place finisher, although the top two, Seppala and Canada's champion Emile St. Godard, were exciting enough to watch. In third, and winning the handicap prize, was 19-year-old Roland Lombard, destined to leave a lasting impression on sled dog racing.

Meanwhile, a group of Laconians got together to see what they could do about local organization and promotion of the annual major sled dog race. Alex Belford, Charles Lyman, Edward Lydiard and Arthur O'Shea formed the Laconia Sled Dog Club and took over the sponsorship of the contest. Substantial cash prizes attracted teams from all over New England and Canada, and the Laconia race rapidly became the most popular sled dog event in the East. Its stature prompted its new billing in 1936 as the World Championship Sled Dog Derby, and a $500 silver bowl was added to the cash prizes. As is traditional, the huge trophy required three wins before permanent possession was awarded. Not until 1963 was this accomplished.

The first series of World Championships ended in 1938, thanks mainly to warm weather and rain. The race was called off after one day's run on a course fraught with bare roads, sand and slick icy patches. World War II was long over before Laconia re-established its prestigious series of sled dog derbies.

Although the sport was suspended during the war years, New Englanders, like Alaskans, found ways to keep their dogs active. Demonstrations and exhibitions helped with the home war effort. In 1942 the New England club sponsored a wheeled rig race, with the dog teams pulling their training carts for the benefit of the "Bundles for Britain" program. Many New England mushers went to war with their dogs, contributing their unique talents to the special sled dog unit commanded by Colonel Norman Vaughan of Hamilton, Massachusetts. A roster of some of the men attached to this unit reads like a list of entrants in a New England Sled

Dog Club who's who: Ed Moody, Dick Moulton, and Vaughan himself had driven dogs for Admiral Byrd, and with them were Bill Belletete, Tat Duval, Don Shaw and Bill Shearer, all known as sport racers on the New England trails.

The mud season encountered by the unit overseas did not deter them. A V-letter home from three of the musher-soldiers told how they maintained their teams: "The New England Sled Dog Club is now holding Spring Training in western France," they wrote. "The early morning dew makes excellent snow conditions!"

The first sled dog race in the lower 48 at Ashton, Idaho, had been blessed with more and deeper snow than anyone really wanted. Fifteen years later, with athletes from all over the world gathered for the 1932 Winter Olympics at Lake Placid, New York, unseasonable rains had melted all signs of snow. The resort area's landscape ranged from dull gray to brown.

Among those bemoaning the situation were a dozen dog drivers. A sled dog race had been allowed by the International Olympic Committee as a demonstration sport to be staged by the host country. Entries for the race included winners of championship races, five drivers from Canada, seven from the United States. Leonhard Seppala and his colleague, Harry Wheeler, from the Gray Rocks Inn in Quebec were there; so were Shorty Russick, Emile St. Godard and Earl Brydges, Canadians who had been giving New Englanders a lot of good competition during the regular racing seasons.

The New England Sled Dog Club had twenty teams at their Olympic tryouts at Wonalancet. In order to qualify, a member needed a top racing record in club events. Weather forced postponements but finally the 25-mile race was run. Official representatives at the Olympics would be the Chinook Kennels first team, driven by Norman Vaughan, and Moseley Taylor's first team, driven by another antarctic veteran, Roger Haines. Young Dick Moulton, a future champion, wanted to drive the Chinook Kennels team, but was ruled ineligible due to his job as trainer-handler for the Seeleys. The distinction between amateur and professional for this race seems to have been liberally interpreted, for although Moulton was ineligible, veteran professional drivers Seppala, St. Godard, Russick and Brydges could run.

Lake Placid had been the scene of sled dog races annually since 1928, races which were dominated by Leonhard Seppala's first-class Siberian Husky dog team. For the Olympics a new 25-mile trail was put in, to be run in two heats. February 6 and 7 were the designated days for the race, but on January 20 few of the 307 athletes from 17 nations thought that the Games could even be held. The Northeast's infamous "January thaw" had removed all traces of snow. Conditions were so bad that the United States chose its bobsled, ski-running and speed-skating teams without holding preliminary trials.

On January 31, however, 307 prayers were answered with a heavy snowfall and the ski teams had their first racing and jumping practice in weeks. On January 25 another five inches of snow fell, and on the 27th, some rain but also more snow. This essential ingredient of the Winter Olympics was still in such meager supply, however, that the headlines on the sports page of the New York *Times* for January 29 heralded six inches of snow at Lake Placid in a way that snow is not usually welcomed.

By February 6 there was enough snow for the sled dog race. Beginning at 2:15 P.M., the NBC network broadcast the start of the race, with drivers and their teams leaving the line at three-minute intervals. In the next day's *Times* Arthur Daley described the first heat:

> "Emile St. Godard of The Pas, Manitoba, gave Canada a lead in the sled dog demonstration race today when he drove his team of Russian Wolf-hounds and Malamutes in ahead of Leonhard Seppala of St. Jovite, Quebec, a Canadian resident but an American citizen.
>
> "Twelve teams competed over a 25-mile course and they will travel the same route tomorrow, the total time to count in the point standing. St. Godard was timed in 2 hours, 12 minutes and 5 seconds; Seppala was clocked at 2 hours, 13 minutes, 34.3 seconds.
>
> "One of Seppala's Siberian Huskies collapsed five miles from the finish line and had to be carried back on the sled, so that the American competitor covered the final five miles with only six dogs drawing his sled.
>
> "Roger Haines of the United States who was fifth, dropped unconscious at the finish line from sheer exhaustion. Running up the hills in back of his sled had sapped his strength and stamina."

In the *Times* for February 8 a photo showed the handsome Emile St. Godard clinching the sled dog race for Canada at the finish of the second heat. There was also a photo of the only woman in the race, Eva Seeley, with her leaders, Holly and Gripp. Mrs. Seeley had sponsored herself as driver of Chinook Kennels' second team so as not to miss competing in this once-in-a-lifetime international event. Seppala and his Siberians were second.

As a demonstration sport, the sled dog races were a grand success. Huge crowds gathered to watch the colorful and picturesque dog teams. They walked out along the trail and jammed the highways at trail crossings. What they saw was a fine representation of the best of the dogs and drivers of 1932. The Canadian drivers, interested in developing a super-fast sled dog that could win races, favored crossing huskies or Malamutes with various speedy hounds. The dogs' appearances figured very little in their breeding programs. Americans, on the other hand, bred their Siberian Huskies not only for speed and endurance but also for looks and behavior. Their concept of the sport embraced an intelligent, versatile dog which would be reproducible. Although Emile St. Godard and his "Canadian Greyhounds" dominated some New England races in the early 1930's, Leonhard Seppala's Siberians were usually right on his heels and occasionally they beat him.

In the decade and a half that Canadians and Americans had been meeting regularly in sled dog races, some good rivalries had developed, some interesting dog breeding had begun. Racing those dogs in the Olympics aptly demonstrated the state of the art.

Racing Sled Dogs in the Great Lone Land

Distances are great in Canada, this vast, second-largest country in the world. Perhaps reflecting a familiarity with endless horizons, Canadian dog drivers have tended to favor long races. From one of the earliest recorded races, a non-stop 400-mile jaunt, to the current 150-mile Canadian Championship at Yellowknife, Northwest Territories, Canadians have averaged more miles per race than any other dog drivers.

Although Alaska and the lower 48 states can well claim to have originated and perpetuated organized sled dog racing in the early twentieth century, Canada's recorded racing history stems even from the middle of the nineteenth. Henry Yule Hind, leader of the Assiniboine and Saskatchewan Exploring Expedition, reported on a 400-mile freight race held in 1857 between Fort Garry, Manitoba, and Crow Wing, Minnesota. Sixteen three-dog teams, each pulling a hefty 300 pounds of freight and provisions, began the long race on November 30, 1857. Six of them managed to finish, 12 days later, and Hind was pleased to come in third.

When Colin Thompson, a fur trader, managed the Hudson's Bay Company business in The Pas between 1883 and 1890, sled dog racing on Christmas Day was a highlight of the long winter. Thompson had a lead dog, Bill, one of the company's "train-dogs." Bill had never been beaten fairly in a race and pressure from the Indians to match their dogs against the company dogs was constant.

Thompson described the first races for the *Calgary Daily Herald* in 1924:

"The Reverend James Settee, an aged native Indian missionary of the revered Christian memory, in charge of Devon Mission "The Pas," and myself, originated the first annual dog racing event, by offering prizes as follows: First Dog Train in got two yacht cotton shirts (no cash being in use in those days); Second, one shirt; and Third, a pair of common moccasins or the equivalent.

"The racing distance was from the Hudson Bay Street gate to the Carrot River Point and return. My dog train, driven by capable men, always won the race, but the honour was their only prize. For this event, every available dog was commandeered to make up trains of four, and as many as twenty dog trains competed in the first Pas dog races."

By 1916, Canadians had acquired the desire to breed and develop a better sled dog. The grudge and fun races that had started many a dog-puncher-turned-racer's career were now viewed not only as entertainment for the drivers and townspeople but for visitors as well. Sponsoring organizations naturally had an interest in the increased attention a big dog race would bring to their town. The money prizes—$1,000 for first place at The Pas—were a great incentive to dog drivers to enter and to win.

The first Dog Derby at The Pas began on March 17, 1916. The trail led over 150 miles of snowy tundra and it took the fastest driver, Albert Campbell, 24 hours and 47 minutes to run it. Three years later his brother, Baptiste Campbell, won the race. The following year, 1920, it was Baptiste and Albert placing first and second in a one-thousand-mile race from The Pas to Minneapolis.

The 1920 derby featured the first appearance of what was then a strange-looking rig. Walter Goyne, known as "King of the Trail," drove an Alaskan-style team hitch, with dogs paired up along the tow line and pulling an Alaskan racing sled with a short basket and long runners. Canadians had been driving a freight hitch up until then, with dogs hitched between two traces, single file, and pulling a toboggan. Goyne's team so outdistanced the others that no one was waiting for him when he finished the race. He went to the church and rang the bell, the traditional signal that the teams were coming in, all by himself.

Goyne's Alaskan racing hitch immediately became popular in Canada and from 1921 on it was the only way to go and to win.

Races in The Pas were expanded in 1922 to 200 miles, to Flin Flon, north of The Pas, and back. In 1924 Shorty Russick, a Russian immigrant who did a little bit of everything in the north country, mushed 200 miles from Cold Lake and entered the race. Russick's first sled dogs were a litter and their mother which he got from Jack Hayes, second-place finisher in the 1916 race, to keep him company on his long, lonely trapping trips. He had tried his hand at racing in the American Dog Derby in Idaho earlier that winter, finishing fourth. That race had cost Russick his great lead dog, Mohegan, who broke his leg in the heavy crust of snow. So he

105

brought another dog up front, Murphy, and two weeks later Murphy led the team to victory in the non-stop, 200-mile race at The Pas. They ran the course in 23 hours, 42 minutes, at an average speed of well over eight miles an hour. This record lasted until Earl Brydges outran it and his racing rival, Emile St. Godard, in 1930.

Russick's dogs were something he called Wolfhounds, basically a hound but with collie, perhaps some setter, and maybe even some of northern Manitoba's ubiquitous "scrub husky" mixed in. Russick attributed his success with these dogs to their long legs and to the high-energy diet he fed them on the trail. Chopping up hamburger with hard-boiled eggs and mixing in bacon fat, Russick prepared the dogs' meals in advance of a race. Trails were not specially packed, so rangy dogs who could break through drifts had an advantage.

"It was a lot different from the races of today," Shorty Russick observed years later. "We broke our own trails and the only thing that mattered was the man who got back first."

Racing in The Pas succumbed to the Great Depression in 1931, but far to the southeast another series of sled dog races had begun in Canada. Initiated by New Englanders, the Eastern International Dog-Sled Derby, first run in New Hampshire in 1922, moved in 1923 to Quebec City. The course was 38 miles long and run in three heats, a total of 114 miles. Eastern Canadians were wildly excited about the new sport and their partisan shouts urged their countryman, Jean Lebel, to victory in 1923.

Much of the success of this series, which lasted through 1939, was due to W.R. Brown, president of the paper company in Berlin, New Hampshire. The company used sled dogs for freighting during their logging operations and, according to Arthur Walden, were hampered in finding good dogs because Scotty Allan had bought up the best for duty in World War I. The conjunction of Brown's problem with Walden's promotion resulted in Brown's sponsoring sled dog races "for the encouragement of production of a type of useful sled-dog with sufficient coat to withstand severe cold, with good feet for traveling over snow and ice, with proper conformation for hauling loaded sleds, and to encourage breeders." The $1,000 first prizes and the $500 gold cup donated by Mr. Brown for a three-time winner, however, tended to encourage the crossbreeding of the fastest dogs the drivers could find. The resulting light, fast, long-legged hound mix won many of the races, but had little value for hauling freight. Even so, the new sport captivated Mr. Brown, for his company sponsored a team each year. Jean Lebel drove and won for the Brown Corporation in 1923; between 1928 and 1930 Leonhard Seppala drove with Brown sponsorship, but won only once. Seppala's Siberians placed second to St. Godard's crossbred hounds the other two years.

JEAN LEBEL AND HIS TEAM OF "CANADIAN GREYHOUNDS," winners of the Eastern International Dog-sled Derby, Quebec, 1923.
Courtesy Cascadian Kennels

When this series of races ended just before World War II, Emile St. Godard and his fleet hounds had won six times.

Canada's far-flung provinces were the scenes of several isolated sled dog races before World War II. In Banff, Alberta, Shorty Russick and his team took a $1,000 first prize in 1923. In 1924 Russick won a 150-mile non-stop race in Big River, Saskatchewan. In little towns like La Tuque, Quebec, smaller races paid more in scarfs, neckties, shirts and pipes than in cash, but they whetted the appetites of the dog drivers for more and bigger races. During the late twenties and thirties an International Sled Dog Race was run at Ottawa, Ontario; at Val d'Or and Ste. Agathe des Monts, Quebec, the winter carnival sled dog races attracted drivers from New England.

By the early 1940's, gasoline rationing and the need to conserve practically everything brought another halt to sled dog racing all over North America. Many of the mushers were in the service of their countries and so were many of the dogs. In its brief three and a half decades of official existence, however, the sport of sled dog racing had captured the fancies of hundreds of drivers and thousands of fans. Perhaps during the war they were unable to race their teams, but they could think, they could plan out their breeding programs and racing techniques for the future, they could dream about the ultimate, the unbeatable dog team. For they had yielded to the same magic that gripped a youthful Danish soldier who was taught how to drive a dog team in Greenland as part of his military duties.

"Nobody who has been admitted to that mystery," admitted Kurt Olson, "is ever quite the same again."

5

Gone with the Dogs

There are just two seasons here in Ely . . . winter, and then a brief time when the dog sledding is poor.

ELY, MINNESOTA, RESIDENT, 1974

The Post-war Sled Dog Boom

Within a few months of the armistice marking the end of World War II, Earl Norris, who had trained dogs for the Army during the war, staged a sled dog race in Anchorage. In Fairbanks, Andy Kokrine, younger brother of the 1940 champion, won the first post-war race there. Back home in New England, ex-sergeants Bill Belletete and Tat Duval joined some eight other drivers when the New England Sled Dog Club resumed its winter schedule. The American Dog Derby was run again in Idaho.

There may have been only four sled dog clubs in North America, but the post-war sled dog boom was gathering momentum. For every person initiated into the mystique of driving a team of sled dogs, several others, friends or relatives, would join in as handlers or organizers.

By the close of the 1960's the number of sled dog clubs throughout the world hovered at around fifty; by 1975 over 115 organizations had something to do with dogs pulling sleds. Although the cold and snowy states were the focus of activity, dog teams of one sort or another padded about in almost every state of the Union. Even in Hawaii a team trained on the beach. The sport spread to Europe, where a few Siberian Huskies imported from major United States kennels found themselves part of what a Dutch enthusiast called "sleddogsport."

Notions about an international organization which could standardize all this sled-dogging activity came to the surface in 1966. During the early 1960's, Bill Wilson of Maine and Mrs. Elizabeth Nansen of Ottawa had spoken of their concept of such an organization to several other dog drivers, who responded eagerly. First officially proposed by Canadian J. Malcolm McDougall at a meeting of the New England Sled Dog Club, the new organization was formed in late April, 1966, at Niagara Falls, New York. This historic meeting was attended by veteran and not-so-veteran sled dog drivers and officials from as far away as Alaska and Canada. The result: the International Sled Dog Racing Association, known as ISDRA, "dedicated to the sport of sled dog racing on a worldwide basis by promoting public interest, encouraging cooperation between clubs, and assisting in the standardization of rules and race management procedures."

As the number of clubs and races increased, ISDRA divided its voluntary services according to geographical areas. Regional and at-large directors were elected by a growing membership in nine ISDRA regions: Alaska, Western Canada, Eastern Canada, Northeast United States, Mid-Atlantic, Central, Plains, West, and Europe. During 1975 well over 200 sled dog races were held, with some clubs emphasizing large, professional races, others more interested in providing smaller competitions for dog drivers and their families. In each region, distinctive races characterize the status of the sport for the majority of drivers in that area.

"Sleddogsport" accommodates people and dogs of every conceivable description or background. For the professional, regional rivalries demand continual striving for a better team. Once a regional champion has done well in races in his own area for a few years, he can venture up the professional race ladder, aiming at driving his team in one of the championships. For the weekend racer or amateur, there are family-oriented club races, one-dog races for pint-sized mushers, lead dog contests, weight pulls, overnight or longer trail expeditions, races with wheeled rigs or cross-country skis, benefits, expositions, or any other excuse anyone can think of to get outdoors, especially in the middle of winter, with a dog.

Alaskans Rediscover Dog Sledding

Alaska's ubiquitous sled dog, once of vital importance in the growing state, had succumbed during the three decades after World War I to the faster miracles of modern mobility. First the train, then the airplane and finally the snowmobile took over tasks which were once the sled dog's sole province. By the time the 1950's slid into the 1960's, the sled dog population in most Alaskan villages was less than the snowmobile population.

It took sled dog racing to counteract this propensity for mechanization. The resumption of organized racing at Anchorage and Fairbanks immediately after World War II awoke latent dog-driving tendencies in many Alaskans. By 1954 the villagers of Tok had initiated their annual series of races. Other villages held local contests to determine who could drive which dogs the fastest and the champ would be sent, with the best village dogs pooled to make up one terrific team, to the big races at Anchorage or Fairbanks. Increased prestige and money prizes at these races, and then the excitement and native pride generated by the running of the thousand-mile Iditarod Trail Race, imparted to the willing sled dog more glory and value than he had ever before enjoyed. In 1971 Governor William A. Egan of Alaska made official what sled dog drivers had known for a long time: he declared that henceforth sled dog racing is the state sport. By the mid-seventies Alaskans supported some twenty sled dog clubs and over seventy scheduled races.

Alaska is where the sport of sled dog racing began and Alaska is still where a team of sled dogs evokes the most enthusiasm. Alaskans talk about races all year. Training begins in the fall and by November short preliminary races are held in village after village. From Anchorage and Fairbanks to such places as Tok, Tanana, Huslia, Unalakleet and Bethel, the competition begins. Slowly the best teams take shape and the drivers calculate their chances of entering and winning at least one of the big ones.

The most attention is focused on the World Championship at Anchorage and the North American Championship at Fairbanks. The furor surrounding the arrival of the world's best dog drivers and the prospects of sharing in some $22,500 of prize money, elevates these events to a combination of the World Series and the Irish Sweepstakes. During the races, Alaskans remain glued to broadcast accounts, and progress is measured only in terms of how fast a favorite team is running the course.

From a tender beginning as a one-dog children's race during the 1936 Fur Rendezvous, Anchorage's Rondy now features one of the toughest and longest championship courses. The teams barrel out from the starting line in front of City Hall, navigate through city streets, loop far out into the wilderness, cross streams and lakes into the foothills of the

Chugach Mountains, finally finishing back where they started, 25 miles later. By the end of the third day of racing, dogs and drivers have covered 75 long, gruelling miles. In 1975, 21 teams ran in the Rondy, most of them driven by veteran Alaskan trail and race drivers, but including three intrepid mushers from the lower 48.

Five weeks later, toward the end of March, the North American Championship is run in Fairbanks. A direct descendant of the pre-war Trophy and Sweepstakes races, the post-war North American course has a unique champion making-or-breaking wrinkle. For the first two days the teams race the same twenty-mile cross-country course. On the third day, the dogs figure they are almost home as they approach the familiar finish. But in order to complete the race they must turn and lope another ten miles.

To a driver who can win both Alaskan championships in the same year goes an even greater distinction, for he is then known as "Dual Champion." A team and driver must exhibit an exceptional degree of ability and depth in order to accomplish these back-to-back victories. Sled dog racing's Dual Championship represents a major achievement in the sport, similar to horse racing's Triple Crown or the Grand Slam in tennis. Thirty years of racing have yielded only six Dual Champions, and only the two giants of modern racing, Alaskan George Attla and Dr. Roland Lombard of Massachusetts, have won this title more than once.

Potential champions begin as young as three years old in Fairbanks, and many of the young mushers are following in their father's or mother's tracks. Juniors can advance through five classes, beginning with a one-dog hitch and progressing, with age and experience, to a seven-dog team at age 16. This "little league" provides a continuous supply of new but experienced drivers to the senior ranks. Junior championships are held at Anchorage, Fairbanks, Tok and Nome, and in Alaska, the Junior Championships are not taken lightly.

Women, too, have their separate championships in Alaska, a tradition which dates from the 1929–35 Fromm Trophy Races at Fairbanks. Although women have been allowed to run in the men's championships since World War II, men are still precluded from running in the women's. The Women's World Championship course at Anchorage is 12 miles long, and must be completed three times. Alaskan women have dominated the race, with many of them winning more than once. Multiple winners include Kit MacInnes (four times), Roxy Brooks and Barbara Parker (three in a row each), Sheri Wright, Shirley Gavin and Carol Lundgren Shepherd. Never far from the top are former champions Natalie Norris or Rosie Losonsky.

Up in Fairbanks, however, the Women's North American Champion-

GARETH WRIGHT WAS MORE THAN READY for the resumption of sled dog racing in Alaska following World War II. In 1950 he won the 100-mile Fur Rendezvous with Venus on lead. *Courtesy Natalie Norris*

THE CHUGACH MOUNTAINS FRAME THE TRAIL at Anchorage's sled dog races. *Maxine Vehlow*

JAKE BUTLER WITH HIS TYPICAL VILLAGE DOGS, Anchorage, 1950. Butler and Earl Norris swapped victories in the 1946–1949 Rondy championships.

Courtesy Natalie Norris

NATALIE NORRIS, just after crossing the finish line. She won the Women's World Championship in 1954.   *Courtesy Natalie Norris*

TEAMWORK: LOUISE AND DOC LOMBARD helping Anne Wing harness
up in Alaska in 1968. *Robert Levorsen*

THE FIRST "OUTSIDE" WINNER IN THE WOMEN'S WORLD
CHAMPIONSHIP, Anne Wing of New York, in 1968.   *Robert Levorsen*

DONNA MUDGETT BRUCE, transplanted from New Hampshire to Alaska,
racing in the Women's World Championship in 1970.   *Maxine Vehlow*

ship is usually associated with Jean Bryar from New Hampshire. A successful driver in New England and Canadian races, Jean Bryar fulfilled a dog musher's dream in 1962 and ventured to Fairbanks for the championship. She won none of the daily heats (of 10 miles each on the first two days and then 14 miles on the third day), but maintained such consistent, fast times that she won the race overall. The next year she won all three heats and the year after that she sped around the 34-mile course at close to 17 miles an hour, tying diminutive Effie Kokrine's 1954 three-in-a-row record. By 1975 Jean had an unprecedented string of six victories.

Other major heat races in Alaska include the Alaska State Championship at Kenai-Soldotna and the Tok Race of Champions. Both these races attract Outside teams who are racing in Alaska, and recently the Yukon Territory champion from Whitehorse, Ed Bauman, raced at Tok. The State Championship race course is known as a rough one, as the trail is often soft, and traverses numerous small hills. Running alongside a busy highway for part of the distance, the trail offers good spectator viewing but a variety of diversions for lead dogs. Teams race 16 miles from Soldotna to Kenai one day, then back the next. Recent State Champions are George Attla, Roland Lombard, Charles Belford (another veterinarian from Massachusetts and son of the founder of the Laconia World Championship race) and Orville Lake (veteran Alaskan musher and race official).

If the Soldotna course is known to be soft and hilly, the Tok course perhaps makes up for some of it, being relatively flat and usually good and hard. Tok's Race of Champions is located some 200 miles down the Alaska Highway toward home for the lower 48 mushers, and marks the end of the regular racing season for most southern drivers in Alaska.

Alaska's re-dedication to the sled dog was furthered during 11 days in January and February, 1975, with a re-enactment of the heroic 1925 serum run. Several of the sons of the original relay drivers took part, traveling the same long trail from Nenana to Nome. Two of the original drivers, Edgar Nollner and Edgar Kalland, toyed with the idea of re-running their routes, but finally decided to let younger drivers go. Fear of epidemic was absent from the modern run, and it took the commemorative mail packet six days longer to cover the distance.

When serum run drivers, both in 1925 and in 1975, reached the town of Ruby, far down the Yukon River, they were mushing along the final sections of the Iditarod Trail. Winding over one thousand miles from Knik (near Anchorage) north through Iditarod to Ruby and then west to Nome, the Iditarod Trail was the major winter route from Alaska's south-central coast to the gold fields of the Interior and the Northwest. Part of this route was run in 1967 for the Iditarod Trail Centennial Race, celebrating the Alaska Purchase, and then the race promoters and the

117

JEAN BRYAR, FIRST "OUTSIDE" WINNER OF THE
WOMEN'S NORTH AMERICAN CHAMPIONSHIP in Fairbanks
in 1962, stopped by Johnny Carson's show to explain about
sled dog racing.
State of New Hampshire Photo, Courtesy Jean Bryar

THE SCRAMBLE RACE IS PART OF THE FUN AT THE FUR RENDEZVOUS.
Bella Levorsen wound up with a fist full of two-dollar bills
and a bump on her head. *Robert Levorsen*

dog drivers began to visualize opening up the whole trail for the longest sled dog race in the world.

Much of the trail was densely overgrown and had to be broken out. The U.S. Army Corps of Engineers, plus civilian volunteers, worked on the trail and were scheduled to pack it with snowmobiles during the month prior to the race. Joe Redington, Sr., primary organizer, aimed for a $50,000 purse, $12,000 to go to the winner. Checkpoints at the old roadhouses along the trail were established, where times were recorded, rest and food were available, and any injured or tired dogs could be left off. A U.S. Air Force veterinarian was in charge of watching the health of the dogs. Only basic survival gear was carried on the sleds, food for men and dogs being cached ahead of time at the roadhouses.

This ambitious event attracted drivers from all over Alaska for the first race in 1973. Thirty-four dog teams left Anchorage on March 3, headed for Nome, 1,049 miles away. While Joe Redington wrestled with purse problems, the dogs and drivers encountered 25-foot snow drifts and then bare ground. Ice with nearly three feet of water standing on it, temperatures to fifty degrees below zero, aggressive moose and curious wolves characterized the trail, and they took their toll. Twelve teams dropped out of the race, and no team finished with all dogs in harness.

At Nulato, more than halfway along, blizzard-wracked dog drivers were greeted by school children who not only helped to mark the trail, posting inspirational signs ("Keep on truckin'," "Nome or bust") but they provided welcome help in caring for the tired teams.

Pre-race speculators, looking at the results from the old 408-mile All-Alaska Sweepstakes, predicted that the teams would travel about a hundred miles a day and that the race would be won in about ten days. George Attla foresaw "a great camping trip." Others thought that nobody would make it. The trail committee's treasurer, of a practical nature, announced a fund-raising lottery for guessing the exact time the winner would take to reach Nome.

Twenty days after the start of the race, dark horse Dick Wilmarth of Red Devil trotted into Nome beside his tall, rangy dog team. Singling out his leader, five-year-old Hotfoot, for special praise, Wilmarth acknowledged, "If it had not been for him, I'd still be out there."

Crowds of ecstatic Alaskans slowed the winner's progress through the streets of Nome, and Wilmarth, although he did not find out until later, was nearly arrested. Some newsmen and city officials were planning to alert the chief of police to a 1905 law still on the books, requiring lead dogs to wear a bell. The surprise was foiled, however, when an admiring woman dashed out to the team and hung a victory necklace of bells over Hotfoot's head.

119

TO WIN THE RONDY LEAD DOG CONTEST a team must run
the course correctly, by voice command, in the fastest
time. Chuck Lewis gives it a try, 1970.   *Maxine Vehlow*

END OF THE 1,049-mile trail in Nome, 1973. Winning musher Dick Wilmarth of
Red Devil trots through town in a flurry of snow and school children.
His team, with Hotfoot on lead, completed the trail in twenty days.
Mike McDermott, Courtesy Northern Dog News

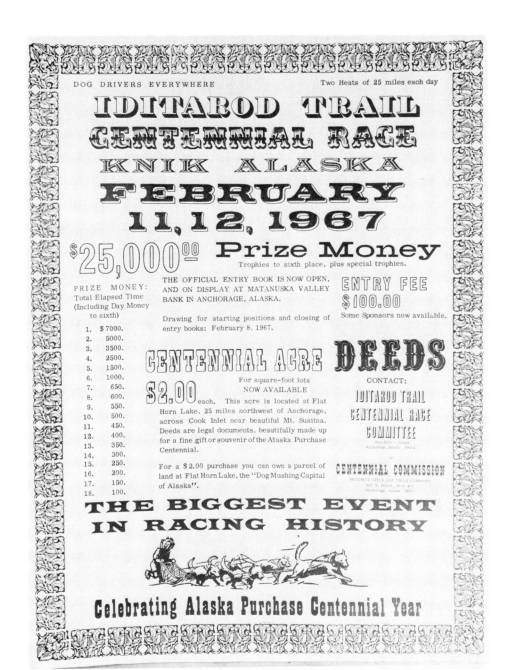

FIFTY-NINE MUSHERS ENTERED THE 1967 IDITAROD TRAIL CENTENNIAL RACE; Isaac Okleasik of Teller won it. *Iditarod Trail Annual*

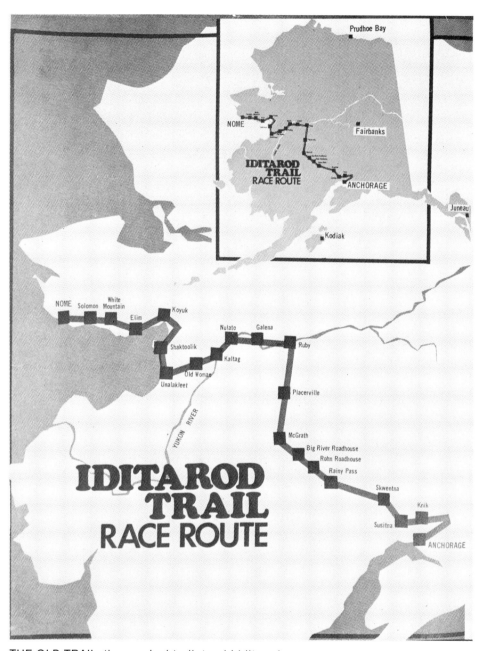

IDITAROD TRAIL RACE ROUTE

THE OLD TRAIL, the crooked trail, to old Iditarod:
The pioneers who laid it down, the very first who trod
The muskeg of the creekbeds in search for yellow stuff
Are now no more. But then, it does seem sensible enough
To think that from productive digging, far off in the blue,
They're laying down their picks to watch the mushers coming through.

Reuben Gaines

A Sled Dog in Every State

In the contiguous south 48 United States, sled dog drivers are no less enthusiastic about their sport than are those from "Seward's Icebox." Although sled dog club constitutions generally contain a formal sentence to the effect that "the Object of the Club shall be to promote interest in the breeding, training and racing of sled dogs and to promote the sport of sled dog racing," the fact is that the clubs are organized so that dyed-in-the-wool sled dog drivers can have races to satisfy that unrelenting urge to drive their dog teams. Even in states with no snow, clubs hold races with the dogs pulling wheeled rigs. In states with no clubs, individuals must be putting together small teams for fun, for one of the leading harness makers claims to have sent equipment to every state.

With its rules reflecting those of the original Nome Kennel Club, the Northeast's New England Sled Dog Club served as a model for new clubs that were formed in such profusion in the late 1960's and early 1970's. New England's sled dog scene is typical of the rest of the United States.

Training and qualifying sessions begin in late autumn in New England; the first scheduled club race is held on the last weekend of the year. Club races provide classes for every musher from age five on up, and in recent years well over one hundred teams have gathered at Tamworth, New Hampshire, for the season's traditional opening race. From then on until March a family with sled dogs is busy every spare minute: training during the week, racing each weekend.

New England races are sometimes associated with a town's winter carnival, but more often the race itself is the major attraction. Several towns besides Tamworth host the sled dogs year after year: Fitzwilliam, Peterborough, Pittsfield and Kingston in New Hampshire; Stowe and Shelburne, Vermont; Gardner, Massachusetts. Purses are moderate, mainly serving to help defray the mushers' expenses. Although the Amateur Athletic Union and ISDRA have agreed that an amateur dog driver can race with professionals as long as he does not accept any winnings, in New England the two classes are kept separate so that students, especially, will not jeopardize their amateur standing.

New England is the site of the oldest of the World Championships, at Laconia, and plans are underway for a new race, a cross-country trek of several hundred miles through the deep snow belt of northern New Hampshire, into Maine, and back.

In the mid-Atlantic states there may not be much snow but the enthusiasm and dedicated organization of the drivers more than make up for that. They have even been known to hold a No-Snow Derby, run, as the majority of mid-Atlantic races are, with the dogs pulling wheeled rigs

123

"THE OBJECT OF THE CLUB SHALL BE to promote interest in the breeding, training and racing of sled dogs and to promote the sport of sled dog racing."   *L. Coppinger*

THE FACES OF ALASKA reflect the pride and the joy of Dick Wilmarth's (center) victory in the first long Iditarod Trail Race.
Smirnoff and Associates, Anchorage

rather than sleds. Five clubs, located throughout the region, joined to form the Mid-Atlantic Sled Dog Racing Association (MASDRA), thus expanding the limited two- or three-race schedules of the individual clubs and also helping to standardize rules and procedures. Members are awarded points according to their season's race record. The MASDRA championships are closely contested, from the senior classes right down to the most determined one-dogger.

A high spot of the MASDRA season is the annual Mint Julep Classic, usually held on a frozen grass base. It may seem a long way from Mint Julep Country to the Land of the Midnight Sun, but the Mason-Dixon Sled Dog Racing Association welcomes over one hundred teams to its southern spectacular.

Slightly north of MASDRA territory, a club called the Canadian-American Sledders represents dog drivers from western New York and southern Ontario. Since 1962 they have held races throughout New York, and they earned a bright feather for their caps by hosting the organizational meeting of ISDRA at Niagara Falls.

Although the emphasis in this region, as in the Northeast, is on family-oriented weekend races, several professional meets have been developing. The reasonably reliable supply of snow in the Adirondack Mountain region is irresistible to sled doggers, and past successes at Lassellsville and Speculator, New York, have attracted good money, good trail makers, and hence some of the best teams.

Two major clubs and a half-dozen top professional races dominate the sled dog racing picture in the Midwest. The Great Lakes Sled Dog Association had its beginnings in the early 1950's when one ex-G.I., A. Cecil Houghton, owner of two Siberian Huskies, was lecturing on the high school assembly circuit about Greenland and the Eskimos. In a school near Detroit, Houghton responded to a raised hand and was informed that the student's uncle had a kennel of Alaskan Malamutes and an army surplus sled. From such beginnings do sled dog clubs grow.

The Great Lakes Sled Dog Association's racing circuit includes races just about every weekend from January through March, the biggest being the Midwest International Championship at Kalkaska, Michigan. Over fifty of the best teams from the United States and Canada compete for two days on an eighteen-mile trail for a total purse of $5,000.

In St. Paul, Minnesota, a Winter Carnival Sled Dog Race in 1963 with a $1,000 purse inspired a growing group of mushers to form the North Star Sled Dog Club. Today, Minnesota supports some dozen races each season, half of which are professional and worth well over $16,000 combined, to the drivers. The area's biggest race is mid-January's All American Championship at Ely, put on by the Ely Sled Dog Committee

RIGHT AFTER WORLD WAR II, STILL IN HIS ARMY
PANTS AND BOOTS, Kent Lawrence of New Hampshire
drove a team of honorably discharged sled dogs.
Courtesy Lorna Demidoff

TAT DUVAL'S DOGS WANTED TO REST, so the teams of
Lorna Demidoff and Short Seeley also got to sniff
the snow. Lorna Demidoff was the first woman ever to win an
official race.   *Bernice B. Perry, Courtesy Lorna Demidoff*

ANOTHER HUSKY JAM IN NEW ENGLAND around 1950, caused by Lester Moody (far left), Freeman "Jack" Frost and Vernon "Brud" Gardner. *Courtesy Lorna Demidoff*

WEARING AN EXTRA TUGLINE FOR A BELT, Bill Shearer surveys his Siberians at a New England race, circa 1950. *Bernice B. Perry, Courtesy Lorna Demidoff*

127

A TIGHT CORNER FOR DOM BLODGETT'S COONHOUNDS
in a New England race.
Charles L. Booth, Courtesy Cascadian Kennels

NEW HAMPSHIRE'S MT. CHOCORUA HAS WITNESSED
THE SEASON'S OPENING RACES in New England for
several decades. Gus Fallgren of Massachusetts and
his Siberians head across Lake Chocorua in the
early 1970's. *Lisa Fallgren Uloth*

NO-SNOW RACING IN NEW JERSEY, 1972. Linda Phillips of the Siberian Husky Club of Greater New York with Phillips' Kamchatka, C.D.X., on lead.

Courtesy Virginia Harrison

TRAINING IN OHIO: Laura McVay, age 18, daughter of ISDRA'S Central U.S. Director, Scott McVay.

Warren Strauss, Courtesy Elaine Gish

MUSHING IN MICHIGAN: Champion Tom Mathias.   *Courtesy Vern Roberts*

ON A STEEP ROAD CLIMB IN THE MINT JULEP CLASSIC at Thurmont, Maryland, Ray Giteles raced to third place. *J.J. Durick, Jr., Courtesy Ray Giteles*

CAREENING AROUND A CORNER AT 8500 feet above sea level, Rick McHardy tries to smooth out a rough course at the Palm Springs Aerial Tramway Race, 1974.

S. Pendergrass, Courtesy Jim Uhl

TRAINING DOGS IN THOUSAND OAKS, CALIFORNIA, 1972.

Greg Lewis, Courtesy Jim Uhl

and the Chamber of Commerce. The trail covers 16 miles and is run on two successive days. The drivers at Ely are the best from Alaska, Canada and the United States, and in 1975 they vied for a purse of $6,500. Racing in the Paul Bunyan Classic at Bemidji, Minnesota, the week before Ely, most of the drivers will then go on to Kalkaska. The best will begin extending their training mileage in preparation for the World Championship either in Laconia or Anchorage. Wherever they go, the top professionals pursue the best in trails, officials, competition and prizes. A good year can bring in well over $10,000 to a winning team.

Smaller races are also important in the Midwest. The Trail Breakers Sled Dog Club in Ohio, the Wisconsin Trailblazers and even the St. Louis Sled Dog Club sponsor races in towns like Burton and Litchfield, Ohio; Stiles and Green Lake, Wisconsin; and around St. Louis, although Missouri mushers depend more on wheels than on runners.

In the West, five of the 18 sled dog clubs are in California. California's long history of sled dog racing dates back to post-World War I days when Scotty Allan and Fay Delezene promoted the sport at various resort areas. It is hard to imagine what those veterans of Alaskan trails would have thought about the Palm Springs Aerial Tramway Race, one of the most unusual races on the continent. Beginning at 2,500 feet above sea level on Mt. San Jacinto, two dog teams at a time board the tramway for the twenty-minute ride to the upper station at 8,500 feet. Teams are limited to three to five dogs due to the size of the holding area at the upper station and to the dangerous mountain course. When five teams are assembled, at about noon, and sixty spectators at a time have also been unloaded, the race begins. The teams must run the 2½-mile course twice, negotiating sudden, sharp turns and threading their way through awed groups of spectators. Four preliminary one-day races, on two succeeding weekends, precede the championship. This last race of the series pits the winners of the preliminaries against each other. When it is over, the Palm Springs Aerial Tramway Champion has a title and an experience unique in sled dog racing.

In the northern Sierra Nevada Mountains of California, another long series of annual races takes place. Near Lake Tahoe, a demanding trail often takes the teams up 2,000 feet, an arduous enough task. Attesting even more to the skill and endurance of the drivers and dogs is their ability to come back down, safely. More than one driver has commented that just to finish one of these races, "You know you've got some kind of dog team!"

This kind of serious racing is traditional in the West, due not only to the historical precedent, but also to the examples set by the long series of races at Priest Lake, Idaho, and Truckee, California. Several thousand dollars

CURRENT PRESIDENT OF ISDRA, DENTIST JOHN RUUD, has won the Pacific Northwest Championship at Priest Lake, Idaho, five times.   *Mally Hilands*

"CHILKOOT HUSKIES" ARE HALF HUSKY, HALF SETTER AND GREYHOUND, and are a main reason that Art and Dorothy Christensen of Oregon enjoy sled dog racing. On a snowy day at Lake of the Woods, Oregon, 1973. *Mally Hilands*

BELLA LEVORSEN, author of several publications on sled dog racing and wife of former ISDRA president, racing at Hobart Mills, California, in 1973.   *Mally Hilands*

HIS TEAM TRAVELING AT FULL TILT, BOB LEVORSEN drove to first place in the 1973 race at Lake of the Woods, Oregon. Levorsen was president of ISDRA from 1970 to 1974. *Mally Hilands*

in prize money has been offered since the early 1960's in races at Tahoe, and Montana's new four-race circuit boasts a minimum of $11,000 in purses. Mileages on these western courses also is impressive: eighteen- to twenty-mile trails over roadless terrain require top-notch teams and driving. An eastern musher venturing west for competition must realize that superiority in New England or New York is one thing, but racing against a seven-dog limited team which averaged 19.5 miles an hour in an 11.7-mile heat is something else.

Surrounding the bigger races in California, Oregon, Washington, Idaho, Montana, Wyoming, Colorado and Utah, dozens of club races keep dog drivers busy from early November through March. Variety of terrain gives to western sled dog racing a distinct character. For years, races in Colorado added to the holiday atmosphere of the Christmas markets, traditional European Yuletide exhibitions which were held in little mountain towns like Georgetown. Westerners get everybody involved, with big classes for smaller teams, and extra events even for non-drivers, such as igloo-building and banquets. The ambience of western sled dogging is definitely upbeat.

Although Hawaii is not properly one of the lower 48 states, and although no official sled dog club exists there, it does have at least one dog team. Hard-packed beach sand is ideal for running dogs, and it is a rare sled dogger who would let the amazed stares of palm tree tourists affect a scheduled training run.

From the Yukon to Labrador

A sled dog driver traveling from race to race in Alaska or the lower 48 would find the scenes homogeneous. In Canada, though, a driver from Quebec would find another world were he to face the 150-mile vastness of the trail at Yellowknife in the Northwest Territories. Distances between major racing areas are so great in Canada that distinct local differences in the races have evolved. In Quebec and Ontario, racing has been influenced by the style in the lower 48, with two-day, ten- to twenty-mile races being most popular. In the wide provinces to the west and north, longer endurance races have been traditional. While drivers in the eastern provinces have been breeding their huskies with hounds to get super-fast racing sled dogs, the working trappers of the west have favored their larger and stronger, but slower, freighting huskies.

The "richest dog derby" is in the sprawling Northwest Territories. Held in late March as part of the annual Caribou Carnival at Yellowknife, the Canadian Championship Dog Derby carries a purse of $10,000 and attracts the best of the long-distance teams. Leading up to the championship are smaller community races and a hundred-mile preliminary with a $3,000 purse at Fort Smith, to the south. In 1975, 19 dog teams started the fifty-mile championship course that stretches out along Great Slave Lake. Three days later, 13 of them had made it through below-zero, increasingly windy weather, and finished the 150-mile event. Three of the drop-outs were teams from the lower 48.

Races in the Northwest Territories are open to entrants from any-where, and the influence of racing teams is making itself felt. Until 1974 the honest working sled dogs in the Caribou Carnival usually wore freight-type collar harnesses and were hitched single file with traces along each side of the team. When drivers began winning with Alaskan-style racing harnesses and the tandem hitch, the teams were transformed, at least superficially. Now, Siberian Huskies are interbred with hounds and Eskimo dogs, racing sleds are preferred, and training specifically for the races changes the winter routine for dogs and drivers.

Canada's farthest-west province, the Yukon Territory, is the scene of the annual Sourdough Rendezvous race in Whitehorse. The race de-mands less in miles from a dog team (three fifteen-mile heats) but more in a certain kind of endurance from the driver. The race is held during a week of a celebration that only the fittest can survive. Dubbed by Jane Gaffin in the Whitehorse *Star* as "The Yukon's 72-hour Endurance Test," the Sourdough Rendezvous carnival is a sure cure for cabin fever, claus-trophobia and bad tempers. A dog driver who can survive the celebration and win the race as well is a champion of immeasurable qualities. He has also earned his $1,500.

In British Columbia, the Wells Winter Whoopie Sled Dog Races, the Fort Nelson Trappers' Rendezvous, the Fort St. John Mukluk Rendez-vous, the British Columbia Championship at Valemont and the Vernon, British Columbia, race, are part of the developing circuit. In Alberta, races at Fox Creek and Fort McMurray award close to $10,000 in prize money. Saskatchewan has two big races, one at the winter festival in Fort Qu'Appele, the other in Prince Albert, the Saskatchewan Championship.

The World Championship sled dog race at The Pas is the highlight of the season in Manitoba. Drivers from Outside are discouraged from en-tering, for the entrants are mostly trappers by trade. The teams are used to long-distance, hard, daily traveling. The total purse for this three-day, fifty-miles-a-day race in 1975 was close to $5,500. Other events for dog drivers at this Northern Manitoba Trappers' Festival are a $1,200 freight race and a junior race worth $200 to the winner. Manitoba's growing sled dog circuit includes other races at towns like St. Norbert, Moose Lake, Cranberry Portage and Winnipeg. Winnipeg's new Cana-dian National Sled Dog Classic attracts the best drivers from central

TOM HINDMARCH, 1975 CHAMPION AT WHITEHORSE, ran
the fifteen-mile trail in well under an hour each of the
three days of the race.   *Jim Beebe, Whitehorse* Star

JACK MEAKIN, ISDRA DIRECTOR FOR WESTERN CANADA, and
his registered Siberian Huskies, winners of the Winnipeg
Festival du Voyageur races held on the Red River in 1972.
The leader and two point dogs are Canadian champions.

Hugh Allan, Courtesy Loboden Kennels

Canada and the Midwest, having grown in a few brief years from a little three-mile race to one of the fastest seventeen-mile trails in Canada. Strung out along the trail in the vast, flat prairie, the dog teams look to observers like miniatures and appear to be barely making headway.

Ontario's sled dog season is as ambitious as any in the United States, beginning in early November with a wheeled race championship in Ottawa and culminating with the annual Towers International Sled Dog Derby and the Nugget Classic in North Bay. The Northern Ontario Sled Dog Club sponsors some seven or eight of the approximately 14 races held in the province, and most of the purses total at least $1,000. United States drivers, mostly from the Midwest, take part in Ontario's races, in towns such as Limerick, Verner, Owen Sound, Perth, Barrie, Capreol, Clarence Creek and Penetanguishene. At Sault Ste. Marie, thousands of spectators gather to watch drivers from both sides of the border guide their teams over a hilly, thirteen-mile trail, for two days. A Canadian tobacco company lent financial support for several years toward a challenge trophy and cash award for the top point-scorer in the Northern Ontario Sled Dog Club's sanctioned races.

Quebec also has a full racing season, beginning with one-day races and rapidly working up to the first big race of the season. The Eastern International Sled Dog Derby at Quebec City has been a major race for decades, and now is the earliest major race in a long professional circuit. Many of the best eastern, mid-western and Canadian teams meet in Quebec in mid-January for a first good look at each other. Reporters estimated that fifty thousand racing fans lined the course in 1975 to watch René Gingras and Jean-Marie Corbin of Quebec, Charlie Belford, Dick Moulton, Lloyd Slocum and Jean Bryar of New England, and Harris Dunlap and Don Light of New York, plus 28 other professional teams, run 16 warm, rain-soaked miles during Saturday's heat and 16 hard, fast miles when the temperature dropped on Sunday.

Canadians took seven out of the top ten places, Slocum came in seventh, and third-place finisher Dick Molburg of New Hampshire related how winner Charlie Belford negotiated part of the course: "I was completely out of control coming down the power line hill and just plain scared, but Belford skied down the hill on the soles of his boots!"

The Border Race at Stanstead has featured an unusual sled dog course which crosses from Quebec into Vermont and back. Val d'Or and Ste. Agathe des Monts, favorite racing towns of the pre-war mushers, have recently been re-introduced to the sled dog racing results columns.

Much of the success of sled dog racing in Quebec has been due to the influential Laurentian Sled Dog Club, reorganized in 1973 and now known as l'Association d'Attelages de Chiens du Bas Canada (the Lower

A HUGE QUEBEC BARN DOMINATES THE FINISH of
the Stanstead-Derby Line Border Race.   *Emily Groves*

A DOUBLE START IN ONTARIO, with a Canadian team
on the left, a U.S. team on the right.   *Leona Hutchings*

"MAC" MCDOUGALL in 1972, one of Canada's best mushers and a founder of ISDRA. *Charles L. Booth, Courtesy Cascadian Kennels*

A SAMOYED TEAM RACING IN SWITZERLAND. *Hans Keusen*

Canada Sled Dog Racing Association). The club sponsors a dozen local races in Quebec each year, at which the drivers can train and test their teams for the important mid-season races in Minnesota and Michigan, and then the late-season races in Laconia, New Hampshire, and Rangeley, Maine.

Dog drivers around Halifax and Dartmouth in Nova Scotia formed the Nova Scotia Sled Dog Club in 1974. Snow can be scarce in this ocean province, but sled doggers rarely let the lack of snow discourage them. Nova Scotia's Department of Recreation supports the new organization, and while the three- or five-dog teams racing as part of local winter carnivals cannot yet match the old-time color of the western teams, the drivers seem to have a good idea (most of the time) where they are headed.

In Canada's farthest east province, rugged and rocky Labrador, dog teams were for years synonymous with travel. The handy snowmobile, however, began supplanting the sled dog population, so much so that by 1972 the annual Easter games at Nain were the first with no dog teams. To correct this situation and to restore the art of sled dog driving to Labrador, Nain's Kemutsik Association has been working toward a $1,500 purse for a long race from Davis Inlet to Nain.

The resurgent interest in sled dogs across Canada has closer ties with Alaska's rediscovery of the sled dog than with the sled dog boom in the lower 48 states. Keeping the tradition and talent extant is important to people who are losing touch with skills that not so long ago were essential to life and livelihood. From the Easter races at Nain to the Canadian Arctic Winter Games on the Yukon River, sled dog races are a major attraction for old-timers and youngsters, for natives and settlers, for participants and spectators. Isolated northern communities are brought together during the winter contests, and although the competition is tough, the brotherhood of the North prevails.

Sleddogsport Comes to Europe

While Canada's sled dog races are isolated due to distances and small population centers, Europe's are separated by national borders, quarantine restrictions and some definite and disparate philosophies as to types of dogs and races. The Swiss Club for Northern Dogs, organized in 1959, was the first to promote the breeding and development of the northern breeds; its approach to sled dog racing is different from the majority of

North American clubs. Races are strictly limited to northern purebred dogs. Members are dedicated first to the concept of raising pure lines of their recognized breeds: the Siberian Husky, the Alaskan Malamute, the Samoyed, the Greenland and Canadian Eskimo Dogs, the Karelian Bearhound, the Finnish Spitz, the Norwegian Elkhound and the Akita. Some of the earliest imports of Siberians into Switzerland had been crossbred with the Greenland Husky, and to prevent this from continuing, the Swiss Club for Northern Dogs adopted its strong rules against crossbreeds. Although Europe's central dog registry, the Fédération Cynologique Internationale, allowed the offspring of, for example, an Alaskan Malamute and a Siberian Husky to be officially registered as polar dogs, breed advocates have successfully eliminated these crossbreeds from the Swiss stud books. The basic assumption of these European sled doggers is that every breed has been developed for a specific task and purpose; the best way to develop the capabilities of a northern breed is to keep it pure and to improve its select talents by racing.

To get the teams running, the first Swiss Sled Dog Camp was organized in 1965. Club members outnumbered the dogs, 25 to 11, but it was reasonable that the aspiring mushers had to learn about forming and training teams before the dogs could learn dog team discipline. A primary promoter of this new sport has been Tom Althaus, who spent a year in Colorado as an exchange student and absorbed the enthusiasm of the western mushers for sled dogs. When he returned to Switzerland, he had a Siberian Husky pup with him.

This dog, and a few others that had been imported from the United States, formed the breeding stock of the Siberian Husky in Switzerland. The reaction of Europeans to the striking Siberian was not unlike that of New Englanders in the 1920's when Leonhard Seppala brought the first of the breed from Alaska. Breeding and racing engrossed dozens of Europeans and by the mid-1970's there were hundreds of huskies in western Europe. The sled dog camp rapidly became an international event, attracting novice teams from Switzerland, Germany, Holland and Italy. Drivers from England, Norway and Finland have also attended, but the dogs had to stay home because of return quarantines of from four to six months.

Not everyone in Europe thinks sled dog racing should be limited to purebreds. In Holland, airline pilot Lew van Leeuwen and his wife, Els, believe that "a sled dog is a dog that wants to run in front of a sled." The van Leeuwens, exposed to Alaska-style racing as the result of his frequent trips to Anchorage, have been foremost promoters of sleddogsport in Europe. Coached by Earl Norris of Anchorage, the van Leeuwens were responsible for introducing basic methods and proper equipment of competitive racing to much of Europe.

To allow for the racing of unlimited teams, the Trail Club of Europe was formed in 1973, modeled closely on ISDRA guidelines. Members held two open races in 1974, a Swiss Open Championship and a European Championship (in Germany), with sixteen-mile trails for two days of racing. Borrowing techniques from America, Europe's best races feature a big trail map for the spectators, showing which team is where. Loudspeakers, food and drink stands, and excellent press and television coverage complete the picture of a major sports event.

The race calendar for central Europe comprises open and limited races sponsored by the Trail Club of Europe, in Switzerland (Koblenz and Saignelégier), Germany (Reichswald, Latrop and Bernau) and Austria (Tannheim). Four races restricted to northern breeds are put on by the Swiss Club for Northern Dogs, in Switzerland (Savognin, Splügen, Gadmen and Lenk), and an Open German Championship race in Todtmoos is limited as to number of dogs but not to breed.

Teams tend to be smaller than in North America, and for good reason. Land is scarce in Europe and a kennel of over 15 dogs is considered huge. The price of dog food and gasoline would cause Americans to shudder. Dutch dog drivers have to travel a thousand miles to race in Switzerland, so large dog trucks carrying 12 to 18 dogs and using a gallon of gas every eight miles are prohibitively expensive. Races for three- and five-dog teams have predominated, but the sport being what it is, teams of from eight to 12 dogs are more frequently being seen in the open races in central Europe as dog drivers aim for the summit.

In Scandinavia, dog mushing has evolved naturally from a past rich in outdoor winter life. Setting out on a Sunday cross-country ski run or for a frosty overnight camping trip, Scandinavians would hitch a dog or two to a toboggan-like sled, called a "pulk" in Norwegian, to carry their gear. More often than not, the dog would be a hunting dog, a German Wirehaired or Shorthaired Pointer, a Giant Schnauzer or a German Shepherd. Long-legged and strong, the hunting dogs were deft at pulling a small load, and they frequently joined their owners for volunteer ambulance work along the cross-country ski trails. Clubs like the Norsk Trekkhundklubb (Norwegian Sled Dog Club), founded in 1931 for people who enjoyed cross-country skiing with a dog, organize the volunteer work. Today some 28 clubs have a membership of about three thousand.

When Els van Leeuwen visited Norway, she was impressed with Scandinavian ski trails. She met many skiers with dogs pulling toboggans loaded with picnics or camping gear. Small cabins along the trails provide shelter, and at least one trail leads all the way to Lapland.

Sled dog racing in Scandinavia, then, stems from a tradition based on a cross-country skier with a small toboggan and one or two dogs to pull it. A race was held at the 1952 Norwegian Olympic Games, and Norway's Seppala Memorial Race, the oldest and longest sled dog race in that country, is a pulk race. This commemorative race consists of two heats, the first about 19 miles, the second about 31. The toboggans are weighted with camping gear according to how many dogs are pulling, about fifty pounds per dog. Dogs and drivers spend one night camped out. The winner in 1971 traveled light, with one dog, a pointer. A Northern Championship race has also been run under rules and classes established by the Norwegian Kennel Club. Drivers from Norway, Sweden and Finland have competed in this two- or three-dog, nineteen-mile race.

One of Sweden's races, a three-day, 75-mile trip through the wildest part of the northern mountains, requires map reading, since no trails are packed, and competitors must camp out for the full course of the race. Often the teams will be separated into two classes, one for hunting dogs, one for northern breeds. In spite of the recent surge in the Siberian Husky population, in Scandinavia hunting dogs still predominate.

With the arrival and subsequent breeding of the first Siberian Huskies in Norway, Sweden and Finland, American-style sled dog racing began in Scandinavia. In 1960, the Norwegian explorer Helge Ingstad and his daughter, Benedicte, received two Siberian pups selected by Leonhard Seppala and donated by Jean Bryar. Benedicte Ingstad visited the Swiss Camp for Northern Dogs in the late 1960's and the information and enthusiasm she brought back to Norway were so persuasive that by 1973 the Norwegians were ready for American-style racing. They then went to Sweden and introduced what they called, appropriately enough, the "Nome style" of racing.

The first Siberian Husky arrived in Finland in 1965 and by 1968 there were enough huskies and enough interest in racing for the new Siberian Husky Club of Finland to hold its first sled dog camp. An ardent promoter of the races is Dr. Esa Mäntysalo, the professor of physics who keeps a dog team to haul scientific instruments to the ice fields. The Finnish Championship now consists of a fourteen-mile trail, run under ISDRA rules in two heats by teams which are limited to five or six dogs. Women's races, races for the youngsters, and Scandinavian-style ski-joring races are also part of the activities.

Despite American influence on sled dog racing in Europe, the sport is flexible enough to accommodate traditions and philosophies from both sides of the Atlantic Ocean. A breed club in Bad-Sooden, Germany, sponsored both Scandinavian and American-style races, with separate classes for purebreds and crossbreds. No matter which style of race, however,

the proceedings reflected a decided Old World flavor due to their surroundings: miles of well-groomed trails that spread out into the forest
around the story-book castle used as headquarters.

In adopting an already-established sport, Europeans have benefited
from the experiences of North Americans. They have consulted often
with veteran dog drivers and they have sought the help of ISDRA with
respect to organizational details, race rules and standards. Some European racers are interested in achieving ISDRA sanctioning for their races.
This would place the best European drivers on the list of point winners
toward ISDRA's International Championships. With this system in full
swing, neither national boundaries nor the world's great distances would
preclude the crowning of true international sled dog racing champions.

And then, North Americans might do well to adopt some tricks which
are customarily European. In Holland, for example, a most sensible
footwear is worn for feeding the dogs or cleaning the kennels: wooden
shoes.

Back Across the Bering Strait

If the Siberian Husky, whose name reflects his origin, is indeed responsible for capturing the imaginations of inspired dog drivers all over the
world, what are his cousins up to in their native land? Have they been
developed as racing huskies or has this natural breed suffered official
displacement by Soviet "factory" breeds? In fact, neither. Individual
breeders of the Chukchi dog in Siberia maintain the natural superiority
of these dogs for the work they have done for centuries. The isolation of
these regions has worked in favor of Siberian breeders and their working
dogs.

Sled dog races are held in the Kolyma region and probably wherever
else there are dog teams. Heats for some of these races are at least 31
miles long, but no statistics are available since they are usually not recorded. The object is solely to see which team wins.

On the inspiration of Mayor Robert H. Renshaw of Nome, the Soviet
Union was invited to participate in the 1974 Iditarod Trail race. The
invitation was communicated by Governor William A. Egan: "Because
sled dogs and their drivers have performed a similar role in heroic service
in Russian history and because of Alaska's ties of heritage with Russia, it
would be appropriate if the Iditarod Trail Sled Dog Race could include
participation from your country."

As yet, no Russian team has joined the race, but when they do, evidence
is that they will fare well. The Kamchatka sled dog, a natural Siberian

breed, was clocked at over twenty miles an hour on a short, five-mile course, with unloaded sled. With a normal load, teams travel for several days an average of 60 to 75 miles a day in Siberia. The 1975 Iditarod Trail Race was won at an average of 62.5 miles a day. It would be anybody's race.

World Championships: The Pas, Laconia, Anchorage

Like many of the sporting world's purported global championships, the world championship in sled dog racing is not a select international event with national champions competing for a world title. In fact, sled dog racing has three "world championships." The winners of these races, however, can be said with confidence to be the best racing sled dog drivers in the world. Not only are the courses of championship quality, but the competition is the stiffest. The races are open to any top driver who wants to enter and over the years those few who are indeed the very best have proved it by winning, often more than once, at least one of the world championships. To win all three in any given year would be next to impossible, for the Anchorage (Alaska) World Championship Sled Dog Race, the Laconia (New Hampshire) World Championship Sled Dog Derby and the World Championship Sled Dog Race at The Pas (Manitoba) are all held within a week of each other. Only one man, Roland Lombard, has even driven in all three races, and there was a twenty-nine-year span between his runs.

The 150-mile race at The Pas is the oldest of the World Championships, sporting its lofty title right from the beginning. "Nowhere in the world is there a race like this," declared local editor Grant Rice, reviewing proposals for this first long cross-country race in 1916. Drivers in Nome's All-Alaska Sweepstakes might have taken exception to this claim, but they didn't.

Besides its notable longevity, the race at The Pas has several outstanding features. The course is twice as long as the other world championships. It begins on a frozen river and includes varied and difficult terrain. Fifty miles a day by dog team is challenging enough, but at The Pas the ability of the drivers to make no errors in selecting and running the best dogs is tested by a rule which limits their teams to nine dogs. Drivers must pace their teams over the long course, considering the stamina of each dog and balancing this with the need for speed.

Another of the fine tests of championship quality at The Pas is the mass start. As many as 25 yelping dog teams have lined up on the river ice near the town, and when the starting gun is fired, they break en masse, each team striving for a front position before the river narrows. A driver who can thread his animated dog team through this bedlam three days in a row and keep a reasonable pace for the rest of the long race deserves his $2,000 first prize and his title of World Champion sled dog driver, The Pas variety.

In its sixty years of races, The Pas has attracted an international array of the best dog drivers. Three-time Alaska Sweepstakes champion Leonhard Seppala raced there once with his Siberians, but was beaten. Shorty Russick and his mixed husky team set a record for what was a 200-mile non-stop event in 1924, arriving back at the finish line 23 hours, 42 minutes after he had left—an average speed of over eight miles an hour. The next year Emile St. Godard and his team of mixed Wolfhound and Malamute dogs began their awesome feat of winning five times in a row, finally capitulating in 1930 to Earl Brydges.

Economic conditions and then World War II caused a seventeen-year hiatus in the running of the race at The Pas. It was revived in 1948 as part of the Northern Manitoba Trappers' Festival, with a freight race as the main attraction.

Some of New England's best drivers, mushing far afield for the first time, arrived in The Pas in 1957. Dr. Roland Lombard was on his way to future victories in Alaska and so was Jean Bryar. Lombard won the race at The Pas that year, and Bryar's two teams (one driven by Quebec's champion, Emile Martel) finished second and third. Another American took first in 1958, when former The Pas resident Art Allen of Iowa returned "home" and set a course record while out-racing the 1956 champion Ernest Jebb by eight minutes. Since then the World Championship at The Pas has been the province of local drivers.

The course record was set in 1971 by John Calvert of The Pas, running a team of mixed breed dogs; in 1975 the winner was Bob McPhail. Even though the trail was smooth and fast, his time was about an hour slower than Calvert's record run.

Most of the dogs in this World Championship are working dogs, most of the drivers are trappers, supplementing their income with prize money. Manitoban sled dogs have changed little since the gold rush days, exhibiting the thick, unruly coats, wiry strength and wide, tough feet of a true working husky. Their hound ancestry is also visible. Capitalizing on these authentic representatives of their turn-of-the-century ancestors, a European film company shot scenes of the race in 1974, to be used in a motion picture version of Jack London's *White Fang*. Three Canadian dog drivers and 22 dogs then traveled to Austria for some more filming. In spite of their international stardom, the huskies will no doubt be kept "honest," for the length and requirements of the championship race at

A POPULAR WAY TO GO HIKING IN EUROPE, with an
Akita pulling a "pulk." *Hans Keusen*

A PLEDGE TO THE FLAG HALTS THE DOG DRIVERS FOR
A MOMENT at a pre-race ceremony at Laconia, N.H.,
in 1969. Drivers from all over the U.S. and Canada
participate in this World Championship.
Charles L. Booth, Courtesy Cascadian Kennels

FOUR DOG TEAMS CROSS THE ICE ON LAKE
OPEECHEE during a World Championship at
Laconia, N.H. *Mildred A. Beach*

WORLD TRAVELER LOWELL THOMAS came for the World Championship Sled
Dog Derby in Laconia in 1962, and as honorary judge started the field of 28
drivers on their way. Left to right: Mrs. Thomas, Laconia's Mayor J. Oliva
Huot, Mrs. Dolores Bridges (wife of Senator Styles Bridges), Lowell
Thomas, and three Queen candidates, Marlee Moulton, Helen Bolduc and
Jean Belair. *Earl O. Anderson*

The Pas precludes selective breeding of these scrub huskies into a fast sprint animal.

People associated with the World Championship Sled Dog Race at The Pas have managed to stay out of the friendly but spirited controversy about World Championships that exists between the people in Anchorage and those in Laconia. A former Laconia resident living in Alaska in the early 1960's expressed distress in a letter back to the Laconia *Evening Citizen* that radio announcers at the annual Alaskan Championship Sled Dog Race in Anchorage had suddenly elevated this race to World Championship status. After all, Laconia had hosted sled dog races since 1922 and claimed the title from 1936 on. During the ensuing verbal blizzard between the two towns, Anchorage claimed a longer, tougher course, keener competition and greater prize money. Laconia insisted that age has its privilege, and cited greater representation by top drivers from several states and Canada as the essence of world championship. A four-time Laconia winner who has also raced in Alaska, Dr. Charles Belford of Massachusetts, perceptively stated in 1964 that Laconia is a speed test, Anchorage one of stamina; both are championship quality.

Settling such disputes of local pride will never be as straightforward as settling on the winner of a race. Six seconds over a 56-mile trail is not a comfortable win, but it is a win. Such was the margin of New Hampshire's Dick Moulton over Maine's Lloyd Slocum at Laconia in 1973. Moulton, veteran sled dog driver and two-time Laconia champion, held a lead of two minutes and 37 seconds over Slocum at the end of the first day's heat. Slocum, 1972's winner and at forty years old still a practising marathon runner, stepped up his pace and won the second and third day's heats. On the third day he even set a record of one hour, ten minutes, 58 seconds for the eighteen-mile trail. His amazing finish, however, was just not enough to overtake Moulton's lead, and Moulton had his third World Championship title.

The 1974 race had to be cancelled, for there was no snow in the Sled Dog Capital of the East. In 1975, Moulton returned and coasted to victory, nine long seconds ahead of Harris Dunlap of New York, two minutes, seven seconds ahead of Slocum.

Moulton thus tied Charlie Belford's record of four Laconia championships, although Belford retains the distinction of being the only three-in-a-row winner. Belford was the second champion to retire the Laconia trophy, the original one having gone home with Keith Bryar of New Hampshire after his wins in 1960, 1962 and 1963.

The dog teams at Laconia are predominantly husky. Moulton's team is based on the Alaskan Husky, that mixed husky breed which originated in Alaska and has been so successful everywhere. Some of Canada's long-

AFTER THE 1960 WORLD CHAMPIONSHIP AT LACONIA: Governor Wesley Powell, World Champion Keith Bryar, and Honorary Judge Leonhard Seppala.   *Earl O. Anderson*

KEEPING TRACK OF THE TEAMS IN THE ANCHORAGE WORLD CHAMPION-SHIP, 1970.   *Maxine Vehlow*

FORMER CHAMPION JAKE BUTLER handled the team for Isaac Okleasik of
Teller at the 1970 Rondy. *Maxine Vehlow*

153

legged, racy hound blood is also evident, and often Moulton's Walker Coonhound-husky crossbreeds run up front. Slocum, a protegé of Roland Lombard, has developed a line of Siberian Huskies from some of Lombard's purebred stock, although his team also includes a good deal of Alaskan strain.

When Canadians race at Laconia, which they do frequently, floppy-eared, hound-type sled dogs appear. Ever since the 1920's and the Eastern International Dog-sled Derbies in Quebec, when the Canadians found that their mixed hound breeds could outrun even Seppala's Siberians under many conditions, the so-called "Quebec Hound" has been the backbone of the fastest Canadian teams. At Laconia, the Canadians are never far from the top and in 1967 they ran away with the race. Eddy Sylvain of Quebec came in first with two of his countrymen right behind him.

The only Alaskan to challenge dog drivers in this most southern of the world championships was Jerry Riley of Nenana. He entered in 1965 but landed in Laconia during Belford's three-in-a-row; he was second by seven minutes.

The World Championship at Anchorage, known as the Rondy, has been distinguished by challenges to Alaskan mushers from Outside. It has also fostered one of the longest and closest rivalries in the world of sports. At the first official World Championship in 1960, 24 Alaskan drivers were joined by the two veterinarians from Massachusetts, Lombard and Belford. Lombard succeeded in winning the second day's heat, but the Outside mushers were, finally, outrun by Alaskans Cue Bifelt, Wilbur Sampson and Leo Kriska. At the end of the three-day, 75-mile race, only 74 seconds separated the first three teams. This means that the third-place team had lost an average of not quite one second per mile relative to the winner. There is no time for relaxing in a sled dog race.

George Attla of Huslia had two Rondy wins to his credit when Doc Lombard, after five attempts, became the first Outsider to win there, in 1963. Since then the Rondy has been dominated by this rivalry, with the up-and-coming Attla and the veteran Lombard battling year after year over split seconds. By the close of the 1975 season the score was Lombard, 8, and Attla, 5.

Several of the best drivers from the lower 48 have recently raced at Anchorage, attracted by the prestige, the challenge and the prizes. Besides Lombard and Belford, Ozzie Bayers from Minnesota and Merv Hilpipre from Iowa have made creditable showings, with Hilpipre finishing third behind Attla and Lombard in 1975. The only Canadian to run in the Rondy scratched his team after the second day, but Canadians have their eyes on this race. As their race circuits produce faster teams, Cana-

INSPECTING THE DOGS (and the photographer) at the 1974 Rondy.
Maxine Vehlow

dians will be counted among the contenders in the Rondy.

World Championships are long, exhausting races. The one at Anchorage is held at the end of the long, exhausting, fun-filled two weeks of mid-winter celebration, the Fur Rendezvous. The annual fur auction is still a main attraction, complementing this farthest-north World Championship sled dog race. It is certain that in no other world championship could a sled dog pick up the extra booty that Darrell Reynolds' team did in 1969. Coming down Fourth Avenue toward the finish, his lead dog spotted a white fox fur lying in the road ahead. It had just been dropped by a buyer at the auction. As he ran past, the leader scooped it up gingerly in his teeth and proudly carried his own prized trophy across the finish line.

A true world championship sled dog derby, in the purest international sense of the term, is somewhat of an impossible dream, at least for the near future. To simulate such a contest, ISDRA has devised a point system for its sanctioned races. This allows the organization to determine its annual Gold, Silver and Bronze Medal winners. A race is fully sanctioned and driver points are awarded only if the race meets certain uniform standards as specified by ISDRA. After the race is run, points are awarded to the drivers, based on their final position, the length of the course, the number of competitors and the size of the purse. Up to four races a year may be used to accumulate annual points. It follows, then, that the top drivers in the biggest races will set the pace. Gold Medal winners to date: George Attla in 1972 and 1975, Roland Lombard in 1973 and 1974.

George Attla has raced outside of Alaska, but not, as yet, in either of the other two world championships. Only two dog drivers have accomplished wins in two separate World Championships: Doc Lombard and Emile St. Godard.

POST-RACE PLEASANTRIES IN ALASKA. Doc Lombard, the Fur Rendezvous Queen, George Attla and Leo Kriska.   *Maxine Vehlow*

6

Renowned Dog Drivers and Their Dogs

Driving dogs, in my opinion, is an art, the qualifications for which must be instinctive in the individual as they cannot fully be acquired. There are persons who have been years in the North who remain inferior dog drivers, while others who have been in the country for only a short time instinctively control their dogs to much better advantage. The qualifications necessary in a good dog driver would appear to be an even temperament, patience, energy, and the ability to curb the more boisterous instincts of one's team without recourse to violence.

INSPECTOR C.E. RIVETT-CARNAC, 1938

The Dog Mushers' Hall of Fame

Walking encyclopedias, especially if they are good at spinning yarns around their facts, are infinitely more informative than the printed ver-

157

sions. Dog mushing harbors colorful veterans with libraries in their heads, but none so visually oriented as those who run the Dog Mushers' Hall of Fame. Long-time dog mushers Joe and Violet Redington of Wasilla, Alaska, inaugurated the Hall of Fame in 1966. Inside the restored wooden frame building that is the museum in Knik are portraits of sled dog racing's finest, the men and women and the dogs who are remembered for their accomplishments in the sport. Inside the Redingtons' heads are stories about races and exploits to back up and bring to life every portrait in the hall.

Organized to salute Alaskans and others who have gained fame in dog mushing circles, the Hall of Fame's first honored musher was Leonhard Seppala. The 12 other drivers elected to date: Scotty Allan, three-time winner of the All-Alaska Sweepstakes; George Attla, multi-champion of the big Alaska races; Percy Blatchford, driver for Jacob Berger in the second All-Alaska Sweepstakes but more famous, according to pioneer Nome resident Carrie McLean, "for his dependable mail delivery by dog team"; Fay Delezene, a top contender in the early Alaskan races and winner of the sixth All-Alaska Sweepstakes; John Hegness, driver of Judge Albert Fink's racing team and winner of the First All-Alaska Sweepstakes; John "Iron Man" Johnson, record-setter on the trail between Nome and Candle in the third Sweepstakes; Dr. Roland Lombard, an Outsider who by 1975 had won at Anchorage and Fairbanks a record 14 times; Earl and Natalie Norris, leaders in organizing and supporting sled dog racing in post-war Alaska; Raymond Paul, native Alaskan and the first three-time winner of the Anchorage World Championship; Fox Maule Ramsay, whose two teams of newly-imported Siberian Huskies placed first and second in the spectacular third running of the Sweepstakes; Emile St. Godard, champion musher from Canada and winner of the 1932 Winter Olympics demonstration sled dog race; Eva B. "Short" Seeley, pioneer breeder and promoter of northern dogs and racing in New England; and Clyde "Slim" Williams, who in 1932–33 drove a dog team a record 5,600 miles from Copper Center, Alaska, to Washington, D.C., to promote an international highway between the lower 48 states and Alaska.

A special section of the Dog Mushers' Hall of Fame honors those non-racers who have contributed significantly to the history of sled dogs: Ben Downing, who laid out the first mail trails between Dawson in the Yukon Territory and Alaska and then drove them dependably for years; Colonel Marvin R. "Muktuk" Marston, who drove dog teams over a thousand miles during World War II, battling recalcitrant administrators and overwhelming blizzards, to organize the Eskimos into the Alaska Territorial Guard, and who also was a prime backer of the first long Iditarod

Trail Race; Carrie McLean, friend and supporter of many of the early Nome drivers; General William "Billy" Mitchell, enthusiastic sled dog fan since his days as a young lieutenant when he drove sled dogs in connection with his work on a telegraph line across Alaska; Dr. Joseph H. Romig, who practiced medicine by dog team in isolated Alaskan villages at the turn of the century, and whose experiences are related by Eva G. Anderson in *Dog Team Doctor;* Raymond L. Thompson, long-time editor, author and promoter of the lore of sled dogs; and Judge James Wickersham, Alaska judge and later congressman, author of *Old Yukon–Tales, Trails and Trials*, about his experiences traveling around his vast Third District by dog team.

Two sled dogs have been elected to the Dog Mushers' Hall of Fame, one from the distant past, one from the recent: Togo, a male Siberian Husky who led Leonhard Seppala's team for many long years, including the race to Nome in 1925; and Nellie, a female Alaskan Husky, leader for George Attla and Roland Lombard, a dog with exceptional speed, courage, stamina and intelligence. A new Canine Hall of Fame will make room for more of these outstanding dogs whose understanding and capacity to give are perhaps even more important than their speed.

The relationship between a sled dog driver and his dogs is unique in history and in the world of sports. The dependence of the driver on the dogs, of the dogs on the driver, is like no other sport. A well-trained team is virtually priceless to its owner. Every dog in the team is important, although a driver often favors his leader, for there is no question that to the leader falls an extra measure of responsibility for the whole outfit. To the driver, too, falls the task of bringing the best out of his dogs. It is no accident that the exceptional lead dogs belong to the exceptional drivers.

Even among the greats in the Hall of Fame, several racing drivers (and their dogs) stand out as superior. Not only are their racing records impressive, but these drivers have been able to bring an uncommon talent to their sport and to advance it in several distinctive ways. Besides those already honored in the Hall of Fame, others have made or are making extraordinary contributions to sled dog racing; they will be the recipients of future honors.

Leonhard Seppala and Togo

No dog driver has the status, the renown, the respect of his colleagues as does Leonhard Seppala. His fame has lasted far beyond his brief national acclaim following the race to Nome against epidemic. His greatness has long outlasted his success as a racer. Before his death in 1967 at the age of 90, Seppala had been made an honorary member of four prestigious organizations: the Siberian Husky Club of America, the International Siberian Husky Club (which was originally chartered as the Seppala Siberian Husky Club), the New England Sled Dog Club and the Norwegian Sled Dog Club. In Norway, the Norsemen's League awarded Seppala its medal for his part in the development of Alaska and as an outstanding citizen of the United States. The longest sled dog race in his homeland is named the Seppala Memorial Race.

The longest sled dog race in North America is also named for Seppala, and when 34 dog teams left the starting line in Anchorage on March 3, 1973, bound for Nome, in the first thousand-mile Seppala Memorial Iditarod Trail Race, no driver wore the Number One. Starting position Number One had been reserved in memory of the most distinguished dog driver of all time. Constance Seppala, his wife, Queen of the 1915 All-Alaska Sweepstakes, was there as a special guest of honor.

In 1961, at a testimonial banquet with the Alaska Press Club, Lowell Thomas introduced the 84-year-old musher with the sparkling blue eyes as "the greatest dog team driver that ever lived."

For Leonhard Seppala was an original, an innovator, a pioneer. There was no aspect of dog driving he left untouched. Even today, almost one hundred years after his birth, many of the Siberian Huskies that race the trails are descendants of Seppala's Siberians.

At the turn of the century young Seppala left his native Norway, his father's fishing boat and his apprenticeship with a blacksmith, and joined the hundreds of men seeking their fortunes in the gold fields of Alaska. He soon discovered that a steadier, if less spectacular, way to make money was to have a dog team and to freight supplies to the miners. Within a few years Seppala had a reputation as one of the best of the dog-punchers.

His life swerved onto a new trail when, inspired by the excitement of the new sled dog races in Nome, he entered and won his first race, at age 36. The next year, 1914, he entered the All-Alaska Sweepstakes with a team of young Siberian dogs that he had been training for the explorer, Roald Amundsen. He finished last of four, with a leader named Suggen, but he was hopelessly hooked on sled dog racing. In 1915, 1916 and 1917 he won the Sweepstakes with good margins, having obtained permanent possession of the Siberians when Amundsen's North Pole trip was cancelled. Seppala's appreciation of the imported huskies was immediately apparent, and years later he wrote, "Once more the little Siberians had proved their superiority over the other dogs and I was proud to have been their driver and to have brought them in in such good condition."

His continuing successes put him on top of the list when the chairman of Nome's Board of Health was looking for fast teams to go for the

160

TOGO, LEADER OF SEPPALA'S TEAM FOR TWELVE YEARS, and canine hero of the serum race to Nome in 1925. *Seppala: Alaskan Dog Driver*

LEONHARD SEPPALA, a legend in his own time. *Courtesy William L. Shearer, III*

WILL ROGERS, LEONHARD SEPPALA, WILEY POST AND JOE CROSSON, 50 miles south of Fairbanks at Harding Lake on August 15, 1935. Four hours later, Rogers and Post perished when their plane crashed. *Courtesy Harris Dunlap and Ivan Beliveau*

DICK MOULTON, WHO LEARNED HOW TO DRIVE SLED DOGS IN THE DAYS OF WALDEN AND SEPPALA, finishing his three-day, sixty-mile run to first place in the 1971 World Championship at Laconia. The black and white Attla is on right lead. *L. Coppinger*

diphtheria serum being relayed in from Anchorage. Seppala's leader by then was Togo, a son of Suggen. Togo, destined to become a hero as the result of his valiant leadership across the trackless treachery of Norton Sound, began life as a spoiled, hard-to-handle pup. He was born north of Nome, in Little Creek, an offspring of some of Fox Ramsay's Siberian imports. Part of his early training included running free beside the big team, which he loved, but one day he ran into a team of tough Malamutes and was badly chewed up. Perhaps this is one of the ways a future lead dog learns part of his lessons, for Togo became the best passer Seppala ever had. He was a master at keeping his team well out of reach of any other dogs on the trail.

After the successful life-saving race to Nome, Seppala and Togo toured the East Coast. In 1927 he took his whole team to New England and proceeded to win race after race. He won New England Sled Dog Club races in Maine and New Hampshire; he won Eastern International Dog Derbies in Quebec; he won races in Lake Placid, although Canada's great Emile St. Godard did beat him for first place in the Olympic race. Everywhere he went, if he was not actually racing, he was talking dogs. Many a future dog driver learned the basics, the fun and the dangers of driving sled dogs, just by listening whenever "Sepp" was around.

Eastern mushers became just as enamoured of the Siberian Huskies as was Seppala, and, with his help, selective breeding programs were started at several kennels. Seppala was looking for a slightly larger dog without diminishing the alertness, grace and lightness of foot that contributed to this natural breed's success in racing. Coloration was not of primary importance to Seppala, although he did prefer lighter coats, and as his program developed, very light grey to white dogs predominated.

In addition to the dogs, Seppala introduced to the East at least two innovations in racing. To New Englanders, familiar with the single-file freight hitch brought from Alaska by Arthur Walden, Seppala's method of hooking the dogs in pairs with a single leader looked strange. Nothing bodes better for an innovation than success, however, and this double tandem hitch, with occasional slight modifications, is standard in races today. The other novelty presented by Seppala was the driver's more active participation in the race. Although dog-punchers and long-distance racers usually ran beside their sleds, the sprint racers would stand on the runners of their lighter racing sleds, jumping off only to run uphill. Seppala broke through this prevailing concept and instigated a pedaling motion with one leg, as though on a scooter, timing his push with the dogs' strides to keep the sled moving at an even rate.

Seppala and his wife returned to Alaska in the mid-thirties, and then, after retirement, moved to Seattle, Washington. In 1960 the chipper little man flew to Laconia to serve as honorary judge at the World Championship Sled Dog Derby. He was 83 years young, and still delighted with the sled dogs. He reflected on his 45 years of dog driving, his quarter of a million miles by dog team, his 43 silver cups and eight gold medals, and the people of Laconia knew they were witnessing a giant of the sport.

There is more, of course, to Seppala's story. Beyond the trophies, the Seppala-strain sled dogs, the inspired dog drivers, the innovations and the contributions to the sport, there lies the quality of the man. In a sport where handling dogs well is a necessity, the best still pay tribute to Seppala's skillful relationships with his dogs. In a sport where some try to win with pressure and punishment, Seppala's unequalled triumphs were achieved with kindness and encouragement. A driver could be running a good race, but he knew if Seppala were in it, chances were good that the little Siberian team would go flying past, almost soundless. "He just clucked to them every now and then, and they would lay into their collars harder than I've ever seen dogs do before," asserted one awed competitor. "Something came out of him and went into those dogs with that clucking. He passed me every day of the race and I wasn't loafing any!"

Harry Wheeler, with whom Seppala set up a kennel in Quebec, described Seppala in his fifties: "I've seen that great Alaska musher get up early in the morning, hitch up 11 dogs, drive 60 miles and return home for a late dinner, ski 20 miles in the afternoon, eat a good evening meal at Gray Rocks, dance every woman in the ballroom until 12 or 1, and for good measure, and for the entertainment of all, turn a few handsprings."

After a long day, related Wheeler, Seppala would reach for his parka and cap and go out to his dogs one more time before retiring, to check on their comfort. Out would go that little weather-beaten Alaskan, a man who pinned his faith and his life on the good health, endurance and loyalty of his dogs.

Scotty Allan and Baldy

Until a lead dog named Fat Albert received nationwide celebrity status during the running of the 1974 Iditarod Trail Race, Leonhard Seppala and Togo were the best known musher and lead dog outside the sled dog world. Except, possibly, for Baldy of Nome and his master, Allan Alexander "Scotty" Allan. The story of Baldy, as written by Allan's colleague, Esther Birdsall Darling, was widely read by the younger set.

Baldy, a flop-eared mongrel, bred in a mining camp for freighting work, joined Scotty Allan's kennel at about the time Allan was helping to establish the Nome Kennel Club and the All-Alaska Sweepstakes races. Baldy's

SCOTTY ALLAN, "KING OF THE ARCTIC TRAIL," and his remarkable leader, Baldy of Nome. *The Great Dog Races of Nome*

first race was at the head of a three-dog team driven by Allan's son, George, in what was probably the first organized junior race. Baldy's attention to the duty at hand, his dependability and loyalty, elevated him rapidly to the position of leader on Allan's big team. The stories of his great leadership ability and his several rescues of his master have singled him out from hundreds of other northern dogs whose achievements are equally inspiring but whose masters did not happen to work with a writer.

One of the most famous incidents occurred during Baldy's first big race on lead. He had been promoted to leader only the night before, as the result of the untimely death of Allan's regular lead dog. Racing in Nome's Solomon Derby and amazed at how well his new leader was doing, Scotty Allan leaned off his sled at one point to check a runner and hit his head on an iron trail stake. He spilled unconscious into the snow.

Darling described the lead dog's reaction in *Baldy of Nome:* "At last the instinct that all was not right was too strong for Baldy. Stopping suddenly, he looked back and discovered that they were driverless . . . and knowing that the time for action had come, that his supremacy as a leader must be acknowledged, and at once, firmly held his ground." Baldy turned the team and ran back over several miles of trail to where he found his pale and bleeding, still unconscious master. Licking his face and scratching at his chest, Baldy revived Allan and, at a mumbled request, again turned the team and continued on with the race. It sounds like a fictional ending, but the record books show that Scotty Allan's dog team with its new leader was the first team in to Solomon and held the lead all the way back to Nome, the winners.

When a person makes a success in a chosen endeavor, information released to the public often refers to at least one incident from that person's youth that proves an early interest in the chosen profession. Childhood being what it is, such connections, although often thin, are usually not hard to make. In the case of Scotty Allan, a reporter would gain a wealth of fascinating material about animals when he investigated the champion dog driver's youth. Not only did young Allan win the Grand National Sheep Dog Trial in Scotland with a remarkable Border Collie named Dandy, but he was schooled in the training of horses. It was this latter ability that led him to the United States with a Clydesdale stallion to be delivered to his employer's client in South Dakota. He landed in America in 1887; Leonhard Seppala was ten, and still in Norway.

Scotty Allan journeyed to Alaska, attracted by news of the gold strike in the Klondike. This short man with the thick Scottish burr in his speech, the deep blue eyes and the light hair, thrived in this land of adventurers. Around him were men of action from many different countries, dependent in large measure upon animals. It was not long before Allan had a wife, a baby and a dog team, and with his uncanny knack with animals, was well on his way to being a first-class dog-puncher. His first leader was called Dubby, a Mackenzie River Husky from the stock of the Hudson's Bay Company. Dubby led the team the day his venturesome owner decided to sledge across the Bering Strait to Russia. Shannon Garst, writing in *Scotty Allan, King of the Dog-Team Drivers,* described Allan's thought process:

> " 'There wasna any reason or sense to what I did, but when I came to Cape Prince of Wales there was Siberia looming off the nor-west. In the clear Arctic air it dinna look more than about thirty miles, so I decided to gae across and take a look.'
>
> "It took him eighteen hours, much of the time in the dark, to get across, and part of the way was on moving chunks of ice and through heavy snow."

Allan visited with some Siberian Eskimos and then headed back to Nome, impressed with the self-sufficiency of these people.

Scotty Allan joined with Judge Albert Fink and other Nome citizens to organize the All-Alaska Sweepstakes, the first official series of sled dog races anywhere. From these races emerged a new kind of hero in the far North, the racing sled dog driver. In preparation for these 408-mile non-stop races, Allan put his team and himself into training. He watched everybody's diet, gave up smoking and even practiced going without sleep. He must have done something right, for in the first eight years of the Sweepstakes, Scotty Allan never finished lower than third and had three firsts and three seconds to his credit. His dog team consisted of lop-eared freighting dogs, mongrels, and he was proud of their ability on the racing trails.

In more than one race, however, Allan could look back over his shoulder and see John "Iron Man" Johnson's long string of Siberians slowly gaining on him. Johnson's great black and white leader, Kolyma, with light, penetrating blue eyes shining out from a jet black and white face mask, would set a tireless pace. Kolyma, a wonder even among the dog-wise people of the North, led a team of culls from Fox Ramsay's other two imported Siberian Husky teams to a record-setting win for Johnson in 1910.

The handwriting was on the wall for the mixed-breed freighting teams. Johnson's Siberians beat Allan's team by nine hours in 1914 and then Leonhard Seppala and his Siberians wrapped it all up in the final three years of the Sweepstakes.

167

Arthur Walden and Chinook

When sled dog racing started to catch on as a winter sport in New England and Canada, however, the speedy little Siberian with the great endurance had not yet been introduced outside of Alaska. Crossbred dogs still held the inside track. Arthur Walden and Emile St. Godard won many races in New England and Canada during the 1920's; Walden's dogs were the big golden Chinooks, a freighting dog, and St. Godard's were hound-husky crosses, bred for speed.

For his part in the promotion of the sport in New England, Arthur Walden holds that inevitable title, "Father of New England Sled Dog Racing." For nearly twenty years he traveled all over the Northeast, including Canada, driving his teams in races and exhibitions, at schools and fairs. For much of that time his famous dog, Chinook, was on lead, or at least a welcome companion at ball games, lectures, promotional visits. Breeding Chinook with a mixed Eskimo husky bitch, Walden selected out the yellow pups that most closely resembled their father. With a breeding program that included not selling any dogs that could reproduce, Walden developed his unique dogs and sold them as sled dogs or pets.

In 1928 Arthur Walden, age 56, with his craggy, New England-granite face, with a squint and a vision in his eyes that spoke of many a long trail, ventured from New Hampshire and his special breed of sled dog, from his New England Sled Dog Club, from the races and the farm where he and Chinook taught dog driving, and joined Admiral Byrd's Antarctic Expedition. His position was that of dog handler and his chief assistant was Chinook. Chinook, one hundred pounds of aggressive masculinity and distinctive personality, with a stout-hearted endurance and great intelligence, had been showing his age for about a year. Although Walden hardly expected the dog would long survive the expedition, he was not prepared to lose his dog quite the way he did. On January 24, 1929, the Manchester (New Hampshire) *Union Leader* carried the following story:

"CHINOOK, WORLD FAMED DOG,
REPORTED DEAD ON ANTARCTIC ICE FIELDS.

"Chinook, Walden's famous veteran of many sled dog races is now believed dead on the ice in the Antarctic. The Wonalancet dog, according to reports, wandered off across the ice fields and is believed to have succumbed to the rigorous climate . . . Throughout New Hampshire and Canada and even to several European countries where his fame as a sled dog leader spread, Chinook's death will come as a blow to dog lovers, especially in the North country where he was considered as a pet and more often treated as a human being than a canine."

ARTHUR T. WALDEN, dog-puncher, sled dog racer, founder of the New England Sled Dog Club, and dog handler for Byrd, with his favorite dog, Chinook, about 1922.

Courtesy New England Sled Dog Club

169

Walden returned to New Hampshire and remained a popular speaker on sled dogs. His life touched all the aspects, from dog-punching to racing, from kennel manager to explorer. He brought the spirit of the gold rush dog team from Alaska; he instigated sport races a continent away from their original home.

He lived to be 91 years old, straddling the animated decades from the 1870's into the 1960's. Without Arthur Walden, the lore and the lure of the sled dog would be much less than it is.

Short Seeley and the Wonalancet Kennels

A large measure of the success of the Siberian Husky and the Alaskan Malamute as purebred sled and show dogs goes to a small, sprightly woman known as "Short" Seeley. When Arthur Walden left New Hampshire to go with Admiral Byrd, he left his Chinook Kennels in the more than capable hands of Milton and Eva Seeley. The enthusiasm and complete professional dedication which the Seeleys lavished on northern dogs influenced (and still does) the status of these dogs all over the world.

At Wonalancet during the late twenties the Seeleys established a school for dogs and dog drivers. The graduates of this school, both canine and human, have gone on antarctic expeditions, served in the United States Armed Forces, and made names for themselves on the sport racing trails. The kennel and training school at Wonalancet must be the oldest such privately-run operation anywhere, and as recently as 1955, Short Seeley supplied dogs for the United States Navy's Operation Deepfreeze in Antarctica.

The dogs favored by the Seeleys were Alaskan Malamutes and Siberian Huskies, and it was primarily through their efforts that a true-to-type Alaskan Malamute was recognized by the American Kennel Club in 1935. The Seeleys organized the Alaskan Malamute Club of America, and kept the New England Sled Dog Club in business after its first president went to Antarctica. Mrs. Seeley herself was one of three women who raced the New England trails during the 1930's. The society pages of Boston newspapers often featured photographs and stories about Miss Millie Turner of Beverly Farms, Massachusetts (who sang, *We're Off to See the Wizard* to her dog team), Mrs. Lorna Taylor of Boston (who later married a Russian prince, Nicholas Demidoff, whom she met dog racing), and Mrs. Short Seeley, (the only woman to race sled dogs in the 1932 Winter Olympics).

In more recent years Mrs. Seeley has maintained her kennel at a minimum while traveling all over the country as a judge for the American

SHORT SEELEY, A GIANT IN THE WORLD OF SLED DOGS.
Bernice B. Perry, Courtesy Kenneth Saxton

Kennel Club and working on books about her life and her dogs. In what must be a record of continuous operation, those almost fifty years of running Chinook Kennels, Mrs. Seeley has estimated that she has seen over "two thousand dogs go through these gates." The accomplishments of these dogs and the achievements of the kennels have been nationally recognized. Admiral Byrd visited in the early thirties, and a plaque was dedicated to all the sled dogs that served on the Byrd Expeditions. In 1971, Senator Norris Cotton of New Hampshire read a tribute to Short Seeley into the *Congressional Record,* citing in particular her excellent contributions to the world of northern dogs. The New England Sled Dog Club and the International Sled Dog Racing Association have both named her to honorary membership. A thread of service to her country by means of her dogs runs through her life, and is unequalled.

In Wonalancet, an eastern version of a sled dog museum exhibits memorabilia relating to the sled dogs' contributions to history. Mrs. Seeley has collected equipment from the earliest days of Chinook Kennels, from the antarctic expeditions, from the vast lore of northern dogs. Meanwhile, far to the northwest, in Alaska, Mrs. Seeley has been honored by election to the Dog Mushers' Hall of Fame, one of only two women to be so distinguished.

Emile St. Godard and Toby

The young, good-looking Emile St. Godard burst onto the racing scene in 1925. The Pas, Manitoba, was his home town, but for the next ten years he was the man to beat throughout Canada and the United States. Even Leonhard Seppala found it difficult to overtake, the racing husky-hound crosses on St. Godard's dog team. These dogs, sleek and long-legged, were bred specifically for speed. If the temperature did not plummet or the snow drift too deep, they were virtually unbeatable. In 1925 they won the 200-mile, non-stop race at The Pas and the three-day, 40-miles-a-day Eastern International Dog-sled Derby at Quebec. St. Godard holds the world's record in the races at The Pas, having won five in a row. By 1928 he was a three-time winner of the Quebec derby, and although Seppala beat him in 1919, in 1930 he returned to the top and set a new record in the race.

Competition in the eastern races heightened in 1927 when Leonhard Seppala arrived; St. Godard had to keep alert in order to stay ahead. The two champion mushers drew huge crowds of excited sled dog fans whenever they appeared in a race. In the 1932 Olympics, the St. Godard-Seppala rivalry caught the attention of Arthur Daley, sportswriter for the New York *Times:*

172

EMILE ST. GODARD AND HIS SHORT-HAIRED, LONG-LEGGED, WINNING TEAM OF "CANADIAN HOUNDS," at The Pas in 1927.

Foote-James, Manitoba, Courtesy Team and Trail

DOC LOMBARD AT THE 1974 RONDY with Jill (part Labrador) and Vixen (part Siberian) on lead; racy dog just behind Lombard is half Saluki. *Maxine Vehlow*

173

"Lake Placid, New York, February 8, 1932.

"In the colorful sled dog race it was a Canadian team that was victorious as Emile St. Godard, the veteran Manitoba musher, emerged the victor over Leonhard Seppala of the United States . . . these two keen rivals, less than a minute and a half apart after the first 25 miles yesterday, again staged a bitter battle over the second 25-mile route today. St. Godard proved that his Russian Wolfhound-Malamutes were the faster dogs when he finished first once more, compiling a total time of 4 hours, 23 minutes, 12.5 seconds. Seppala, famous for his race with death to bring the antitoxin to Nome, was clocked in 4 hours, 31 minutes, 1.8 seconds for the 50 miles."

Another St. Godard record has yet to be duplicated: his victories in the four big championship races at Laconia, Quebec, Ottawa and The Pas. During his relatively brief racing career, he entered more than fifty sled dog races and won over half of them. He was never far from the top. Nominating him to the Dog Mushers' Hall of Fame, Short Seeley commented that Emile St. Godard "was one of the most sportsminded sled dog racers ever."

He learned his sport as a freighting driver, hauling supplies to trappers, traders and miners in the bush country of northern Manitoba. When he got serious about sled dog racing he quickly adapted from the working "scrub huskies" to the racing hound-husky crosses that had been the mainstay of Canadian teams for years. His leader, Toby, a clever, battle-scarred dog, was a grey husky-hound cross. He was the hero of St. Godard's victories, cheered by crowds as he crossed the finish lines, revered by school children with that special appreciation children have for remarkable animals.

Following the death of Toby in 1934, the magic seemed to vanish from racing for St. Godard. He died young, of pneumonia, at the age of 43. Yet his solid success as a sled dog driver, his winning smile that made him a favorite, are still remembered.

Roland Lombard and Nellie

Emile St. Godard's flop-eared racing hounds may have looked like odd sled dogs to Siberian fans in New England, but as he raced them in the 1929 race at Laconia, an even odder-looking team was making a first mark in sled dog racing for its youthful owner, Roland Lombard of Maine. Lombard, later to win time and again in the biggest races with long teams of Siberian-Alaskan Husky crosses, was right on St. Godard's

DOC LOMBARD AND ONE OF HIS LEADERS, "OLD HELEN."
Courtesy Lorna Demidoff

DOC LOMBARD, ALASKA, 1973. *Rondy 1973*

DOC LOMBARD'S TEAM OF SEPPALA SIBERIANS RACING IN NEW ENGLAND, circa 1950.

Bernice B. Perry, Courtesy Lorna Demidoff

heels with a motley five-dog crew. On lead, a cocker spaniel-collie farm dog; behind him, a German Shepherd cross and a mixed husky; filling out the team, two Siberians borrowed from Seppala. Lombard's third-place finish was fast enough to win him first-place handicap money, $1,000, which went a long way in those Depression days toward his schooling for a career as a veterinarian.

Once his new veterinary practice was set up near Boston, Massachusetts, Lombard returned eagerly to sled dogs. His early teams were made up of purebred Siberians, the fruits of a half-dozen New England kennels that had been breeding from Seppala stock for almost three decades.

In the late forties and well into the fifties, "Doc" Lombard and his wife, Louise, ran their Igloo Pak Kennel dogs in dozens of New England races. By the mid-fifties Lombard, along with Charles Belford and Keith Bryar, represented the best in dog driving outside of Alaska. These mushers were known as New England's "big three," whose dominance of New England races has yet to be equalled. When the New England club could scarcely contain their blazing fast teams, Lombard, Belford and Bryar ventured to bigger races in New York, Canada and finally to Alaska. Lombard was the first to take sled dog racing back to the state where it started, driving in his first Alaskan race in 1958 at the age of 46. He was also to be the most successful Outsider in Alaskan championship races, giving every sled dog driver in the state a tough run for his money for many, many years. His kind face, lined with a lifetime of smiles, became well known in Alaska. Although he remained an Outsider, his gentle manner, considerate words and fine racing record won him the respect of the farthest-north Americans.

Lombard won his first Alaskan race on his second attempt. This he did at Fairbanks, in the North American Championship, the first Outsider to challenge successfully in the fifty years of Alaskan sled dog racing. From 1958 to 1975 Doc Lombard won six North American Championships, placing second in six others. Down in Anchorage at the Fur Rendezvous World Championship it took him until 1963 to win his first one, and he was the oldest driver to ever win the Rondy when he did it. He had also won the North American that year, and so added the coveted title of Dual Champion to his laurels. In the next 12 years Lombard kept returning to Alaska, and kept proving his talents, winning eight more World Championships. In 1964 and 1967 he re-earned the Dual Championship an extraordinary second and third times.

Lombard's lead dog in most of these victories was a 48-pound black and white Alaskan Husky named Nellie. Trained in Huslia, the little Alaskan town famed for its sled dogs and their drivers, Nellie attracted

Lombard's attention in 1962 while she was running lead on champion George Attla's team. Lombard's professional admiration for the dog resulted in the first sale of a sled dog for the then unheard-of price of $1,000.

According to Attla, "She just never made a mistake on commands. It was like driving a car; you made every turn you wanted to make." Nellie had all the good traits, she worked enthusiastically, she had "heart." She helped Lombard to his unprecedented 14 Alaskan championships. The year that both Doc and his dog were elected to the Dog Mushers' Hall of Fame, Lombard commented to the Boston *Globe:* "Nellie is very special. She not only has speed, courage and stamina—because these championship races are long distance—but Nellie is highly intelligent."

Nellie represented the finest in a canine evolution that had been occurring in Alaska since Seppala left with his Siberians. A purebred Siberian strain had been developed there, but so had an unregisterable breed called the Alaskan Husky. The toughest of the survivors from the gold rush days, the fastest of the winners in the early races, were interbred with Siberians, with Malamutes, with Eskimo dogs, with wolves. When the New Englanders brought the best of their Seppala Siberians back to Alaska to race, it was the best of these husky-type dogs that beat them.

Although his once-in-a-lifetime leader, Nellie, was gone from his team by the 1970's, Doc Lombard's was still the team to beat. He earned racing's top awards in 1973 and 1974, the International Sled Dog Racing Association Gold Medal.

Roland Lombard's contributions to sled dog racing extend far beyond his racing record or his abilities with dogs. During his career he has aided more than one aspiring musher with dogs and advice, spending hours talking, explaining, teaching. The more serious of the new drivers who visit him are slowly included in fall training activities, and several of New England's better drivers learned the basics from Doc.

Another major contribution was his early belief in the idea of an international organization for the sport. Serving as the first president of the International Sled Dog Racing Association, from 1966 to 1970, he and a small group of intensely dedicated people gave unselfishly of their time and money to make this infant idea into a reality. In 1973 he was awarded an honorary membership in the association, in recognition of his substantial devotion to so many aspects of his sport.

Charles Belford and Timmy

Right behind Doc Lombard to Alaska came the other noted Massachusetts veterinarian-dog driver, Dr. Charles Belford. Known as

CHARLIE BELFORD AND NANA, half Siberian, half Malamute. No matter where he was on the trail, Belford's exhortation, "Come on, Nana, let's go home!" would inspire the dog to a home-stretch pace.

Bernice B. Perry, Courtesy Lorna Demidoff

"Sonny" in Laconia where his father was not only a prominent businessman, but one of the first to have a Seppala Siberian, and an enthusiastic race promoter, young Belford drove in his first sled dog race at age ten and won. Alec Belford "always kept dogs," according to his son, and when Leonhard Seppala arrived in New England, nothing would do but to obtain some of these original sled dogs, adding them to the kennel of prize coonhounds. Belford remembers creeping downstairs late one evening to eavesdrop on his father and Seppala "talking dogs" in the kitchen. Later he spent several winter vacations training Seppala dogs at the Gatineau Kennels of Harry Wheeler in St. Jovite, Quebec.

In 1937, just before the difficult job of giving up his dog team in order to concentrate on his training as a veterinarian, the 17-year-old Belford entered the World Championship at Laconia. He was the only American driver in a field of Canadians, and he finished not far from the top.

World War II and his schooling over, Belford set up his practice in Deerfield, Massachusetts, and began building the best racing team possible. By the early 1950's his Siberians were cruising along the New England trails at 12 to 13 miles an hour. Soon, his deliberate and careful training techniques, coupled with his uncanny ability to select good dogs, brought his team up to consistent 14- to 15-mile-an-hour runs. During these years he set a still-unbroken record for the number of races won on the New England circuit.

The life span of a good sled dog is far shorter than a driver's career, and part of the agony of this sport is wishing that a good old lead dog was still around to go with a new, fast team. Belford's favorite leader was Timmy, a pure white, registered Siberian Husky. Besides the obligatory qualities of speed and intelligence, Timmy possessed an extra measure of leadership, responding quickly to the merest suggestion of a command. "I could thread a needle with him," Belford says with great admiration, and more than one dog driver of the fifties remembers Timmy.

Charlie Belford returned to Laconia to race in 1956 and won his first World Championship. Up until then his remarkable racing record included several New England Championships, two in Lake Placid and several more at the big races in Quebec. Timmy beat Belford to Alaska, on loan to Doc Lombard in 1958. Following the Quebec race in 1959 the old leader was retired, still a champion. In 1960 Belford made his first long journey to Alaska, but neither he nor Doc Lombard were able to out-race the rangy Alaskan dogs. They both were impressed by the Alaskan racing huskies and they both recognized the possibilities inherent in introducing this varied Alaskan blood into their closely-bred Siberians.

Back at Laconia in 1964, 1965 and 1966, Belford showed the results of his breeding and training program and won the World Championship an unmatched three times in a row. He then donated his magnificent trophy back to the race, to be awarded in perpetuity in memory of his mother.

It has been said that Charlie Belford has a little bit of the sled dog in him, that his ability to walk through someone's racing kennel and spot the best of the fastest is nothing short of amazing. He is also recognized as a top trainer of sled dogs, pulling more speed out of a team than anyone else. He attributes much of this not only to knowing his dogs, but also to his tightly regulated training schedule. A would-be driver who can fit his schedule in with Doctor Belford's, who shows skill around dogs, can learn more than enough to put together a first-class dog team. Quick, serious and professional, Belford is also very fond, as are all sled dog drivers, of "talking dogs." With a bright twinkle in his blue eyes, he tells stories on himself and others, compares notes and remembers amazing details about dogs he drove way back when he was ten. He has been an inspiration to more than one young driver, and a "Belford dog" is an inspiration to any dog team.

The legacy of Lombard and Belford will live for a long time not only in New England but in the rest of the sled dog world. Learning from the experiences of the first generation of mushers, from pioneers like Walden and Seppala, these New Englanders carried the sport and the Siberian Husky to their finest limits. When they had perfected the best racing Siberian they could, they took him back to Alaska to prove their proficiency—and found that during the intervening years Alaskan mushers had not been concentrating on the Siberian Husky. Races were being won not only with the Alaskan Husky, but also with the village dogs of the Interior. The New England drivers recognized the potential for crossbreeding these indigenous Alaskan dogs with their Siberians, and their new breeding programs rapidly achieved another superior racing animal. Team speeds in New England increased to 16, 17 and 18 miles an hour for a twenty-mile course.

Carrying on in the tradition of Goosak and Ramsay, who imported the first Siberian dogs, and of St. Godard and Seppala, who bred their favorite dogs for greater speed, Lombard and Belford did much to improve the quality of racing husky teams in the Northeast. While they were at it, they set quite a few records all the way from New England back to Alaska. Before these records can be broken a new generation of dog drivers will have to match them, will have to approach their limits and then go past.

Jean Bryar and Brandy

Meanwhile, no one is standing around just watching. Especially not Jean Bryar, who during the sixties and seventies has become the foremost

181

woman sled dog trainer and driver in the world. Although her husband, Keith, is remembered as the third factor in the Lombard-Belford-Bryar hegemony, Jean was no back seat member of the Bryar team. She worked her way through the New England circuit, usually finishing near the top, against some of the toughest competition New England has ever had. Having developed one of the best Siberian Husky racing teams in the Northeast, the Bryars made the big jump to Alaska with the other New England champions in the early sixties. They, too, were entranced by the abilities of the Alaskan dogs, and in 1962 they bought a superb example of this racing husky, a leader named Brandy. They paid $1,001 for him.

During the next few seasons either Keith or Jean drove Brandy at the head of a team that won several of the most important sled dog races in North America. In 1963 they captured the Eastern International at Quebec, the World Championship at Laconia, and the Women's North American Championship at Fairbanks. The Laconia victory gave Keith Bryar the distinction of being the first driver to win three times in this World Championship (1960, 1962 and 1963), and he retired the original silver bowl. In Alaska in 1962, 1963 and 1964, Jean paralleled Doc Lombard's wins in the Men's North American with wins of her own in the Women's. In 1964, she drove to a second place in the Laconia World Championship, right behind Charlie Belford. This marked the highest finish for a woman driver in the history of that race. Keith took several cracks at the Men's North American, finally winning it in 1965 by a scant 2½ minutes over Doc Lombard.

A dog to match their talents, Brandy was the mainstay of the Bryar team during these years. In his pedigree were dozens of lead dogs, including one named Kit who was not only Brandy's grandmother but the famous Nellie's as well. It takes more than pedigree or blue eyes to win consistently in the races, however, and Brandy had the necessary qualities. Speed and endurance are the physical characteristics, but responsiveness, desire and courage are equally important. When this great sled dog died in 1969, he left magnificent memories in the minds of people who had seen him race. He also left his progeny, and his superior Alaskan lineage is still producing sled dogs and leaders of select capability.

Following Keith Bryar's successful bid for the Men's North American Championship in 1965 and his subsequent retirement from racing, Jean Bryar maintained the Norvik Kennels in Center Harbor, New Hampshire, and expanded her racing schedule. Coordinating her training and racing talents with those of another champion driver and veteran dog musher, Dick Moulton, Jean has gone on to secure her own reputation in the sporting world. Selecting only the most challenging professional races

JEAN BRYAR'S FIRST-CLASS DOG TEAM, BRANDY ON LEAD, heading for fifth place in the 1965 Laconia World Championship.

Charles L. Booth, Courtesy Cascadian Kennels

DICK MOULTON WITH BRANDY, ONE OF THE MOST ADMIRED ALASKAN HUSKIES. Brandy was bred in Alaska and raced all over North America with the Bryars of New Hampshire. He was a fine companion as well as a leader of exceptional skill, and is still referred to by mushers as the ultimate racing sled dog.

Charles L. Booth, Courtesy Cascadian Kennels

for their teams, Bryar and Moulton have left well-defined tracks wherever they have competed.

What can a combination like this accomplish? The results from a year such as 1973 tell the bare bones of the story: at Quebec, a first for Moulton; at Ely, another first; at Kalkaska, a second for Moulton, fourth for Bryar; at Laconia, Bryar handled the team and Moulton drove to his third World Championship; two weeks later they were in Fairbanks, where Bryar took her fifth Women's North American title and a week later Moulton came in third in the Men's division, right behind Harold Greenway of Fairbanks and Doc Lombard.

Bryar's unprecedented six wins (through 1975) in the Women's North American, against the best women drivers in Alaska, will be tough for anyone to equal. She has the determination and the flexibility of an all-time great sled dog driver. In her first try at the North American, for example, Bryar's lead dog was of a breed never before known to qualify for such a position, a small, long-haired Border Collie. She tends to pamper her dogs a little more than some of her colleagues think is necessary, but her achievements as a racer and trainer justify her techniques. Tall, slim, energetic and personable, Jean Bryar is completely dedicated to her dogs. During the off-season she manages her kennel and works with a real estate firm in a summer visitor haven on the northern shores of Lake Winnipesaukee. When the cool mornings of fall arrive, it is back to the business of training the puppies and stretching the veterans' muscles for a new racing season.

Dick Moulton and Attla

Of all the best sled dog drivers still racing, only one has the long, varied, high-scoring career that Dick Moulton has. Moulton is not flashy, he does not burn up the courses or startle with innovations. But he wins races. When all the records are in, when all the greats are compared, Dick Moulton is certain to be ranked with the masters. This tall, tranquil man drives the steadiest races of any. He knows his team, knows his competition, knows his job.

And well he should. His career with dogs spans almost five decades, "officially" beginning when he was nine years old and hitched a couple of pets to a sled. Young Dick Moulton was rarely seen without a dog, and around Meredith, New Hampshire, he was known as "Pooch." Before he had finished high school he was working as instructor and trainer for the Chinook Kennels, under the direction of the Seeleys. He raced the Chinook Kennels team on the New England circuit and then had a chance to fulfill the impossible dream of many boys growing up during the thirties.

Admiral Byrd, preparing for his third Antarctic Expedition, was again relying on the Chinook Kennels for his sled dogs. On the Seeleys' recommendation, Moulton was chosen out of hundreds of applicants to accompany the expedition as assistant sled dog handler. Among the duties of the dog drivers was a three-month, 1,400-mile trek, one of the longest ever made in the Antarctic. The expedition was shortened due to the impending war, and back in the United States, Dick Moulton entered the Army. Even here Moulton and dogs were inseparable, for he became part of Norman Vaughan's "Voyageurs," the special sled dog branch of the Arctic Search and Rescue Unit.

In the history of the world, the number of people who have been able to make careers out of driving a team of sled dogs is understandably small. For all practical purposes, today it is an anachronistic activity. Yet where it has been needed, no other method of travel would have served as well. Having made his early career in more practical aspects of driving dogs, Dick Moulton, in the tradition of Leonhard Seppala and Scotty Allan, turned to racing.

His dogs are Alaskan Huskies, mixed judiciously with racing hounds, his record is outstanding. His trademark in a long race is his consistency, his knack of keeping his team close enough to the winning pace so that by the last heat the dogs still have enough drive to finish well. "He does it by holding his team back the first two days of a three-day race," reason the other drivers. Perhaps. But often his first heat will be very fast.

Dick Moulton's favorite leader is a hound-husky cross named Attla. Attla resembles a hound, with short hair and floppy ears, but he is all sled dog on the trail. As with so many of the great leaders, Attla claims the admiration of his driver by exhibiting qualities beyond his speed and stamina. Again, Moulton refers to the dog's responsiveness and loyalty as elevating him to the status of that "once-in-a-lifetime" leader.

It would be hard to estimate the number of miles Dick Moulton has traveled by dog sled. Compared to most mushers, it would be unapproachable. Considering that mileage and the time spent watching, thinking, figuring, behind his running team, Moulton's achievements follow smoothly. In 1968 he received the "Musher of the Year" title from *Team and Trail,* a foremost monthly sled dog publication. In 1971 he beat the best Canadian and United States drivers in four of the biggest races, at Ely, Kalkaska, Ottawa and Laconia. By 1973 he had stretched his victories at Ely's All American Championship to three in a row. He also won at Quebec and Laconia that year, and finished third at Fairbanks. In 1975 he equalled Charlie Belford's four wins at Laconia. Then he took all his dogs to Fairbanks and placed sixth, behind George Attla and Charlie Belford, but ahead of Roland Lombard.

Doc Lombard is in his sixties, Doc Belford and Dick Moulton are in their fifties. Once in a while they consider retirement from this "most gruelling of all sports." But autumn usually finds them all out on the training trails, often on the same one, and in spite of their impressive records, they are still working for that ultimate dog team.

George Attla and Tuffy

George Attla, in any other sport, would also be past normal retirement age. In his early forties now, Attla has also spent his life driving sled dogs. Driving Attla was a desire to overcome a debilitating boyhood bout with bone tuberculosis. Struck down by this notorious crippler of native Alaskans when he was only eight years old, George spent more of his next eight years in the hospital than out. During a two-year stretch in the Tanana hospital the young Athabascan learned English, and that represented the total of his schooling. When he finally returned home, halfway through his teens, he was pronounced cured, but his right knee joint had been permanently fused.

Attla returned home to the small village of Huslia, where sled dogs are a large part of life. Near the confluence of the Huslia River with the Koyukuk, Huslia is about fifty miles south of the Arctic Circle. Its people do use snowmobiles for hunting, trapping and hauling wood, but they are partial, as are many interior villagers, to sled dogs. Culls from his father's team and a new birch sled had been part of young Attla's therapy during his times at home. He worked so hard at strengthening his inert muscles that he gained a degree of control over his right leg. The fusion operation enabled him to walk without crutches and gave him also the ability to assist his dog team from the back of the sled with a mighty push of his good leg.

Since 1956, when Jim Huntington mushed all the way from his trapper's cabin near Huslia to the Dual Championship of sled dog racing, the little Indian village has commanded great respect from those who know sled dogs. Huntington was the third Alaskan to achieve Dual Champion status, the first from Huslia. Bergman Sam, the second "Huslia Hustler," won at Fairbanks in 1957 and in 1958 George Attla decided to give big-time racing a try, at the Fur Rendezvous. By the end of the first day's heat Attla had set a new course record and the official time showed him with an advantage of two minutes, five seconds over Gareth Wright, Alaska's first Dual Champion and a speed demon from Fairbanks. On the second day Wright beat Attla by two seconds. In an all-out effort on the last day, pedaling and pushing and not relenting for an instant, the 24-year-old Attla pumped his way to his first major victory.

Attla's racing record since then has become legend. Five times he has won in Anchorage, four times in Fairbanks, and numerous other times all over Alaska. He is also the only Alaskan musher to have competed successfully on the growing professional circuit in the lower 48 states. In 1972 he won the Midwest Championship in Kalkaska and the Paul Bunyan Classic in Bemidji; he took second at the All American in Ely. In 1975 he came back and won the All American.

It is said about George Attla that the only dogs that can beat him are ones he has trained. This could well be, for Attla has an international reputation as a trainer of sled dogs. He trains dogs that win, and his forte is leaders.

Leading the trapline team of Sidney Huntington (Jim's brother) outside of Huslia in 1958 was a young, golden-red dog known as Tuffy. There is not much public glory in guiding a working team day after day, but Huntington's team was known well in the village for its ability to cover great distances no matter what the weather. Like the rough but promising bush league pitcher who gets a chance to try out in the majors, Tuffy found himself traded to George Attla in 1961, in a deal involving several dogs. Attla tried him on lead, but trotting was Tuffy's customary pace. Not wanting to force the dog, Attla hitched him back in the team, just ahead of the wheel dogs, where he could learn to run.

Learn he did, and by the next racing season he was up front again, sharing double lead with Attla's other star, Nellie. The two leaders sparked Attla to victory at the Rondy in 1962, following which Doc Lombard bought Nellie. At the end of the 1963 season, Tuffy and five other dogs were sold to Keith Bryar, and Tuffy ran a brilliant lead for him in the 1964 and 1965 North American races. A leg injury developed into a back condition for the now middle-aged dog, and so Bryar bought an ultra-sound machine and ministered to his sore but valuable champion. Retiring after the 1965 championship, Bryar turned his team over to Billy Sullivan of Soldotna. Running on lead for Sullivan in the next year's Rondy was the irrepressible Tuffy. Showing his stiffness but also his courage, on the third day of this 75-mile race Tuffy ran from the starting line on three legs. Nevertheless, he managed to keep his team of over a dozen dogs stretched out until he loosened up. He then led them in to a good second place, right behind Joe Redington's son, Joee.

Bill Sturdevant of Anchorage purchased Tuffy in the spring of 1966, and with the veteran leader came one used ultra-sound machine. Although many noted mushers predicted that the dog's career was over,

ALASKA'S CHAMPION, GEORGE ATTLA, and his long string
of dogs in the 1971 North American.   *Nelson's Studio*

Tuffy ran the two 25-mile heats in the 1967 Iditarod Trail Centennial Race, coming in second. The next season George Attla looked over his shoulder during the Rondy and whom should he see catching up with him but his former lead dog. It was a strong bid, but Attla beat Sturdevant and Tuffy for the race by a grand total of 45 seconds.

"Retired" to sunny California in 1968, Tuffy ran his last race in 1969, leading Bob Levorsen's limited class team to victory in the East Meets West race at St. Paul, Minnesota. In the starting chute before the race Tuffy put on his trade-mark show of bucking, rolling around in the snow, checking out the dogs behind him. Coming in, he approached the finish in his long, easy lope, and walked about afterward with his head up and his golden plume of a tail waving. Tuffy never wasted time nor energy on tail wagging or yapping for attention. His aloof dignity belied the enjoyment in his eyes, for he reveled in leading teams as big as 16 dogs in a perfect, well-functioning unit. He seemed especially gifted with the ability to pace himself for the utmost endurance in the longest races. His distinguished life ended, quietly, four days after his last race.

Like several other lead dogs "discovered" and trained by George Attla—Lombard's Nellie, Hilpipre's Johnny, Anne Wing's Buster—Tuffy inspired the teams of Bryar, Sullivan, Sturdevant and Levorsen. He was a "leader's leader," still cherished by the men who drove him. Even his wonder leader of 1972, Grover, cannot diminish the stardom of Tuffy in George Attla's memory.

Team and Trail's "Musher of the Year" award went to George Attla in 1969 and again in 1975. The first year the ISDRA point championship was in effect, 1972, he won the Gold Medal. He won it again in 1975, garnering the Silver Medal in the other two years when Roland Lombard beat him in the standings. Attla has been elected to the Dog Mushers' Hall of Fame. All of this has been achieved in his first 17 years of professional racing; at the end of another 17 years he still will not have reached the age of Doc Lombard at his peak.

Known as a champion among champions, George Attla has won the admiration of mushers everywhere. This admiration stems not only from his talents as a racer, but also for his broad concept of what being a champion means. Young Alaskan mushers have benefited from Attla's tutelage in the sport, receiving dogs and training instruction from their idol. With junior drivers and with his dogs, he is a firm disciplinarian. But not too firm, as can be seen from his dogs, a happy, good-natured, willing lot. Attla also sets a fine example as a private man, honest, likeable, professional, competing in and also contributing to his sport. His 1972 book, *Everything I Know About Training and Racing Sled Dogs,* is the first extensive work ever published on the subject.

Attla has few peers as a trainer, handler and racer of sled dogs, but one of them, Doc Lombard, paid tribute to his tenacious racing rival right after his close, nine-second victory over the Alaskan in the 1969 Rondy.

"George is the toughest competitor in dog mushing," said the Doc. "He really has a sense of how to pace those dogs . . . This is a great group of competitors. You can visit with a dog musher over a cup of coffee, then go out and try to get his hide in a dog race and I thought George had mine today. I feel like I've been ridden hard and put away wet."

With a good grip on his sense of humor, Attla's comment about the race, over a cup of coffee, was, "It's going to take me all year to think of an excuse for losing this race!"

Dog-driving Dynasties in Alaska: Wright, Redington, Norris

Renowned primarily in Alaska, but gaining international recognition as word of their achievements spreads even to Europe, are the several family dynasties which seem to be especially characteristic of sled dog racing in the forty-ninth state. More than any other sport, sled dog racing attracts and holds whole families. All age groups can compete in classes tailored to their abilities and desires, and there is plenty of room for fathers and mothers, teenagers and little siblings. With increasing age and skills, a youngster can progress through a succession of classes until he arrives at a senior level that corresponds to the number of dogs on his limited or unlimited class team. This organization is one reason that sled dogging is so popular with families. Another reason is that sled dog drivers get better with age. While swimming's teenagers or tennis players in their early twenties are at their physical peaks, the grand old men of sled dog racing are several decades beyond even the baseball veteran's creaky 38 years.

It is not surprising, then, to witness the ascension of several family dynasties in this sport. And the most outstanding of these related racers grow in Alaska. The tendency for families to race together first showed up in the Fairbanks area during the 1930's, when Joe and Fred Stickman, Andy and Bergman Kokrine, Hortense and Genevieve Parker, and Irene Coulombe and her mother were the drivers to beat. After World War II the founders of the next dynasties began laying out trails for the generations of dog drivers coming along.

Spanning three generations with a champion in each, Gareth Wright's family can claim one of the youngest champions in the current succession. In 1973, at the venerable age of four, Wright's grandson, Raymond "Ramy" Brooks, won his first Junior North American Championship, one-dog class. He was barely able to see over the handlebar of his sled, but young Brooks and his dog got through the three quarter-mile heats in a

191

GARETH WRIGHT OF FAIRBANKS, winner of the 1952 races, and Venus, his lead dog, and the Al Fox Trophy at the Anchorage championship.
Courtesy Natalie Norris

THE BELFORD THIRD OF NEW ENGLAND'S "BIG THREE" MUSHERS during the 1950's. His favorite leader, Timmy, was a purebred Siberian Husky.
Bernice B. Perry, Courtesy Lorna Demidoff

GARETH WRIGHT, ON THE LEFT, AND HIS DAUGHTER, ROXY WRIGHT WOODS
AT THE RONDY IN 1974. *Maxine Vehlow*

ROXY WRIGHT WOODS AT THE FINISH OF THE three-day, thirty-mile Women's
World Championship run in 1974. This was her second victory in this race.
Maxine Vehlow

winning time of two minutes, 26 seconds. He also shared the sportsmanship award. That same year Ramy's mother, Roxy Wright Woods, took the title of Women's World Champion at Anchorage. One week later Grandfather Wright beat both Doc Lombard and George Attla for second place in the Men's World Championship. The next two years Roxy retained her title at Anchorage, and in 1975 she took her second Women's North American Championship, out-racing the formidable Jean Bryar by almost three minutes. Gareth did not race those years, but young Ramy, his dog clearly visible now over the handlebar, drove to another Junior Championship at Fairbanks.

These victories are the result of nearly three decades of immersion in the world of sled dogs. Born and raised in Nenana, Gareth Wright jumped right onto the sled dog bandwagon in 1946, lending some of his dogs to Jake Butler of Gulkana for the first Fur Rendezvous exhibition race against Earl Norris. Wright was fascinated by the possibilities of crossbreeding racing dogs, especially by the formula used by his boyhood idol, Johnny Allen, triple winner of the pre-war Livengood Sweepstakes. Allen had developed a remarkably uniform and fast strain of sled dog by crossbreeding Irish Setters with the local sled dogs. Unable to reproduce the formula, Wright bred some dogs he called Spalamutes, a cross between a Springer Spaniel and a husky. The Spalamutes were a favorite of the spectators and rewarded everyone's attention by sparking his team to victories in the 1950 championships at both Anchorage and Fairbanks. Thus they gained for their driver the first Dual Championship. Two years later Wright and his team (without the Spalamutes) set a total time record for the Rondy, completing the then hundred-mile course at an average of 14.45 miles an hour.

When Lloyd Van Sickle of Truckee, California, won the North American preliminary races during the 1955 season with his Targhee Hounds, Wright bought some of the Irish Setter-Staghound dogs and then went on to concentrate on something he called the Aurora Husky. These dogs were bred from pure setter, some Siberian, and some of the Johnny Allen strain. One of the most famous of these was Jennie, from a registered setter mother and a half-Siberian father. Jennie was a fast, hardy lead dog with short hair, soft ears and light blue eyes. Her ancestry, appearance and ability made her a legend in her own time. Wright and his Aurora Huskies have plagued the top contenders in Alaskan races for two decades, never finishing out of the money and always ready for a good sprint. He won his third World Champion title in 1957, and in 1972 and 1973 he came in second only to George Attla and Carl Huntington. Then he switched his emphasis to his fast family.

How does a sled dog dynasty grow? A successful father includes his daughter in his racing activities, especially in the care and training of the dogs. He guides her interest, gives her the opportunity to put together a team, and then stands back to watch with pride as she enters her first race. Before he knows it, he has a grandson, and the young mother bundles up the baby and rides him on her sled during the long training runs. With a dog sled for a cradle, he might sleep all the way, but he absorbs the magic of a dog team, and his future is assured.

Three decades is a long stretch for anyone to remain in the forefront of any sport, but Gareth Wright has succeeded. What makes his achievements more noteworthy is the fact that he is one of the top racing drivers whose profession, unrelated to the sport, makes year-round demands on his time. While running a construction company, Wright has still managed to develop his own breeds of sled dog and to race them with the best for many years. That his daughter and grandson are as taken with the sport as he is offers an insight into the satisfactions to be gained from sled dogs and racing.

Just outside of Anchorage, across Cook Inlet, is the village of Knik, home of the Dog Mushers' Hall of Fame. Running this National Historic Site are not only Joe and Vi Redington, but their son Joee and his wife, Pam. Knik is also the spot where an old gold trail begins its long route northwest to the mining camp of Iditarod. It was Joe Redington, Sr., who first envisioned a sled dog race from Knik, past his homestead over the old Iditarod Trail. "Mr. Iditarod," they call him, practical dreamer, and founder of another well-known dynasty of dog drivers.

When they are racing, Joe and his three grown sons figure prominently in a dozen Alaskan races each year. Of nine entrants in a preliminary race at Knik in 1975, four were Redingtons, and Joe, Joee, Tim and Raymie filled third through sixth places. Although the boys often beat their dad, Joe is never far behind. And soon the boys will have to be prepared for the next generation to overtake them, for in a recent Junior World Championship, third-generation Redingtons took second and fourth places. One highlight in the family's career was Joee's 1966 victory at the Rondy, when he brought the World Championship home to the U.S. Army's Alaskan Search and Rescue Unit. On lead in that race were two black Labrador-Irish Setter crossbreeds, Happy and Windy. Tim extended the family's hopes for further championships when he ran against the sport's best competition in the 1975 North American and came in third, within two minutes of winner George Attla.

Administrative and promotional support of sled dog racing claim much of the Redingtons' attention, and when they are not racing they are busy behind the scenes. A club called the Aurora Dog Mushers runs several preliminary races early in the season, including an Aurora

TALKING DOGS: Joee, Joe and Ramie Redington, 1975.
Courtesy Team and Trail

ALASKA'S GREAT RACING RIVALS, GEORGE ATTLA, 41, AND DOC LOMBARD, 63, posing with one signed print of a limited edition published to help fund the Fur Rendezvous World Championship sled dog races. *Maxine Vehlow*

Championship in the middle of January. Most of the arrangements for these races are handled by Joe, on the board of directors, Joee, as vice president, and Pam, as secretary. At the end of Alaska's long racing season, the Aurora Dog Mushers have been known to get together and hold a "Dog-Gone Party," a chance to relax, talk about dogs and races, and make plans for next year.

Joe Redington arrived in Alaska from Pennsylvania in 1948, and before he had a homestead he had a sled dog. Knik Kennels numbered forty dogs by 1949, and Redington had a job as a member of the U.S. Air Force's Rescue and Reclamation Unit. Married in 1953 to a girl he had met before the war in Pennsylvania, Joe moved to Flat Horn Lake along the old Iditarod Trail and established a guide business. His 270-dog kennel was part of his business, and his growing children became as experienced with sled dogs as their parents.

Following his successful promotion of the fifty-mile Iditarod Trail Race in 1967, Alaska's Centennial Year, Joe began looking more carefully at the remains of the old trail that passed his homestead. "The old trail is out there, somewhere," mused Joe, and a new dream began to form in his mind. With a few other hardy souls he set out to locate and clear the trail, thinking harder about a long race to Iditarod. They found some of the weather-beaten log tripods marking the trail, but it was tough, if exciting, going. Before long, Joe's plan had expanded from the 500-mile Knik to Iditarod race. Instead of stopping at the ghost town, why not keep on due north to the mighty Yukon, pick up the diphtheria serum run trail at Ruby, and follow it west to Unalakleet and Nome?

With immense determination and enthusiasm, the Iditarod Trail Committee had a thousand-mile trail ready by 1973, and although the promised prize money was not yet collected, 34 Alaskan dog drivers with teams of from nine to twenty dogs began the race on March 3. Of course Joe Redington wanted to be in the race, but he had to let his son, Raymie, substitute for him, for his talents were needed on the fund-raising trail. Raymie had to scratch his exhausted team at Ruby, but Redington success in the race was assured as the prize money was waiting when the first mushers reached Nome.

More of Redington's dream came true in 1974 when he, Joee and Raymie entered the long race with 41 other drivers. "Bad weather with wind chill factors to 130° below zero hit the mushers head-on in treacherous Ptarmigan Pass in the Alaska Range," reported *Team and Trail*, "and the crystalline snow wore the tender pads on the dogs' feet until drops of blood dotted the trail." It took almost 21 days for winner Carl Huntington to get to Nome. The first Redington in was Raymie, after 23 days on the trail, in seventh place. Joee was an hour and a half behind him, in ninth, and Joe finished seven hours behind Joee, in eleventh place. The scope of the race increased that year when two Alaskan women entered, and one musher from Outside.

By 1975 the trail had been greatly improved, aided in part by a grant from an oil company. According to *Team and Trail:*

> "A superbly packed trail was aided by two weeks of mild weather and benign breezes. The mushers were all making fast time from the start, with the 'Father' of the race, Joe Redington, Sr., leading the pack with a first day run of over one hundred miles in 12 hours.
>
> "They pushed to get through the mountain pass before bad weather caught them . . . but the pass came and went, and still the pocket of sunshine followed them."

Joee finished third, spending only 14 days and 15 hours on the trail; Joe came in 24 hours after him. Fine weather and a well-packed trail contributed to the fast times. Although still a go-as-you-please race, in the tradition of the old Nome sweepstakes races, the Iditarod requires each musher to stop for 24 hours at least once, at whichever he chooses of the 23 checkpoints along the trail to Nome.

Tireless, dedicated Joe Redington has done more than establish a race that attracts international attention because of its length and prize money. According to people like George Attla, one of the more important results of the running of the Iditarod Trail is that Alaskans in outlying villages through which the teams run have been thinking more about dogs and less about snowmobiles. Twenty-two dog teams completed the course in 1973, but only one snowmobile. For Alaskan natives, caught since World War II between modern conveniences and the old ways of doing things, the resurgent interest in sled dogs is looked on as a healthy sign, as a positive modern contact with a tradition so important to their way of life.

One of the most influential kennels of sled dogs, world-wide, is that of Earl and Natalie Norris of Willow, Alaska. At their Howling Dog Farm they have raised purebred as well as mixed breed sled dogs, and have also raised a son who came within a frosty whisker of beating George Attla in the 1970 North American. The whole family's racing record over the years has been impressive, beginning with Earl's first win in 1947 when he raced from behind to beat Jake Butler by 18 seconds in the second running of the future World Championship. In 1951 he broke all records with a team of purebred Siberian Huskies on the last day, the fourth heat of what was then a one hundred-mile race. Several triumphs occurred in 1970 when 21-year-old J.P. Norris came in a close second in the North American, Natalie won the Women's North American title, and Earl and his leader took first in the lead dog contest. Highlights of intervening

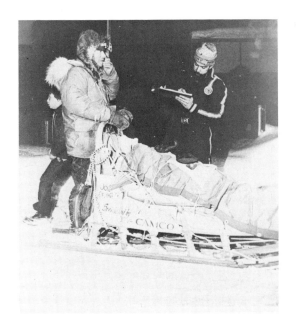

JOE REDINGTON, CHECKING IN ALONG THE IDITAROD TRAIL. *Courtesy Team and Trail*

PUSHING FOR THE FINISH, JOEE REDINGTON shows why the driver is referred to as "the hardest-working dog on the team." *Courtesy Joe Redington, Jr.*

years include Natalie's substituting for an ill Earl and almost beating Jake Butler in 1949; Earl's second and Natalie's fourth placings in the 1952 World Championship; Natalie's first in the 1954 Women's World Championship with a beautiful team of Siberians; and the continual "in the money" runs of Earl, Natalie and J.P. all over Alaska.

Young Natalie Jubin and her 11 dogs left Lake Placid, New York, just after World War II, for the Territory of Alaska. She must have found romance and adventure for she married Earl Norris and she continued with sled dogs. Earl never missed a turn with his team, for during the winter right after the war he pitted his freighting dogs against Jake Butler's. Founding what was to become the Alaskan Championship and then the World Championship was no small task, but the Norrises were instrumental in establishing one of the world's best sled dog races. The Alaskan Sled Dog and Racing Association (ASDRA) was formed in 1949 to run the race; Natalie Norris served as president in 1952.

The Norrises also helped to organize a Siberian Husky breed club in Alaska, and Natalie has traveled all over North America as a judge for the American Kennel Club. Breeding purebred Siberians under the kennel name of Alaskan, with the suffix Anadyr, the Norrises had several show champions on their racing teams. One famous lead dog, Champion Bonzo of Anadyr, C.D., had the distinction of being the first Siberian to be placed Best in Show in an all-breed show. When Europeans began putting together sled dog teams, they bought many dogs from the Norris kennel, and soon most teams in central Europe had at least one Anadyr Siberian, with the rest of the team often made up of dogs with Anadyr ancestry.

Balancing their interests in purebreds with growing demands for good sled dogs, the Norrises encouraged junior members of ASDRA by awarding a registered Siberian pup to promising dog drivers. Their emphasis on teaching young drivers how to care for and race these valuable dogs was designed to contribute to the concept of good sportsmanship for Alaska's future mushers. The Howling Dog Farm, housing well over 200 dogs, became not only a place to see or buy first-class sled dogs, but also to learn dog driving. It was never difficult for Earl to find aspiring dog drivers from Alaska or the south 48 to work with him, in a kind of musher's apprenticeship.

In what could be called the George Plimpton approach to sled dog racing, that is, a rank amateur participating in a professional contest, Virginia Kraft arrived in Anchorage ten days before the start of the 1966 World Championship and headed for Howling Dog Farm to learn some of the basics. She had been assigned to cover the race for a national sports magazine, and decided, despite a total lack of experience, that participa-

EARL NORRIS FREIGHTING UP MULDROW GLACIER ON MT. MCKINLEY, 1949. The leader, point and wheel dogs are Malamutes; the other two pairs are Alaskan Huskies. *Courtesy Natalie Norris*

PRACTICING WHAT HE PREACHES. Earl Norris, a founder of sled dog racing in post-war Alaska, racing in 1969. *Maxine Vehlow*

J.P. NORRIS, FOLLOWING IN HIS PARENTS' BOOTPRINTS, carries on the family's affair with sled dog racing.

Maxine Vehlow

NATALIE NORRIS, ELECTED RECENTLY WITH HER HUSBAND, EARL, TO THE DOG MUSHERS' HALL OF FAME, gives out race times to noted sled dog cartoonist Jon Van Zyle.   *Maxine Vehlow*

tion in the race would enhance her understanding of the intricacies. Earl Norris put her through an accelerated course in how to stay on the sled and the difference between "gee" and "haw," among other things. In spite of the family's regular schedule of training and racing, in full swing at this time of year, the novice musher from Outside learned enough to stay in the race through three 25-mile heats. Four other drivers dropped out, so the training had paid off. Virginia Kraft so impressed the Alaskans with her game participation and talented courage, that along with the traditional lantern award for last place, she was feted at the finish line with champagne and an armful of roses.

J.P. Norris has taught at Howling Dog Farm, carrying on the family tradition. He practices what he preaches whenever he can, driving well in the races. His dad still prefers to race—Earl Norris's 1975 record looked like this: second in the New Year's Day race at Anchorage, thirds at Susitna and an Anchorage preliminary, first in Knik's Aurora Championship (ahead of four Redingtons), second at Anchorage's Exxon Open, sixth at Soldotna's Alaskan Championship, eighth in the World Championship, and eleventh in the North American. This is a commendable season for any sled dog racer, especially one in his fifties. Most of Earl Norris's life has centered around sled dogs; his contributions and those of his family have left lasting impressions on the sport.

TUMULO, A TARGHEE HOUND: part Irish Setter, part Staghound, all sled dog. Bred by L. Van Sickle, owned by B. Allen.
Courtesy Mel Fishback

A PUREBRED SIBERIAN, playing hearth husky today, lead dog tomorrow.
Bernice B. Perry, Courtesy Lorna Demidoff

ALASKAN MALAMUTE CHAMPION KOUGAROK, owned by Kay and J.L. Moustakis, winner of best in show.
Maxine Vehlow

7

"They are only Dogs"

"How far is it," the Arctic explorer asked the Eskimo, *"to that next mountain range?"*

Responded the Eskimo, *"No good dogs, long way . . . good dogs, close to."*

WHO ARE THESE DOGS that pull the sleds? Are they purebreds or mongrels? What sets them apart from other dogs and enables them to work with man under the most brutal of weather conditions? What sort of strange dog is it that yammers and yowls to be part of a team, preferring to work or race rather than rest in a warm kennel?

A dog does not need a written pedigree to enter a sled dog race. He does not even have to be a northern breed, although the majority of dogs on the racing trails are related to the working breeds of the North. Their instinct to pull is strong. More than one owner of a northern dog has been amazed, on hitching his dog to a child's sled, to see his pet put his head down and pull, just as though he were a veteran team dog. The dog could be an American Kennel Club registered Siberian Husky or a "one-quarter husky" mixed breed. He could be an Irish Setter, a Walker Coonhound, or the ubiquitous, nondescript "farm collie." In the search for an unbeatable dog team, dozens and dozens of crossbreedings, inbreedings and line breedings have been tried. Some breeders work within a recognized breed, seeking to refine that breed's natural talents; others select the fastest and strongest of whatever dogs come to their attention, caring more about performance than looks or pedigree.

Siberian Husky

The most popular of the registered breeds for sled dog racing, worldwide, is the Siberian Husky. An uncommonly attractive dog, the Siberian evokes for many the call of the wild, the lure of the North. The finely-chiseled, fox-like head, the pricked ears, the "mask" markings on the face and the expressive eyes, often a light, icy blue, seem to personify the romantic image of the North country. In temperament, Siberians can be affectionate or aloof, playful or serious. They are basically a gentle, protective dog. Stories about their exploits as guardians of children are legion, and a keener companion would be hard to find.

Siberians are bred today for the show ring or for racing, and sometimes for both. The original standard of the breed, accepted by the American Kennel Club in 1930, purposefully described the qualities of the Siberian that made him a fine working animal. The peoples of the Chukchi Peninsula in Siberia had already developed a dog which excelled as a draft animal and a companion; in the hands of Alaskan sport racers at the turn of the century the husky from Siberia was selectively bred to improve these desirable traits.

When Leonhard Seppala took some 44 of these dogs to New England in 1927 and began racing and promoting the breed there, the stage was set for the development of the American Kennel Club registered Siberian Husky. Most of Seppala's dogs figured significantly in the foundation stocks of such influential eastern kennels as Chinook, Foxstand, Monadnock and Gatineau (these dogs from Harry Wheeler's kennels at Gray Rocks carried the suffix "of Seppala"). Seven other imported dogs found their way to the kennels of Elizabeth Ricker, in partnership with Seppala, and to Gray Rocks. The two males in Quebec, Kree-Vanka and Tserko, influenced the registered breed tremendously. In 1946, two descendants of these dogs were sent back to Alaska to Earl and Natalie Norris's Anadyr Kennels, and a new generation of racing drivers rekindled the interest of Alaskans in Siberian Huskies.

Siberians predominated on the best New England teams of the thirties, forties and fifties. Roland Lombard drove Siberians when he won the World Championship at The Pas in 1957 and took second at the North American Championship in 1958. His dogs, especially one named Igloo Pak's Tok, showed excellent Siberian conformation and would have provided tough competition in the show ring. In Alaska in the fifties, Champion Tyndrum's Oslo, C.D.X., led the team of Charles and Kit MacInnes to dozens of victories. Champion Bonzo of Anadyr, C.D., led the Earl and Natalie Norris team in 16 championship races and was never out of the money.

Purebred Siberian teams abound wherever there is racing, and although they are eclipsed in speed by the mixed-breed Alaskan Husky, their racing records are solid. Today's racing Siberian can be a credit to good breeders, for behind the breed statistics (average of 22 inches at the shoulders and 45 to 50 pounds), and beneath his glossy coat (black, grey, white or russet, with various markings), still stands much of the graceful, intelligent, light-footed, speedy husky from Siberia. It seems harder to tell what a blue-eyed dog is thinking than a brown-eyed dog, but when the sporty Siberian is harnessed to a sled his thoughts are transparent. He is all Go.

Alaskan Malamute

The second most popular registered sled dog in North America is the Alaskan Malamute. Superficially, the Malamute resembles the Siberian, with pricked ears, face mask and brushy tail. In fact, the Malamute is a larger dog, bred for freighting, averaging an inch or two more in height and 15 to 20 pounds heavier than the Siberian. A Malamute's coat is either black with white markings, like some Siberians, or wolfish grey. His eyes, almond-shaped and set obliquely into his broad head, are dark. As a sled dog, the Malamute is well known as the workhorse of the North, a superb, dependable animal. In a race he is not as fast as the Siberian, but his power and endurance have kept him a favorite sled dog.

The Alaskan Malamute is one of five breeds of dog that are reputedly native to the Western Hemisphere. A distinct native breed of the Arctic, having evolved from the breeding practices of the Eskimos in the far northwest, he is one of the oldest known breeds of sled dog. Russian explorers were among the first white men to record the Malamute's existence, having found him among the native Innuit tribe of Kotzebue Sound, a people known then as the Mahlemut or Malemuit.

The Alaskan Malamute sled dog contributed substantially to the rapid exploration and development of Alaska, the Yukon and the Arctic. He also figured importantly in polar expeditions and in both World Wars. With the advent of sled dog racing at the turn of the century in Alaska, the breed was threatened by the crossbreeding practices of men who were interested in speed. The Malamute was called upon to contribute his stamina to a variety of smaller, faster racing dogs. At the Chinook Kennels in New Hampshire, however, the Seeleys concentrated on establishing perpetuity for this breed, and succeeded in registering the first one, Rowdy of Nome, in 1935.

Like the Siberian, the Malamute is a highly intelligent, loyal dog, one that loves to work and also loves to lie quietly in his own place. Malamutes are bred for show and for racing, and faster members of the breed have helped to improve the racing skills of the mixed Alaskan Husky. In the North the Malamute is still also used, here and there, for his original purposes of freighting and tending the trap lines.

Samoyed

Less evident on the racing trails but most striking when they are, are the Samoyeds. Pure white with dark eyes and curled, bushy tails, the "Sammy" is similar in size to the Siberian, but gives the impression of more hair per pound than any other sled dog.

Originally bred by the inland Siberian tribe called the Samoyed, the Samoyed dog served as a general-purpose work animal which hunted, drove reindeer herds, and pulled loads at such times as reindeer could not be used. The dogs also acted as companions and watchdogs, and were used for both food and clothing. It was said that a good dog was worth more than a wife to a Samoyed herdsman, and when British explorers first came across this amazing white dog, it took all their bargaining talents to accomplish a trade. In 1899 the first Samoyed dog was exported, to Britain, and from there his popularity has grown. Today's Samoyeds closely resemble the original sled dogs, for attempted improvements on such a dog as Moustan of Argenteau, the American Kennel Club's first registered Samoyed (in 1906), could only have been to this natural breed's detriment.

The best racing and working Samoyeds of recent times have been dogs of medium stature and structure, perhaps somewhat taller than the standard (which is 19 to 23½ inches at the shoulder) but never exceptionally heavy in body or bone. The ideal working Samoyed ranges from 22 to 24 inches, and weighs from 42 to 55 pounds. Males have more "punch" and are ordinarily a more useful size for work, but the smaller, racy females can certainly add to a racing team.

THE SAMOYED TEAM OF BOB AND KATIE LECOUR OF COLORADO.
Rocky Mountain News

VILLAGE DOGS, members of a native dog team in Gambell, on St. Lawrence Island, 1968. *Robert Levorsen*

On the average, Sams possess a more concerned personality than other arctic breeds; they are capable of great loyalty and have a pronounced desire to please. They are somewhat more apt to stand up to pressure than is the typical natural runner, and they often excel in less-than-perfect conditions where other dogs lose heart. They have a native stubbornness and a strong will, which, once turned to the driver's advantage, will keep them working consistently and hard.

Sams have often been used on demonstration teams or in benefits, and one of the West's storied dog drivers, Lloyd Van Sickle, worked and raced Sams for years. His accomplishments with the White Way Kennels dogs, especially with Rex of White Way, gave the breed a charisma in the sled dog world which persists to this day. Although most are not fast enough to compete in speed races against Siberians or Alaskans, the Samoyed's heart and loyalty make him an exceptional dog, and drivers of Sam teams will brook no disparaging comparisons with any other dog team.

Breed clubs, traditionally interested more in show or obedience activities, have begun to recognize racing teams or weight-pulling accomplishments of purebred northern dogs. The Siberian Husky Club of America, the Northern California Alaskan Malamute Association or the Organization for Working Sams, for example, seek to reward those registered dogs which excel at tasks they were originally bred for—pulling sleds or loaded toboggans.

Other Northern Breeds

Other purebred northern breeds used on dog teams, but mostly in Europe, include the Japanese Akita, the Norwegian Elkhound, the Finnish Spitz and the Canadian and Greenland Eskimo Dogs. Only the first two are recognized by the American Kennel Club, but all are recognized by Europe's Fédération Cynologique Internationale and by the Swiss Club for Northern Dogs. The Akita is large for a racing sled dog (averaging 26½ inches and 85 to 110 pounds), but has the double coat, tough feet and love of work that enable him to pull well in cold climates. He is a versatile dog, used for sentry duty, guiding the blind, protecting children and homes, hunting (everything from bear to ducks) and companionship. On the northern Japanese island of Hokkaido he is used for sled work, in Europe he has pulled in Scandinavian-style races, and in California he has been trained in front of wheeled rigs for racing.

The Norwegian Elkhound resembles a small, stocky husky. At 20½ inches and 50 pounds, he is smaller even than the Siberian, and not as speedy over long distances. The Elkhound was bred in Norway for track-

A TEAM OF AKITAS in Switzerland.   *Hans Keusen*

ing and hunting; he is a bold, powerful, agile, fast, dignified, independent animal. He is amenable to intelligent training, serving as a popular "pulk" dog in Norway. The Finnish Spitz is a recognized breed in Europe and Great Britain, used as a sled dog but more popular as a pet. The Canadian and Greenland Eskimo dogs are only rarely seen on racing teams, but a team of Greenland dogs has attracted tourists on the Jungfrau in Switzerland, and Roald Amundsen took one hundred Greenland Huskies with him on his successful South Pole expedition of 1910–12.

Alaskan Husky and Village Dog

The first sled dog races in Nome were run by mixed breeds, and today's best teams are still made up of mixed breeds, although of a vastly different genetic composition. The first racing sled dogs were working animals first, racers second. The Eskimos and Indians of Alaska had their natural breeds of sled dogs when the gold stampeders arrived in the last years of the 1800's, but there were nowhere enough dogs to support the thousands of men and women traveling around the territory. As a result, large, strong dogs were brought from the lower 48 states, mixed in with the northern dogs, and the result was mongrel sled dogs, like those of Scotty Allan. These were the dogs that won the early All-Alaska Sweepstakes races, but were rapidly replaced by the faster Siberian Husky on the racing trails. Then, as sled dog racing became popular and profitable in Alaska, drivers bred their working stock with the fastest native dogs they could find. These tough hybrids provided a speedy tenacity, and when interbred with the bigger Alaskan Malamute' or the Mackenzie River Husky (the biggest of the natural sled dog breeds, from Canada), produced a racing sled dog to suit most of the early competitors.

The most frequent canine winners of sled dog races are Alaskan Huskies and another indigenous Alaskan marvel called the Village Dog. Neither of these types are purebreds, but they are recognized as distinct, nevertheless. The Alaskan Husky is essentially a mixture of northern dogs, and would be called simply a "husky" in Alaska. The Village, or Indian, Dog is the chief racing dog in Alaska now, basically a northern dog, but in his background is anything from domestic stock to wolf, whatever the interior villagers of Alaska had around.

Alaskan Huskies, bred mainly by white men, reveal their dominant arctic genes in their appearance: a nicely marked face, curled tail, pricked ears and perhaps blue eyes. The larger examples of this type have been bred from Malamutes, Mackenzie River Huskies, or even wolves. The smaller ones reflect their Siberian Husky or Samoyed background.

JOHN LYMAN of New Hampshire with his Irish Setter dog team. The sight of these lanky red dogs strung out along the trail always causes amazed comments from the spectators.

Charles L. Booth, Courtesy Cascadian Kennels

A LITTLE OF EVERYTHING goes into the husky teams in small Alaskan villages, but village children find that racing is a fun winter sport.

Robert Levorsen

Siberian-Malamute crossbreedings yield the most common Alaskan Huskies, but there can also be Eskimo or Greenland Husky, or any other of the northern breeds, mixed in. The average Alaskan Husky stands from 24 to 26 inches high, weighs between 50 and 70 pounds, and can be quite handsome. He is taller than the Siberian, lighter and rangier than the Malamute, and faster and stronger than almost any other breed on the snowy racing trail.

An Alaskan Village Dog comes from an Eskimo or Indian village, is often hopelessly nondescript, but he can travel a mile in close to three minutes. He completes a twenty-mile race at better than 17 miles an hour and still looks forward to tomorrow's trail. His color can range from every known solid color to a pinto, a typical husky marking, or a collie or shepherd coat. He is lanky, light, and often his ears do not stand up. He is tall, from 23 to 25 inches at the shoulder, but weighs only 45 or 50 pounds. He is probably unimpressive in appearance to anyone except a racing driver. His beauty is in his gait.

Because of genetic isolation between villages, the strains of sled dog developed in each area can be quite different. In the lower Yukon region, for example, the Village Dogs show the influence of some large hound breeding, and have been too big to race. As the breeding of fast dogs has become important, though, some of the differences are disappearing. Other characteristics are taking over, and certain villages are known for certain types of sled dogs. A typical dog from Tanana is mahogany brown, with a finely-chiseled, racy-looking head, and tough feet. In Bethel, the dogs are bigger, resembling Malamutes. Ever since the mid-fifties, when Jim Huntington surprised the racing world by winning the Dual Championship with a dog team from Huslia, the dogs from that area have become deservedly famous for their racing abilities.

Neither Huntington nor George Attla can definitely pin down the origins of the Village Dog, but they are aware of variations from village to village. According to Attla, "The average production of good dogs in Huslia is much higher than any place I have been to. I have gone to a lot of places and gone through a lot of dogs, just buying dogs generally, but I still get my best percentage right in Huslia." The Huslia strain, shared with the other Koyukuk River villages of Allakaket and Hughes, contains some hound, collie and Labrador Retriever, since that is what was in the village. They are fast, strong sled dogs, and have earned the title of "Huslia Hustler" for several of the local racers.

Efforts to keep track of sled dogs in their own registry are more popular in the lower 48 states than in Alaska. The Alaskan Husky Club provides a registry for the non-pedigreed Alaskan Huskies, and the International Sled Dog Racing Association is developing guidelines for registering sled dogs. Qualifications for dogs in these registries are based on performance, as in the Border Collie registries, and not on appearance. A dog's ancestry becomes significant and valuable only when he can prove himself on the trail or as a producer of other good sled dogs.

Special Sled Dog Breeds

South of Alaska, other dogs have been interbred to make up special sled dog breeds. Arthur Walden's Chinook, the Targhee Hounds of Idaho and the Quebec Hounds of Canadian breeders are examples of these special racing dogs. The original Chinook's ancestry is somewhat shrouded in public relations mystery, but his offspring, many resulting from a breeding with a husky, served as creditable sled dogs for Walden in eastern races during the 1920's. Chinooks are still bred at a kennel in Maine, and are sold mostly as pets.

The Targhee Hound was originally bred in Idaho, the result of a cross between a Staghound and an Irish Setter. These were fast, sprint dogs, dominating the American Dog Derby for years. They were also capable of hauling a sled full of mail after a blizzard. Targhees still appear on dog teams in the West, not only in their "pure" form but also as offspring of further crossbreedings.

The Quebec Hound, also called the Canadian Hound or the Canadian Greyhound, is a name that describes the dogs resulting from the propensity of Canadians to breed a lot of sleek, racy-looking hounds into their northern sled dogs. These animals have short hair and long, strong legs. Their racing record is exceptional, from Emile St. Godard's many victories in the 1920's through Emile Martel's top team of the 1930's to most of the Quebec teams of today. Quebec Hounds have raced annually at Laconia, placing well up in the standings.

Other Racing Purebreds

Besides these racing crossbred dogs, dozens of drivers have trained and raced purebred dogs that are ordinarily thought of in contexts other than sled dog racing. The Irish Setter, besides being crossbred with huskies, has been run on many a team and done well. His long coat and leg hair hinder him in some snow conditions, but his rangy conformation and endurance enable him to complete a 15- to 20-mile course in good shape,

EMILE MARTEL of Quebec could put a dog team together out of just about any dogs around, and win races. His favorite leader was Jess, a classic example of the "Canadian Hound." *Bernice B. Perry, Courtesy Lorna Demidoff*

often at or near the front. A 25-mile track record was set at Ashton, Idaho, in 1935 by Don Cordingly and seven Irish Setters, traveling at about 13½ miles an hour. Gary Gunkel and his nine-dog team of setters was unbeatable in the West in the 1960's, and in the East, John Lyman's long team of dark red dogs held their own for years against the husky-powered competition of Lombard, Belford, Bryar, Moulton and Piscopo.

Part of the urge to harness up retrievers or hounds in the winter stems from the owners' desires to keep their sporting dogs in shape. These dogs have tough feet that can take the punishment of running many icy miles. When Dom Blodgett of Maine hit the sled dog circuit with a team of Walker Coonhounds in the 1960's, he was merely trying to extend his season beyond raccoon hunting, water races and field trials. Even more startling to racing fans than the sight of the red setters, Blodgett's hounds would start a race in full voice, their deep baying adding an anomalous note to the northern proceedings. Their coats are short but dense, their feet are tough, but the coonhounds tend to wear themselves out during the first day of a race, running like the wind and impossible to slow down. Since hounds are motivated by the chase, by the desire to know what is ahead on the trail, their first day's enthusiasm often turns to disinterest on the second day and by the third day of a big race they tend to be completely bored with the whole event. Blodgett's team has been clocked in a test run at 32 miles an hour, faster than any husky over any distance. Attesting to Blodgett's talents with his hounds: three wins in Quebec, a win at Rangeley, Maine, and as high as third in the three-day championship at Laconia.

Only a few dog teams consist solely of a non-northern breed, although many may have an unusual individual like a Border Collie, a Scotch Collie or a Golden Retriever. In New York, Bob Wehle has had a good team of Pointers, and Gary and Nancy Link of California caused spots before the eyes with their team of Dalmatians. Teams with Airedales and German Shepherds also have appeared on the sled dog trails, as have Belgian Shepherds, Doberman Pinschers, Labrador Retrievers and Weimaraners. If it can run fast, it has probably been on a dog team.

The wild dogs, too, have been interbred with domestic dogs and tried out in harness. Huskies from Alaska are frequently designated as being one-eighth or one-sixteenth wolf, and there have been reports of a few teams, in Alaska and Northern Quebec, of all wolves. During the 1930's in Alaska, a traveling dentist crossed some light, fast, tough coyotes with his racing huskies. In the early 1970's some New York mushers experimented with the feral Dingo from Australia. None of these wild crosses has flourished as a sled dog, but from a genetic or behavioral point of view, they are certainly worthwhile experiments.

THE TREEING WALKER COONHOUNDS of Dom Blodgett, tearing up the trail at Augusta, Maine, in 1971.   *Cynthia Molburg, Courtesy Cascadian Kennels*

A SHEEP DOG LEADS THE TEAM. Jean Bryar's clever Border Collie was one of the first of his breed to excel as a sled dog.

Bernice B. Perry, Courtesy Lorna Demidoff

BOB WEHLE of New York raced a team of purebred pointers, top field trial dogs, with several national field trial champions on the team.

Courtesy Lorna Demidoff

SPOTS BEFORE THE EYES IN CALIFORNIA occurred when Gary Link's Dalmatians raced. *Gary Link*

A LEAD DOG, MINGO, HALF SIBERIAN, HALF GERMAN SHORTHAIRED POINTER.
Steve McCullough, Courtesy Burt Jones

Breeding Practices

In all of these attempts to determine a superior sled dog, whether it be pure or mixed, the breeders are trying to refine the best qualities of the animal with which they are working. They select a type of dog which suits their concepts, an animal with the physical capacity for the job and an attitude which matches their own. Some drivers need "hard" dogs, dogs which ignore everything except the trail ahead; others need softer dogs, sensitive and responsive to the driver's commands. The personality of the driver, too, has a lot to do with how the team runs. The ultimate goal for a serious sled dog racer is the performance of his team, and how close he gets to that goal depends on a host of variables and a smattering of luck. If dog breeders have little formal knowledge of genetics or animal behavior when they start, they can, after years of breeding and training, attain a practical proficiency in these fields.

The whole subject of breeding top dogs, for any purpose, is likely to provoke lively debate, for the priorities of the individual breeders are often different. There are several valid theories of breeding, all with advantages and disadvantages.

Beginners often think that they are going to get something for nothing. One litter of pups is easy enough to get, and presto! instant dog team. There have been good dog teams made up of single litters, but they are not common, and neither are they apt to be the best. If a driver wants to develop his own strain of sled dog, a certain amount of inbreeding has to take place. In order to avoid genetic problems, that is, physical or mental abnormalities brought on by breeding animals that are too closely related, the dogs must be line-bred. In this system, an outstanding dog's genes are brought in from both the mother's and the father's lines. The father of a litter might also be the great-grandfather on the mother's side. Ostensibly, such line-bred puppies will retain those prime qualities of the particular dog that the breeder is trying to duplicate. However, line breeding can also exaggerate bad qualities, so a great deal of attention and experience is necessary to line-breed successfully. Advantages of line breeding include not only perpetuation of a particular desired characteristic, but also uniformity in size, shape, color, or whatever other attribute the breeder seeks. Disadvantages include a reduced vitality, in time, and the stubbornness of some faults in resisting deletion.

Outbreeding, used in conjunction with line breeding, keeps a dog team at its best. This is a system of selecting new pups by breeding two totally unrelated dogs. Breeders will buy or lease a mate from a distant kennel for one of their own dogs, to ensure that the dogs are unrelated. Vitality in the new strain is increased, but uniformity suffers. A lot of pups have to be bred, raised, trained, evaluated, and then either culled or kept. This is a time-consuming and chancy way to put together a dog team, for a breeder can go through dozens of pups before he gets even one top sled dog.

"Breed the best to the best," is the advice often heard in sled dog circles. This system can be an inadvertent substitute for outbreeding, since the best dogs are often ones that are already results of outbreeding, and thereby lies their superiority. Vitality is preserved, but variability is magnified. This loss of uniformity is expensive in terms of pups.

One way of outbreeding which will produce both uniformity and vitality is to cross two unrelated breeds of working or running dogs and then use only the first generation of pups for racing. The Staghound-Irish Setter cross, the Targhee Hound, is an example of this, and so are the Quebec Hounds. A disadvantage of this method is that it requires the maintenance of a breeding stock separate from a racing stock. Some experimentation is necessary, because non-northern breeds have not been selected for pulling or desire to run, and the pups may not have the innate pulling instinct which is so important in a sled dog. Also, a particular physical weakness, such as soft feet or lack of endurance, may dominate such a hybrid.

The best method, in theory, would be to take two unrelated strains of sled dog, inbreed them to purify the strains, and then outbreed, or hybridize them. Unfortunately, existing strains of sled dogs are not unrelated enough, and to try to purify them would take hundreds of animals and a prodigious amount of time. World champion drivers like Lombard, Belford and Bryar in New England, and the noted kennels in Alaska of Julian Hurley, Bob and Libby Wescott, or Steve and Rosie Losonsky, have led the way in crossing the outbred Alaskan Husky with the line-bred Siberian Husky, obviously with a degree of success.

Arriving at a workable variation on this system, other breeders start with a good sled dog and mix in other unrelated breeds, such as hounds or setters. The Spalamute or the Targhee are good examples. Because the hound or setter was not bred for sled dog racing, however, the first generation of pups will often be lacking in some necessary quality. Crossing the pups back with good huskies may result in the loss of some vitality, but, if done correctly and thoughtfully, the missing quality should be gained. Dick Moulton's leader, Attla, is an outstanding example of this approach, Attla being basically a husky but with some lightning-fast Walker Coonhound in his ancestry. Again, this outbreeding system produces a lot of variation, and Attla is still only one dog out of dozens of puppies.

The Alaskan Husky, the mainstay of the best teams across North America, is basically a melting pot of a breed. Such dogs from Dick

Moulton's team might look very much like those from Earl Norris's, but they could be completely unrelated. So many breeds are in the background of the Alaskan Husky that it is a vital dog, showing the advantages of hybrid vigor. Litters from Alaskan Husky breedings are usually highly variable, so a lot of breeding and selecting is required to develop a uniform team.

Uniformity is an advantage in a dog team, for the dogs should all run fairly much alike. Hitching a bigger, longer-gaited dog next to a smaller, shorter-gaited one results in a lot of wasted energy as they work against each other. Power and speed are reduced. If uniformity of coat and eye color are important to a driver, then his problems are compounded as the genetics involved gets even more complex. Leonhard Seppala had some success in breeding not only for slightly larger and faster Siberians, but he was also able to reproduce the light grey coat he preferred. As the Siberian became more and more inbred, however, some racing qualities suffered; professional drivers turned to hybrid racing dogs.

Juggling the many factors related to breeding a best, or even a good, dog team, is part of what makes sled dog racing so fascinating. There is plenty of room in the sport for those who would drive show-quality purebred dogs—anything from a Siberian Husky to an Irish Setter—and for those who care little for looks and only for speed. Sled dog races are too often won or lost by mere seconds for a driver to overlook any slight advantage or skill he can bring to his team. Breeding and selecting the dogs are most important, because no amount of training or race strategy will overcome the weaknesses of the dogs. The best drivers realize that going out and buying top dogs from other kennels can do wonders for their teams and their breeding programs, and that even though the initial cost may be higher, in the long run a thousand-dollar leader or a few five-hundred-dollar team dogs could be well worth the investment.

There is no pat method for breeding a "perfect" sled dog. The priorities and personalities of dogs and drivers set some restrictions, as do the temperatures and the conditions of the trail. Within any breeding program, nature is always ready to interfere. Even with his almost-perfect, first-class team at the ready, a driver has to recognize that even the best dogs have their off days. The set of an ear, the droop of a tail, are subtle signals given by a dog to a master who is wise enough to see. The "Old Fox," Emile Martel, recognized this, and advised the younger drivers, "Races are won by the dogs you leave at home. Never forget: they are only dogs."

RALPH WARD OF NEW YORK, one of the Northeast's more prolific racing dog sled builders.
Courtesy Team and Trail

8

Harnesses of Nylon,
Sleds of Wood

The life style and environment of the Eskimo never did allow him to be much of a perfectionist when it came to sled dog equipment and nowadays in the far-north villages the old ways are as seldom practiced as they are in the 'outside' sled dog world. The Eskimo of the 1970's leaps upon a roll of nylon webbing, or a stack of milled lumber, as delightedly as any harness maker in Minnesota or Oregon. What he makes from this material shows little similarity to what his grandfather made.

LEE AND MEL FISHBACK, 1972

ALL OVER THE WORLD, the gear used by racing sled dog drivers looks very much alike. Why? Because the styles of sleds and harnesses originated by the arctic peoples and the early explorers of the North have been so perfected in time, that it is becoming almost impossible to improve on them. Today's harnesses look much different from

225

those used on sled dogs a hundred years ago, superficially—the basic style is still similar. Nylon now takes the place of leather or skin (although many an Eskimo pup still finds his harness a delectable snack!) and on the neckpiece of a contemporary harness is a pad of waterproof acrylic pile instead of the costly, absorbent sheepskin and wool felt of the All-Alaska Sweepstakes days.

The Dog Sled

It is the same with racing sleds. Nowadays, the tough lashings at the joints can be nylon cord instead of the traditional and honorable rawhide, although this "babiche" is still the trusted favorite for tying the flexible sleds together. Once the only material available in the Arctic, rawhide has proved to be the best material for the job, long outlasting numerous experimental alternatives. Sleds are now built lighter and faster, but the professional racer of today could, and would gladly, drive and perhaps win with the identical sleds used by Leonhard Seppala or Scotty Allan in the great races of the early 1900's.

These racing sleds only roughly resemble the early sleds used by northern peoples. In its earliest form, where wood was available, two parallel logs with crosspieces lashed on, ladder-like, served well to transport the Eskimo during his daily and seasonal movements. Refinements to this design depended on the ingenuity of the makers and the snow conditions. For soft, deep snow, a flat-bottomed toboggan worked best. For soft but not so deep snow, wide runners provided less resistance than a toboggan. For hard-packed, wind-blown snow or ice, narrower runners, supporting low-slung crosspieces, gave the greatest speed. Runners were shod with whalebone or strips of caribou antler. In the interior, Eskimos boiled peaty earth to a thick paste and spread this mudpack evenly onto the runners where the Arctic's fourth dimension, the cold, froze it solidly. Before and at intervals during a trip, heated water would be smoothed onto the runner, resulting in a hard, even glaze. Where wood or bone was not available, Eskimos could still construct serviceable sleds. Runners they shaped out of soaked and then frozen animal hides, and the crosspieces were frozen fish or scraps of meat.

When the trappers and prospectors arrived in arctic regions, they modified some details of sled design to suit their own purposes. The flat Yukon sled, seven feet long and 16 inches wide, was built with the crosspieces, or bed, clearing the ground by only four inches, to keep the load low. Other sleds were longer (12 feet) or wider (22 inches), depending on the terrain and the use. They were all made of wood, with mortised and interlocking

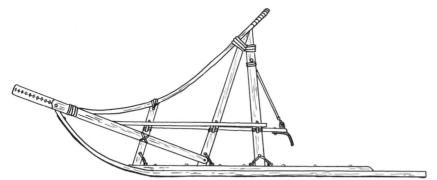

THIS RACING SLED is tied at the joints with rawhide, of mortise and tenon construction, with a leather-covered brush bow and a steel claw brake.   *Mel Fishback*

(DRAWING—Team Terms)   *Mel Fishback*

MODERN RACING EQUIPMENT includes a light nylon gangline, synthetic pile padding in two-ounce nylon webbing harnesses, and small brass snaphooks which resist freezing. *Mel Fishback*

227

side bars (stanchions), and tied at the joints with rawhide strips. This was a firm, tight, but flexible construction. To curve the wood, Indians immersed it in cold water before bending, while white men used boiling hot water, which tended to make the wood more brittle. In later years, sled builders steamed the wood for several hours; this method is still used.

The earliest sleds, or "komatiks," had no extending runners or handlebars for the driver, since the "driver" usually broke trail out front of the team. The dog-punchers at the turn of the century, though, built sleds with these features, enabling them to ride once in a while when the going was easier. For the first races in Alaska the drivers built the first racing sleds, and although an early Eskimo would have recognized its function, he would have been amazed at its light weight and maneuverability.

"Most wonderful of all," wrote Darling in *Baldy of Nome,* "was the racing sled, built on delicate lines, but of tough, almost unbreakable hickory, and lashed with reindeer sinew. It weighed but little more than thirty pounds, 'as trim a bark as ever sailed the uncharted trail.' "

Inherent in the structure of any good racing sled are many fine points that are not obvious to the untrained eye. Certain parts of this simple-looking collection of wooden strips are much thicker or wider than others, and for the best strength and flex, must be set at certain angles. Some of the joints are tight, to permit a twisting action that takes the sled smoothly around curves, while others are loose so that the sled can give way gracefully as it strikes bumps or runs along a steep side slope. A solid piece of hardwood must be used in one place, a laminated (layered) piece may do better in another.

Although in the early days the northern natives and pioneers had little choice in shoeing their runners, the modern Eskimo or Indian dog driver is as selective about shoes as his counterpart in the South. His old training sled has steel-shod runners for the bare patches and warm snows of the early and late seasons, but his best racing sled may sport "P-tex," a super-fast ski-runner surface. From frozen fish runners to the fast poly plastics, each type of shoe has some advantages, some disadvantages. Bare wood runners, coated with ski lacquers, give excellent results, but under normal use require constant maintenance and the wood gets progressively thinner. Spring steel provides the most protection as well as a fast surface for most conditions, except severe cold. Stainless steel is harder than spring steel, but does not wear well. It does provide a fast surface in warm, wet snow or melting ice, but is poor in cold weather as the snow builds up icy bumps on the runner. The plastics work best in the cold and are resistant to rock or gravel damage. The fastest surface available, P-tex, is best used on smooth surfaces, like packed snow, for it is fragile and loses every encounter with a rock. White poly plastic is not as slick but much tougher and is widely used. Fiberglass makes a hard, fast running surface, but maintaining the smoothness and structure takes time and is messy.

Nobody in sled dog racing considers it peculiar that such modern inventions may be found on the same sled that is tied together with strips of caribou skin or moosehide. The best of everything old is combined with the best of everything new—with the emphasis on the old.

When modern racing sleds do vary from one another, usually local environment or personal preference have dictated the differences. People who race in forested, steep terrain prefer a sled that gives more than does the stiffer sled used in open country and on well-packed trails. Outside of Alaska sleds have to turn and track well on the narrow trails and the typical intersecting country roads of the lower 48 states. Here the baskets are built higher off the ground and the bow is steeply upswept to ride over deep snow or bumps. In Alaska, sleds tend to have longer baskets, looser construction, and a longer and more gradual, but higher, upsweep in the bow. Alaskan drivers need stability for hummocky, hard trails. When bumps are a factor, runner length is extended in order to bridge the gaps between the humps more smoothly.

Beyond the requirements of terrain, personal preference also dictates the size and action of a sled. A tall person often likes a higher, wider sled than that preferred by a shorter individual. An agile person can ride a sled almost like a pair of skis and wants a sled that will respond to his motion.

Sleds used for hauling freight are longer and wider than their racing counterparts. Weighing as much as 60 to 100 pounds and extending some 13 or 14 feet from bow to back of runners, the freight sled is built of more, not heavier, pieces of wood. The slats of the baskets extend all the way forward, for maximum load-carrying capability. Wider runners help to distribute the load. Although 500-pound freight runs or passengers on long-distance trips are rare for a dog team these days, freight sleds are still used along trap lines, for scientific trips, and in long races like the Iditarod Trail Race. There may be more wood in a freight sled, but the pieces all correspond to those on a racing sled.

Harnesses

Sled dog harnesses, however, vary considerably between freight and racing models, and to some degree, within those models. A first major improvement in the leather harnesses used by native drivers is attributed to the explorer, Fridtjof Nansen. The design of the harnesses used by the Eskimos he traveled with allowed the traces of the tug line to wear constantly on the underside of the dogs. The improvements he made, causing the harness to pull from the top of the back, resulted in greater efficiency and more comfort for the dogs, and became the prototype for most modern racing harnesses.

A good harness, be it of leather or nylon webbing, puts the pulling strain on the shoulders and chest of the dog, and fits him closely but not so as to bind. A freight harness is heavier and with more parts than a racing harness; it pulls the load from lower down and often has a spreader bar behind the dog to keep the harness straps from chafing his legs. A racing harness is light, about two ounces. It is designed to pull from low on the dog's shoulder blades and his chest, and to permit him as much freedom of movement as possible. Ideally, a racing harness is tailor-made for each dog, to allow for small variations in build even between dogs of similar height and weight. Sled dog drivers spend hours debating the relative merits of minute variations in harness design, and some of them have made small personal improvements on the ones they buy or make.

Towlines and Hitches, Hooks and Brakes

For the lines that hitch the team to the sled, too, individual variations are not only possible but probable, as each driver tries to suit his particular style of driving. The double-tandem or "gang" hitch towline, to which all dogs are hitched in pairs, has become the standard racing arrangement throughout the sport. In parts of Canada mushers have hooked their dogs in a single line with the traces on each side of the dog, mostly because the trails are narrow and difficult to negotiate with two dogs abreast. Even so, drivers in these areas are gradually changing to the gang hitch as races become faster and trails are better prepared with the help of mechanical equipment. Another factor in the changeover is the increasing size of competitive dog teams. A team of fourteen or more dogs hitched in a single line is a long dog team indeed.

The original arctic sea ice hitch is called the "fan" hitch, because each dog is hitched by his own trace to the sled, and the team fans out in front. A slightly longer trace permits the leader a front position, with any lazy dogs given short lines for closer control by the driver.

In Scandinavia, where skiers and dogs have toured and raced for many years, the Alaskan method of hitching is finding increasing favor. The Norwegian system requires long shafts attached to the brakeless toboggan, with bent bows over the dogs' shoulders to keep the shafts from crowding the animals. Rarely is a team of more than three dogs harnessed, and often one suffices for a day or overnight trip. In North

NECKLINES AND TUGLINES TIGHT, Howard Drown's team of purebred Siberians gets off to a good start at Bellingham, Massachusetts, in 1969.

Charles L. Booth,
Courtesy Cascadian Kennels

HAVING A GOOD DRINK AFTER THE RACE, Gerry Couture's dogs are still keeping their towlines taut. *Jim Beebe, Whitehorse* Star

TOO HEAVY A TOWLINE FOR A RACE, but perfect for this team of working Samoyeds in Europe.   *M. Gonin, Courtesy Boots Walker*

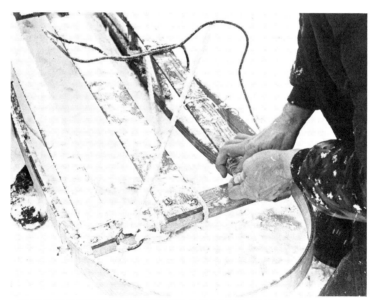

THE BOW ON THE FRONT OF A RACING SLED is mandatory, helps to divert the sled from direct collisions.   *L. Coppinger*

American-style races, however, the skiers who once glided alongside the teams have taken to the runners, and it is difficult to tell from a photograph whether a team picture was made in Sweden, Switzerland or Saskatchewan.

In the racing gang hitch, the most common, all the dogs except the leader are required to have a neckline between their collars and the central trace, so that they are prevented from turning out and perhaps disrupting a passing team. If two leaders are used, they are hitched together by a neckline at the collar. Sled dogs never pull on these necklines, except for those that like to lean outward against them for balance in rough traveling. All the pulling power of each dog is transmitted to the longer tugline or backline, which attaches to the back of the harness over the dogs' hips. These lines are at least four feet long so that each dog can run in close or swing far out from the center line without disturbing the stride of his teammate. Leather for traces and gangline has long since given way to polyethylene rope, a light, strong, colorful way to hitch the dogs to the sled. Thicker line can be used for the center gangline, thinner for the individual tuglines and necklines. With the ganglines of one color, the necklines of another, the tuglines of a third, it is a good deal easier to extricate dogs and lines from an occasional tangle. Brightly colored harnesses and sometimes a team with pompoms attached lend to the air of gaiety on the trail which the old-time Hudson's Bay teams used to exhibit.

Modern collars, too, are made of colorful nylon webbing, and fit closely over each dog's head.

Connecting the necklines and tuglines to the collars and harnesses are metal snap hooks, with brass preferred because it does not freeze shut. Bone or wooden toggles are seen occasionally, but are slower to disengage under the pressure of an excited dog team in a tangle.

Dogs harnessed to the gangline for racing are ordinarily given considerable space between the pairs, so that snow kicked up by one pair does not fly into the lowered faces of the pair behind. Allowing about six feet for each dog along the gangline also smooths out individual variations in gait, reducing the effect of an "up" pair on a "down" pair behind. A perfect racing team gallops in unison, all the dogs rising and falling at the same time, with every tugline taut, each pair of dogs directly behind the pair in front, the necklines slack. Such a team displays the rhythm sought after by every good dog driver, and the proper construction, length and spacing of the tuglines and other equipment are very important in producing this smooth-running assemblage.

Because the driver of a racing team (or any dog team, for that matter) does not use reins to guide or stop his dogs, several forms of control have been invented. Actually, the snow hook, which is fixed to the end of a short snubbing rope, was invented long ago by the Eskimos, who trimmed angular bony parts of arctic animals into anchor-shaped hooks that could be sunk into a soft drift or wedged between blocks of ice. A runaway team could mean death or serious hindrance to the hunter, or injury to a dog. Today's snow hook is made from steel, with as many variations as there are snow conditions. In those places where no snow falls, or where trails go through dense forest or bush, the drivers use brush hooks, a lighter and simpler version of the snow hook. Instead of stamping it into the ground, they hook it to branches, roots, saplings—and even to car bumpers and parking meters, be they close by.

The brake on the racing sled is a modern addition. In the early days, before the driver considered riding on the runners, the sleigh or toboggan was slowed by the driver holding back or pulling to one side on the long "gee" pole installed at the bow of the sled. If a hill was so steep that the driver's weight proved insufficient to slow the descent, he wrapped a rope or chains around the front part of the runners to cause extra friction. Since these early systems had distinct disadvantages, drivers riding behind their sleds devised new and more efficient methods of slowing and stopping. Jack Laonte of Alaska supposedly built the first riding-type sled with a claw brake attached, and in today's races a team is not allowed to leave the starting line without such a brake. While the brake is not in use, it is held up under the basket by a spring, rubber rope, or sometimes by the resiliency of the wooden brake bar itself.

More Tools of the Trade

Individual drivers use a great diversity of miscellaneous gear. Professional drivers often carry a whip, because the majority of Alaskan dogs are taught to respond to whip signals or warnings. Using the whip properly is a great art, and a few experienced drivers can produce an explosion like a gunshot which startles uninitiated spectators as well as the sluggish dog. The whip should never touch the dogs during a race (most clubs limit whip length to three feet) unless a stray arrives to provoke a fight, or in some other emergency in which a quick pop with the tip will discourage a potentially dangerous situation. The driver is not allowed even to snap his whip in the vicinity of another racing team. Drivers who do not carry a whip may depend on whistles, voice commands or "jinglers" (personally invented noisemakers, such as bottle caps strung together) to provide a dash of incentive at a crucial point.

Two other pieces of equipment still of value to the modern long distance racer are boots to protect the dogs' feet, and loin covers to protect their thinly-haired undersides. Contemporary boots are made from boat canvas with rawhide drawstrings, and provide more traction than does leather. Sometimes they are made so that the dog's toenails can protrude, affording him even greater stability. They are tied on whenever an animal has a sore foot, or when the trail leads over sharp ice. Modern racers also use various protective salves on their dogs' feet, for a footsore dog has to "sit on the bench," and it can take days for a raw pad to heal.

When Charlie Evans left Bishop Mountain for Nulato with the package of serum in 1925, his forgetting of the rabbit-skin loin covers for his dogs caused him greater difficulty on the thirty-mile trail than the 64-degrees-below-zero temperature might otherwise have warranted. Modern races, most of them, are short and not run in such conditions. For the thousand-plus miles of the Iditarod Trail, of course, loin covers are standard equipment.

On their sleds, racers carry two kinds of bags, usually made of light-weight nylon. One is suspended in the framework at the back of the sled, where the driver can carry extra gloves, an emergency neckline or harness, and some snap hooks in case a towline parts or is snipped in two by over-anxious canine teeth. The other bag rides on the sled basket, and is designed to enclose a dog with one quick motion by the driver. A tired or injured dog relegated to the ignominy of riding home must be kept well wrapped, partly so he will not cool off too rapidly and partly so he cannot fall or jump from the moving sled.

Racing rules require that the sled be equipped with a brush bow, a curved piece of wood (or tough plastic) at the front which wards off serious collisions with dogs, other sleds, trees or similar impediments to forward motion.

Equipment failures have contributed to some historic racing disasters. One young driver, leading the heat in the Race of Champions at Tok, was forced to drop out of the running when a light-duty snap hook connecting his towline with the sled bridle gave way and released his entire team of 14 dogs. Like all eager racing teams, his dogs accelerated immediately and completed the course long before the sore-footed, sore-tempered musher and his sled. The first driver from the West Coast to compete in the difficult Laconia championship broke his sled brake crossing a curb only one block out from the starting line. That he completed the tortuous course in seventeenth place out of forty teams is a tribute to his fine lead dog that continued to work the course almost perfectly, despite the absence of the usual light tap on the brake which is a driver's signal to alert the team for an approaching turn. Ill-fitting harnesses eliminated many excellent dogs from the running of the first thousand-mile marathon on the Iditarod Trail; like workhorses of old, some of them sustained collar galls and bruised backs, and were removed from the race. Those mushers who watched their dogs led away by officials acquired a new respect for good racing equipment, equipment worthy of the gritty dogs wearing it and pulling with it.

Transportation for the Team

In 1916 Leonhard Seppala's dog team ran the 450 miles from Nome to Ruby to compete in the Ruby Dog Derby. Today's racing huskies travel in luxury. Custom-made dog boxes built on the backs of trucks or trailers can carry whole kennels, often as many as fifty dogs, plus food and equipment. Inside the boxes is deep straw and sometimes a second dog for companionship and extra warmth. Occasionally a driver will have sleeping and cooking facilities for himself and a handler built into a bigger rig. Parked in the staging area of a race, a racer will often leave the door of his van open or drop the tailgate and keep a pot of hot stew simmering for his family or a hungry friend. Transportation for today's racing huskies varies from Merv Hilpipre's multi-thousand-dollar, multi-dozen-dog, four-wheel-drive rolling hotel, which tours the professional circuits from Iowa to Alaska, to Roscoe Bicknell's square-backed Volkswagen, with six pleased Siberians sitting up attentively on the back seats, traveling around New England on weekends. The investment and the scope may be far apart, but the sport is the same and chances are the pleasures of driving the dogs are similar for each man.

No-snow Rigs

Sled dogs are thought of in terms of snow, but a good deal of training, conditioning and even racing takes place without this cold, slippery phenomenon. Although having enough snow is little problem for the Alaska Dog Mushers' Association or the Whitehorse Sled Dog Club, what about for the equally enthusiastic mushers of the St. Louis Sled Dog Club or the Mason-Dixon Sled Dog Racing Association? Even in Alaska, the temperature can be cool enough for fall training before any snow has fallen. In most areas, in fact, the majority of fall training has to be accomplished without sleds.

Dog drivers have invented a handful of methods for keeping their dogs in shape, from free running to huge exercise wheels, from one or two dogs harnessed in front of a brave bicyclist to 16 dogs hitched to a cut-down Crosley chassis. There are drag sleds and snow sleds with wheels

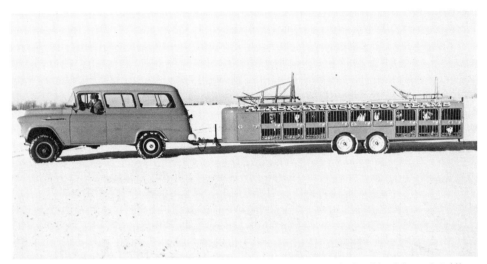

ROY GADDIS OUTFITTED HIS TEAM with this remarkable rig for his driver, Art Allen, to take to the races in the late 1950's.   *Les Burianek, Courtesy Lorna Demidoff*

THE ROLLING KENNELS OF MAC MCDOUGALL, the sled dog world's noted dog truck designer.   *J. Malcolm McDougall, Courtesy Harris Dunlap*

attached; there are light, tubular-framed three-wheeled rigs, some of which resemble Roman chariots.

The type of rig used depends on how many dogs are to be run. A cut-down foreign car chassis is still a hefty load to pull, so a five-dog team would be a minimum. On the other hand, to hitch a team of more than five dogs to a light three-wheeled cart would be asking for trouble. Car chassis with full frames are made into rigs by removing everything from the frame except the wheels, brakes, steering wheel and front seat. A proper chassis rig weighs about 500 pounds when trimmed down, and it is the most popular, versatile, stable vehicle for no-snow training. The specially-made training carts, welded out of tubular metal, generally have only three wheels, the front one being caster-mounted for steering. A 150-pound cart, well sprung, with good brakes and steering, can be driven by an experienced driver with almost any size team. Lighter rigs are limited to small teams, perhaps even to one dog, making individual training easier. A drag sled is built with flat runners that are wider than those on a racing sled, shod with steel, and can weigh as little as fifty pounds. It is useful in rough country, can go on asphalt, leaves, grass, pine needles or through the woods. In Pennsylvania, Betty Padgett believes that the drag sled is the best way to first introduce her young dogs to pull. It does not roll up on the dogs, distracting or frightening them. They can concentrate on pulling.

Actually, a dog driver might very well use all three types of rig during his fall schedule, beginning with a light cart for conditioning a few dogs at a time or putting a new leader into training, progressing to a drag sled for strengthening the pulling muscles and stamina, and then hitching his developing team to a chassis rig so that he can run the whole team together and train for speed and distance.

Build It or Buy It?

In spite of the fact that the harnesses and sleds, the towlines and the rest of a sled dog team's equipment look pretty much the same throughout the sled dog world and still resemble the equipment used decades ago by dog-punchers, there is an important difference that sets sled dog equipment apart from equipment used in most other sports: none of it is mass-produced. A sled maker must carefully select the hardwoods he uses, looking for good straight grains, and then sorting, cutting and steaming each piece for its own particular use in the sled. The pieces are clamped skillfully into forms, assembled into component parts, and then assembled. Minute finishing touches are as important to the way a sled handles as is selection, cutting and fitting of the wood. Time is as impor-

A SPECIAL SLED DOG TRAINING RIG, built by Frank Hall of Michigan. *Frank Hall*

NOT A HIGHLY RECOMMENDED WAY TO TRAIN A DOG TEAM—but effective for brave bike riders. *Jim Mitchell*

FRANK HALL'S SWIVEL SLED, designed to sweep neatly around curves.   *Frank Hall*

QUITE A SLED: The 1000th one built by Frank Hall, finished in the fall of 1973. This is his Kalkaska Cross-country model.   *Frank Hall*

tant as skill, and no factory could put together with machines an implement so fine as a dog sled. The number of high-quality sled builders across North America is small, but they all must share the satisfaction expressed by Frank Hall, who builds sleds in Michigan: "When the sled is all finished and totally equipped with brake, bridle, and so on, the builder can look at it as a beautiful, custom-built creation, with a lot of pride involved. It's a great feeling."

Sled dog drivers often construct their own harnesses and ganglines. Materials are available at hardware stores, tack shops, marine, aviation or mountaineering supply outlets; with a "how-to" book in one hand, making basic team equipment is fairly simple. Many drivers also make their own sleds, although a degree of woodworking skill is necessary. A professionally-designed, well-built sled does a lot to eliminate problems of following the team and staying on. The difference between a homemade sled and one built by someone like Ed Moody, one of the best-known sled builders, can be the difference between a smooth ride on the trail or a jerky one, or between a race won or lost.

Across North America there are less than a dozen regular sources of sled dog equipment, although several racing kennels sell harnesses or other items. All these businesses are owned and run by families or individuals who make the equipment themselves to high-quality, professional specifications. Like ordering clothes from a mail-order house, drivers fill out a form with each dog's measurements for a harness. Ganglines and sleds can also be built to individual specifications. Ed Moody of New Hampshire, who went on Admiral Byrd's Second Antarctic Expedition, and then drove dogs on the New England circuit, has supplied sleds for years to Lombard and Belford and other top drivers. In Alaska, Moody sleds are said to be more sought after than cash as payment for a sled dog. Sled makers do not usually have to advertise, for the demand for good sleds is constant. Once, for example, a new musher, determined to get off to a good start in dog racing, telephoned Ed Moody at his shop to order a sled. He was promised delivery within two years.

If a beginning dog driver, with five dogs, wanted to order a complete outfit of racing sled, harnesses, collars and towline for his team, it would cost him between $200 and $300, depending on the quality of sled. He could spend more. Of course it would be cheaper to buy raw materials and make his own, but he would be missing the refinements inherent in professionally-constructed equipment.

No matter who makes the equipment, the design and form of the whole assemblage still evoke the crudest komatik team of the past. And no matter how fine or colorful the equipment, it is still up to the dogs and drivers to meld their abilities into a going dog team.

SCIENTIFIC PUPPY TRAINING IN NEW YORK. Christopher Dunlap with a fourteen-week old husky.
Harris Dunlap

A PEACEFUL TRAINING RUN, on the dirt roads of Ohio, November 1974.
Leona Hutchings

9

Think Sled Dogs

Dogs are the most intuitive creatures alive. They take the disposition and feelings of their driver. That is why I never let my dogs know I'm tired. At the end of the day when my heart has been nigh breaking with the weariness, I sing to the little chaps, and whistle, so they always reach the end of the trail with their tails up and waving.

SCOTTY ALLAN, 1921

W<small>HEN MORNING TEMPERATURES</small> in sled dog country begin to sink into the sixties, hundreds of sled dogs rise and shake off the summer's lethargy. Modern mushers haul out the harnesses and towlines, check the tires and brakes of their training rigs, and start preparing for the long, full schedule of winter races.

What follows is a veritable avalanche of training, conditioning, traveling, racing. From as early as September through as late as April, a dedicated dog driver spends all his free time with his dogs. When he is not actually working with the dogs he is thinking about them, wondering, mulling, figuring, calculating, deciding, planning; his absorption can be total.

A veteran musher has his own system of selecting for his team, of training and conditioning himself and his dogs. He believes his system is best, but he keeps his senses alert for improvements. A beginner in the sport may have to solve problems about equipment, about dogs, and then flounder around until he finds a technique that suits his aspirations. Yet his dedication is no less complete.

All the mushers and all the dogs have to go through similar processes, be they veterans or novices. Selection, training, conditioning and then scheduling the team's competitions, must be accomplished by everyone involved. Only the extent to which these are carried will vary, with the professional making it more than a full-time job. Yet the weekend or recreational sled dogger also finds his mind frequently returning to a small problem or a large satisfaction. Putting together a dog team involves paying attention both to a myriad of details and to the developing picture as a whole. That a person is interested in dogs as more than sleeping house pets already indicates a desire to know the animals better and to work with them in a common, exhilarating task. The rewards are many and not always predictable. They can be achieved by constant, unrelenting, perpetual thinking—thinking sled dogs.

Selecting a Dog Team

Selection of a dog team usually starts within a particular breed. Although the only real requirement for a sled dog is that he be big enough, fast enough and strong enough to pull sled and driver over a prescribed course in a reasonable amount of time, most mushers favor the northern breeds.

Leonhard Seppala received his first dog team intact: 15 young huskies, most of them females, offspring of the first sled dogs imported to Alaska from the Kolyma River region in Siberia.

Donna Mudgett, one of Alaska's best women drivers, watched the Laconia World Championship racers go by her door as a youngster, and had to give dog racing a try. She hitched her Standard Poodle to a toboggan and off they went. The next year her father bought her a dog sled and she and the poodle finished second in the Junior Championship.

Byron James, an unsuspecting professor in Wisconsin, selected a pair of huskies for his children when they asked for a snowmobile. "Grow your own snowmobile," he suggested, and before he knew it he had 22 huskies.

John Lyman of New Hampshire watched a team of Irish Setters beat a few husky teams and decided that the perfectly matched, long-haired, leggy red setters were for him.

John Ruud, currently the president of the International Sled Dog Racing Association and holder of five Pacific Coast Championships, promised his skeptical wife that one husky was all he wanted—he would certainly never get involved with anything like racing.

Lloyd Slocum of Maine bought his first husky from Doc Lombard, and then he bought four more. The Igloo Pak stock on which his successful team is based came from Siberians bred in New England by Leonhard Seppala.

An experienced dog team can be bought intact, or a potential musher can raise a litter of pups and call that his team. This latter method takes several years, with dogs and driver making mistakes but also learning together. The former method gets the driver on the trail in short order, and has the further advantage of the dogs being able to teach the new master. The degree of success attained on the race course, however, is directly related to the abilities of the dogs and driver, and to the hours spent training both.

Selecting a good sled dog depends on more than selecting a breed, for even within the northern breeds there is diversity between individuals. To qualify as a fast sled dog with stamina, the dog has to be built right and he has to have those interior qualities of heart and desire. Although the set and form of a dog's ears should not have any bearing on how he runs, many drivers, for example Charlie Belford, much prefer prick-eared dogs. Next he might look at the length of the dog's back and the slope of his rump. He will fit his fingers between a dog's front shoulder blades, looking for a minimum space to accommodate the bones as the dog reaches forward in a fast lope. He will run his hands down the dog's legs, feeling the weight of the bone and the muscle, then pick up the feet and look for dark pads. Experience has taught veteran mushers that pink pads are often less tough than dark or what they call lemon-colored pads. The hair on the feet should be short, so it will not collect snow and ice. The coat should be full and dense, but not long and wavy: a sled dog needs insulation against weather, but not much, for he warms up rapidly while running.

Then, a knowledgeable sled dog fancier will step back and look at how the bones and the muscles are put together. He looks for a slightly arched neck, a shoulder slope close to 45 degrees, a good reach in the upper arm, well-set elbows, and springy, strong, medium-length pasterns. The front legs should be let down comfortably, not too close together, not too far apart. A full chest, tapering towards the rear, indicates room enough for lung expansion. A longish back with no roach and no sag, sloping easily in

A LITTLE TROUBLE ON THE TRAINING TRAIL: a tangle of dogs in
the Midwest. *Leona Hutchings*

FAMILIAR SIGHT AT A SLED DOG RACE: the staging area, this one
at Ranch Rudolph near Traverse City, Michigan. *Leona Hutchings*

FULL SPEED FOR THE FINISH—DRIVER OR NOT! *Lisa Fallgren Uloth*

the croup to well-let-down rear legs, gives promise of speed. Length in the upper and lower thighs and shortness in the hock, connected by well-angled bends at the stifle and hock, contribute to a sense not only of good speed but also of endurance in a dog. So does a neat tuck of the abdomen up into the flanks.

Even with all the proper physical attributes, the dog still has to be able to move well, running low and not bobbing, flashing his legs back and forth with no sidewise or crossing-over motions, thrusting hard with his rear end, reaching far forward with his front. Conformation has a lot to do with how a dog runs.

Yet for all the well-built dogs on a championship team, there is always a Magic. Magic's front legs seemed to come out of the same hole, and he ran splay-footed; even Charlie Belford could not figure out where his dog got his speed. There have been other strangely-built dogs that can run fast forever, but they are rare. There are differences of opinion among the best drivers as to the most important qualities of a racing sled dog, but after the debate is over, the proof of the dog is still in the running.

Biologist Kent Allender, a racer from Wisconsin, puts attitude at the head of the list in breeding for performance in his sled dogs. In his search for the ultimate racer, Allender bought foundation dogs with a superior attitude toward racing. "Give me a choice of two dogs, one built like a racehorse, but sour, and the other built like a box with legs, but with lots of guts and desire, and I'll choose the boxy dog and beat you every time."

The age-old qualities of heart and loyalty, those indefinable attributes so well known by people who work with dogs, exist somewhere in a dog's personality. Modern sled dog racers are on the lookout for these qualities, and can apply a certain genetic knowledge in breeding for desire, determination, or a positive response to stress. So many factors are at work, however—genetics, environment, training—that some degree of luck is also part of developing a top-notch sled dog.

Racing sled dogs are generally a friendly, personable lot, getting on well with humans and canines alike. They must not be too friendly, however, especially when in harness, for a stop by the side of the trail for an admiring pat is not of utmost priority to the driver. Jack London notwithstanding, fighting for position among racing sled dogs is unheard of. Spats and conflicts of interest do arise, but they are rare. Sled dogs are bred to work together, and for this reason have been selected for the ability to get on with each other. A bit of shyness or natural reserve is fine, as these traits tend to keep a dog's mind on the job.

WELL-TRAINED TEAMS AVOID EACH OTHER ON THE TRAIL. Bob Corriveau, Sr.,
of New Hampshire.
Lisa Fallgren Uloth

In Training Together

Training a well-built dog with a good racing attitude to run is not much of a problem; it just takes time. In fact, most dogs, once they understand what is expected of them in harness, are eager to run, to pull, to be a part of the team. Training to pull, except in the case of wheel dogs, is secondary to the need for running. Dogs usually learn how to run in harness and how to pull simultaneously, although some do need individual lessons on the art and joy of pulling their share. According to Doc Lombard, "You can't scare a dog into running. They run because they want to, because you've built that into them." Once the team is in motion, the amount of drag on any dog's harness is small. Theoretically, one dog pulling one thirty-pound sled pulls thirty pounds. Actually, once he gets that sled moving on a slippery surface, he is subjected to far less than a thirty-pound tug. Hills, snowdrifts and pavement can all figure in a race, so the racing husky does have to know how to pull.

A dog team, like other sporting teams, consists of individuals filling certain positions. Each position requires slightly different attributes: a lead dog must run out front with confidence and guide the team on turns; behind the leader the two point dogs (called swing dogs in Alaska) also carry responsibility for the guidance and pace of the team; the pairs of dogs behind point are called swing dogs (in Alaska, team dogs), and much of the power and endurance of the team as a whole depends on them. Just in front of the sled are the wheel dogs, responsible for getting the sled going and keeping it on the trail on turns. Some dogs will run only on the right or the left side of the gangline, and thus a "left swing dog" or a "right wheel dog" can become a regular in his position.

During fall training a driver works his new or young dogs at various positions, finding out who runs best where, and with what other dog he gaits smoothly. A young pup may hang back on his neckline and give every indication of not being ready for the team, but then when moved to another position he runs fine. Training a dog to run in harness is usually accomplished by hitching him in, at six to eight months, with a small team of veterans, for a slow, short, fun run. He may already have learned about dog teams by watching the others go out and listening to their enthusiastic din, or he may have been allowed to run free alongside the team. Perhaps he has even been introduced at the age of six or seven weeks to a harness, dragging a string. Whatever the method, the driver must control his own enthusiasm and not ask more from a dog than he can give. Many young dogs have been soured on running by being driven too far, too fast, before they were ready.

In any training session, it is important to let the dogs know that they have done a good job. A pat and a word of praise for each dog is standard operating procedure for an experienced driver. Even if the run has featured more problems than pleasures, the session should end on a cheerful tone. Bella Levorsen, a California musher and the author of a beginner's manual on training, emphasizes this point. "If a dog did not do what you wanted it was because he was either sick or he did not understand. Check for sickness first. If nothing is wrong with him, then you must go to the second alternative and try to think of possible reasons why he doesn't know what you want. Obviously you must find a better way to communicate your wishes to him. Figuring all this out is what makes dog training so fascinating, and makes it so rewarding when you finally succeed."

From out of a pack of runners will come a natural lead dog or two. This dog seems to need to be up front, for his enthusiasm drops conspicuously whenever he has to run back in the team. A first-class leader couples this desire to lead with above-average intelligence, responsibility, and an imperviousness to pressure. His intelligence enables him to learn the commands for right and left turns ("gee" and "haw"), for going straight ("go ahead" or "hike"), or even for an emergency stop ("whoa"), and to detect and respond to nuances in his driver's voice commands. A leader's responsibility relates to things he can do on the trail on his own, how he handles both normal and unexpected situations. He keeps the team strung out at all times, never falling back to be overtaken by the dogs behind him; he keeps well out of the way of other teams when passing or being passed. He keeps the rest of his team out of trouble. Racing today does not usually carry the awesome possibility of crossing dangerous ice packs or sniffing out buried trails, but many of today's lead dogs have shown that kind of ability when an unusual event has arisen.

Harris Dunlap runs a leader training program at his Zero Kennels in upstate New York. He begins with pups as young as 12 weeks old in a field of tall grass with mowed grids. Pups on leashes quickly learn to associate the words "gee" and "haw" with right or left turns, and then they are taught to "go ahead."

In *Training Lead Dogs My Way*, musher Lee Fishback of Montana recommends a step-by-step method similar to that used by obedience trainers, which starts with the dog learning to stand ahead of the trainer on a taut towline and gradually progresses to intricate maneuvering on command, the dog having learned always to work in front of the trainer. The method is based on the trainer having complete control at all times and practicing what the author calls "positive training."

With all the schooling and proper techniques available, occasionally a leader comes along whose talents are so outstanding that he practically trains himself. Such was the case with a Border Collie belonging to Ray Coppinger, a New England driver. Perro ran well enough in the team of Alaskan Huskies, but was continually chafing. Put on lead, he sparkled, but got confused at corners. A ten-minute session in the comfort of the living room, with Coppinger simply turning the dog's head left or right and repeating the commands, served as Perro's education.

Frequently a team will have a double lead, two leaders hitched up front. One may be an excellent command leader but not too keen on being out front alone, or perhaps he is shy of crowds. The other dog might not be good on commands but be an enthusiastic trail leader otherwise. If the command leader is able to shoulder or suggest his way around the turns, the pair adds up to a fine front end and gives more dog team for the same length of gangline.

Hazards on the trail sometimes severely test the mettle of even the best-trained leaders. A moose or an incautious rabbit can tempt a normally obedient dog team to forget all about the scheduled race and to undertake one of their own. Not too many years ago, in California, the lead dog led his colleagues smack into an inviting hot dog stand. The resulting havoc lasted for 11 minutes, while the unenthralled driver tried to separate the cold dogs from the hot ones.

Conditioning

Fall training, especially for the veterans on a team, is more properly a conditioning process. Even if the dogs are exercised during the summer, they still need to be brought slowly to peak racing condition, for a racing sled dog is no less of an athlete than any other sports competitor. The racing dog needs proper exercise and nutrition, and when he is in racing shape, no pet Greyhound could touch him over any distance.

Conditioning is usually accomplished by running small teams two or three miles at a time, gradually extending the distance as the dogs' feet and muscles toughen. Veteran race dogs need fewer conditioning miles than do young dogs, but "putting on the miles" each fall requires daily runs, with young dogs mixed in with older ones, and careful records kept as to each day's progress. Each day's team will consist of different dogs, as today's speedy youngster is dropped to a slower team for more education on the finer points of pulling, or yesterday's older leader is today run at left point in order to add stability to a team of pups.

Not only do conditioning techniques vary, but the desired peak a driver is aiming for differs from driver to driver. Since sled dog races can be ten miles long, or a hundred, or a thousand, teams are usually trained for the specific distance of the race. New England drivers, racing 12 to 14 miles per heat, will often train their dogs for a fast ten-mile run, counting on the excitement of the race to inspire a few more miles from the dogs. Bill Shearer, however, consistently finishing high in New England races during the late 1940's and early 1950's, trained his Siberians for long distances, far longer than they would ever race. He believed that the distance would condition them best, and then in a race he would drive them for speed. In Alaska, George Attla keeps his team off balance: "They never know how far they are going today, whether it will be ten miles or twenty miles. This way I am the one who is setting the pace of the team. But if I went on a thirty-mile run every day, then they are the ones who would be setting the pace."

Serious racing drivers believe that right from the start, the team should be run at a lope, an easy gallop. In this way, dogs are trained to run all the time. If they are not running, they are stopped, allowed to catch their breath, and then "hiked" into a lope again. In a twenty-mile race, with cold weather, packed snow and no steep hills, a team will lope the entire distance, except on fast stretches when the dogs break into a sprinting gallop. For a long race like the Iditarod, a racing team does not often do so well as one trained for long distances. Carl Huntington, winner of the 1974 Iditarod, said he trained his dogs during the race. "I want my Rondy dogs to run. But I want my Iditarod dogs to trot," noted Huntington. He finished seventh in the three-heat, ninety-mile Rondy, and then, with different dogs, first in a twenty-day run along the one thousand miles of the Iditarod Trail.

The Celusniks of Fairbanks train long-distance dogs, a mixed Alaskan breed they designate only as "gen-u-wine Alaskan fishburners." "When we train for long distances, we do just that. Basically, we start off the season with a short course of seven miles. Gradually we build up the distance and the amount of weight. Usually we drag a seventeen-inch truck tire behind the sled which not only creates a drag but keeps the trail in good shape. On long runs we normally go empty sled as the trails do get rough and it eliminates the sled dumping over on slanted river banks. This year we will have about a hundred-mile trail that will be available to all the mushers in our area."

One of the most unusual methods of training sled dogs is that of Lloyd Slocum, an over-forty marathon runner from Maine. In five years Slocum raced his way from entering a novice dog team in his first race to winning the World Championship in Laconia. His method? Year-round conditioning. "I like to run year round—on a fun basis in the off season, and then more seriously in the winter. I run with my dogs every day in the summer." Conditioning, according to Slocum, is a way of life. He points to Olympic champions Frank Shorter and Valery Borzov, one a marathoner, one a sprinter, but both of them year-round runners.

"The point should be unmistakable to anyone who has an understanding of what it takes to get near the top in any keenly competitive sport," states Slocum. "A three-week crash program will not do the trick. Three months is much too short, too, and in most cases three years is not long enough. For many it takes the better part of a lifetime of constant dedication combined with an unfailing belief that you can win, no matter what the competition."

Fifteen minutes of fast, free running every day in the cool Maine evening enable Slocum's dogs to cruise for six miles at 16 miles an hour the first time out as a team, in October. The free runs build their strength as well as their joy in streaking across the countryside. Inherent competitiveness appears as the dogs continually challenge one another in all-out, short sprints. The results? Dogs that love to run, who run from desire, not from fear, and when the going gets tough they do not cheat in subtle ways.

Dick Moulton also emphasizes proper behavior as an important quality in winning sled dog races. "You win races by having the least trouble—no lame dogs, or fights and tangles. To me, there's nothing like training a team to run well. That's the romance."

On a less intense level of training, but scarcely less serious, is Ethel Bacon of Rocky Hill, Connecticut. Out with her two purebred Siberians, she recalls "gliding smoothly along an icy, winding snowmobile trail (midweek, when the woods were quiet). A jet flew over, quite low, and the dogs both looked up without a change in pace, and I also looked up. Until suddenly I thought, no one is watching where we are going!"

Conditioning is not always a smooth operation. A loose team, skylarking down the trail, is part of any dog driver's experience. It is doubtful that a dog driver exists who has not encountered a training session resembling this one, described by Els van Leeuwen in Holland:

> "With my husband Lew away to Sydney for two weeks, I promised to keep the dogs in training until he came back. You may think a ten-dog team is just a little thing but to me it is a lot of dogs!
>
> "The first three times out on the rig went fine but on the fourth run it was rain, rain and more rain. But the dogs weren't quitting so I tried not to. So, under rainy conditions, all went well for the first four miles until I hollered, 'Red, come haw!' which he didn't. What was it that George Attla said in his book—something like the dog is always right? How right he was because Red *was* right—that haw turn was one too early and it led to a dead-end road.
>
> "Well, on we went and doubts are creeping into my soul about this day's training. Red got away with it once but the next turn I found I called out the command again—there was no way he was going to take it! Slowly but surely the ten of them dragged screaming and hollering me on, despite

254

the fact that my feet were on the hydraulic brakes. There was nothing to grab, no trees, nothing but rain which made for a wet and slippery surface. There was nothing I could do but go along with them and try for the next intersection, a gee turn, but that confounded dog, straight on he went down the road and now I was in real trouble. Another 400 meters down the road was a highway, and I just managed to catch a tree with my snub line.

"Now I had to get the team turned around and then, of course, switch leaders—I had had enough of Red! My mind was spinning, 'Why am I standing here with some crazy dogs in some crazy wood, wet, dirty and miserable. Why is Lew in Sydney, halfway around the world, when I need him here?'

"I had promised not to 'ruin' our true leader, Yaddam, but I needed him up front. I switched the dogs around, untangled some for the tenth time and got back on the rig. I even threw in a prayer for good measure before letting them go . . .

"They went perfectly. The sun started to break through and the run back was made without any problems. The dogs were happy, I was happy, and there is nothing like taking a dog team out, rain or no rain, trees or no trees, and leaders or no leaders.

"Sleddogsport is a disease, that's what it is!"

Conditioning the driver for such experiences is practically impossible. But a sled dogger must have an in-born tolerance for the frustrations of putting together a dog team, since the mental and physical stress caused by the process can be borne only by the dedicated. The driver is called the biggest and hardest-working dog on the team, loading and unloading dogs, pedaling the sled or running up hills, and generally as active as any team manager would want to be. Since the first race in Nome, when Scotty Allan and the other pioneer racing drivers began watching their diets and taking regular exercise, better dog drivers have been careful to match their dogs' training program with one of their own. Not many can go to the lengths of Lloyd Slocum, foot-running with his dogs or working out on a track. Some drivers consider that the exercise they get training their team is enough; others may be in shape from participation in some other sport. The wisest watch what they eat, especially during training and racing seasons, and exercise regularly.

What the Sled Dogs Eat

During these periods of increased stress, what the dogs eat dictates to a large degree how well they will run and what kind of shape they will be in at the end of the racing season. Minimum nourishment results in minimum performance. Maximum nourishment is an entirely different story, its scientific precepts painstakingly established but its practice endlessly debated. Wet food, dry food, commercial food, homemade food, or combinations thereof, can all sustain a working sled dog.

In the Arctic, especially along the coast, fish has always been the staple dog food. Walrus or seal meat is regarded as the best, but the natives feed whatever is available, including whale, bear, beaver, caribou or reindeer. Explorers, dog-punchers and early racers often added corn meal, oatmeal, or rice. Fish meal is still a basic ingredient of commercially-made dog food, and the "all beef" that goes into canned food is primarily the leftovers from a processed steer. Usually the whole animal, not just the muscle, must be consumed to ensure a balance of proteins, fats and carbohydrates, in approximately the best percentages for an animal like the dog.

The most popular food for feeding in large kennels is the dry, kibbled dog food which comes in fifty-pound bags. It can be fed dry, with plenty of water available for the dogs to drink, or it can be mixed with water or supplemental nutrients. Doc Lombard feeds a dry dog food, supplementing with a tiny bit of canned meat, liver or chicken, and a sprinkling of vitamins. George Attla feeds similarly to Lombard, adding liver or canned meat and wheat germ oil when he can get it. Going into a three-day race, his dogs receive an extra collation in the morning: some rice, cottage cheese, honey and vegetable oil. Attla's experience has shown him that slightly overweight dogs at the beginning of a triple-heat race will deliver more power during the last day's heat. Gareth Wright and Charlie Belford also feed high-protein commercial dog food, carefully supplementing this balanced diet with the extra protein and fat needed to maintain their hard-working dogs in cold weather.

Another successful Alaskan racer, Joe Redington, Sr., feeds his dogs cookies. They are made of soybean meal and honey and serve both dogs and driver during a long race. Redington's dogs' usual diet is ground-up halibut heads and beaver meat, saved for them by trappers. At the home of the "gen-u-wine Alaskan fishburners," in the winter the long-distance dogs eat a thick mash made of meat scraps, suet, water and bones (cooked for the marrow and then removed). The mixture is cooked well, let cool, and some high-protein dog food added to set it up. At below-zero temperatures, a dog needs a lot of good fuel.

Water for racing dogs makes a difference. Dehydrated dogs cannot digest their food properly nor maintain their physiological well-being. Leonhard Seppala knew this when he left his warm fireside to go out and tend his dogs at night. Lloyd Slocum says he is careful to water late at night when his dogs drink the best. Chances are good that Doc Lombard does the same, for he taught Slocum, and Seppala taught him. Sometimes meat juice or fish meal or even honey is added to the water, and the water is heated, so that the dogs do not use valuable calories to re-warm their bodies after a cold drink.

How to Make the Winter Short

There is no sport like sled dog racing for making the winter go by fast. Beginning with daily or every-other-day training sessions, the driver and his whole family are quickly immersed in a winter schedule of races and traveling and training that would leave other athletes far behind. In most parts of the sled dog world the first race of the season is held at the end of December or the first of January. From then on through March a dog driver faces stiff, sore muscles on Mondays, a growing awareness on Tuesdays that his hurts may be disappearing, Wednesdays spent juggling the team line-up, slightly increased enthusiasm and a little bit of attention at his regular job on Thursdays, and Fridays spent checking and loading equipment. Saturdays and Sundays are packed from dawn to well after dark with traveling to and from the races, and driving the team hard for anywhere between ten and thirty-plus miles.

The dogs usually rest on Mondays, are run on their training trail on Tuesdays, Wednesdays and Thursdays, rest again on Fridays, and race on the weekend. No doubt the winter goes by fast also for them.

In New England the trucks, trailers and vans with the sled dog boxes congregate, on different weekends, in New Hampshire at Tamworth, Rindge, Kingston, Wolfeboro, Jaffrey, Pittsfield and Laconia; in Massachusetts at Gardner, Fort Devens and Maynard; in Vermont at Shelburne, Essex Junction and Brandon. In Michigan the schedule includes races at Ranch Rudolf, Kalkaska, Newaygo, Mio and Grand Valley State College. California and Oregon mushers make for Sisters, Palm Springs, Hobart Mills, Diamond Lake, Susanville, Truckee and Lake Tahoe. In Quebec, the circuit takes the sled dogger to St. Augustin, Neufchatel, Mont Carmel, Quebec City, Stanstead, Amos, Chicoutimi and Val d'Or. Europe's scheduled races are farther flung for any one driver, and European teams have border-crossing problems. In Finland, they race at Hervanta, Kyrkslart, Kuurila, Kerava, Luhalahti, Nikkila and Viljakkala; in Germany, at Latrop and Todtmoos; in Switzerland, at Savognin, Splügen, Saignelégier, Gadmen and Lenk. Races are not always held each year in each of these towns, but these towns represent a sample from the dozens of little-known towns which enjoy the sled dogs and invite them back frequently.

When a driver belongs to a club which sponsors races every weekend during the season, his standing in the club's point championship is affected not only by where he finishes in the races but how many races he attends. Recreational drivers, that is, drivers who have regular full-time jobs and race dogs as a hobby, take advantage of their club's racing circuit. Nine weekend races, one right after the other, is the average club schedule. The competition at these races is good, and the other drivers have similar schedules. Recreational drivers keep fewer dogs than do the professionals; classes limited to three, five or seven dogs give them ample scope to compete without the need to support dozens of sled dogs.

In California, a former president of the International Sled Dog Racing Association keeps 15 sled dogs and runs in as many of the Sierra Nevada Dog Drivers' races as allowed by his schedule as an exploration consultant for a large oil company. During the 1974–75 season Bob Levorsen raced in both limited and unlimited classes, beginning in wheeled rig contests at Prosser Dam with three teams of seven, five and three dogs. Two weeks later his teams were ready to run in the unlimited and limited seven-dog classes at Sisters, Oregon. Two weeks after that the season was in full swing and he ran his big team at Leland Meadows and Hobart Mills, California. Then he passed up a trip to Europe in order to race with George Attla and other top drivers in Colorado's first big professional race, the ISDRA-sanctioned Rocky Mountain Championship at Dillon. Levorsen ran there in the seven- and five-dog classes, then went back to the West Coast for races at South Lake Tahoe, Diamond Lake, Truckee, and an end-of-the-year fun race. His daughter, Daphne, or his wife, Bella, usually run the second-string dogs in the limited-class competitions.

A season for a professional team is not much different, although the emphasis is on racing in the big races, against the best competition. Art and Judy Allen own the Natomah Kennels in Iowa, where they raise Alaskan and Siberian Huskies for racing and for show. Successfully promoting their kennels with excellent racing teams, and keeping their Siberians versatile by schooling them for the show ring, the Allens make sled dogs a full-time, year-round profession. During the 1973–74 season they entered the most important races in their area, including several championships. Between January 12 and February 24, the Allens raced Art's unlimited team and Judy's limited team at Bemidji and Ely, Minnesota; Kalkaska, Michigan; Estherville, Iowa; Florence, Wisconsin and Winnipeg, Manitoba. Several of these races were sanctioned by ISDRA, and the Allens did so well that Art placed seventh in the ISDRA point championship awards and Judy won the Gold Medal for limited class teams.

Traveling farther afield after the best competition he can find is Alaska's champion, George Attla. For the past few years he has raced in the lower 48, proving the quality of his team by winning just about anywhere

RACING THE SLED DOGS IN DOWNTOWN CHICAGO. Fifteen-year-old Grace Masek has raced since she was five. *Courtesy Larry and Helen Masek*

he raced. His 1974–75 schedule included two preliminary races in Fairbanks, a two-day race in Susitna, a sprint in the annual New Year's Day race at Anchorage, and then he headed south. He raced in Ely and Dillon, then trucked back north for the Alaska State Championship at Soldotna, the North American Championship in Fairbanks, and the Race of Champions at Tok. His record: third and fifth in the preliminaries, second at Dillon, first in all the rest. His reward: undisputed championship in sled dog racing, his second ISDRA Gold Medal, several thousand dollars in prize money, and the vast satisfaction that comes with achieving the summit in his sport.

If George Attla represents a successful culmination of decades of experience with sled dogs, then Olaf Swenson must share some of the credit for contributing to Attla's achievements. For Swenson put a lot of thought into his dog team, too, but his results were a far cry from Attla's. Reminiscing in 1944 about his days with the Northeastern Siberian Company, Swenson wrote, "When I first went to Siberia and began buying dogs, I decided that I wanted a sporty-looking outfit. I made up my mind that I would have a white team, composed of especially large, fine, well-matched animals, with fine red harnesses and red sleds. I was going to be cock of the trail and show those natives how fine an outfit could look. I could see that the natives were amused, but they hunted up the dogs all right, and I got my white team. It looked like a million dollars. It would have made the most impressive exhibit any department store could have ever imported to amuse the children at Christmas time. But as a sled team it was no good at all. There were a few good dogs in it, but before long I replaced half of the team with dogs which had stamina and speed and intelligence. For years the natives kidded me about that white team. They'd laugh and say, 'Swenson wants a white dog. He doesn't care whether it's good or bad; he just wants a white dog.' "

Swenson's conclusions about this venture would coincide with any modern musher's musings about his own team: "Driving a good bunch of dogs is the best fun in the world and driving a poor team, the most exasperating."

10

On the Runners

From where I was parked I witnessed Mrs. Demidoff overtaking the team ahead, a neat and interesting performance. Her dogs seemed not at all tired; they were moving right along in close formation, very intent and businesslike.

MARJORY GANE HARKNESS, 1955

The battle of the minds as well as that of the dog teams was evident as Attla said later, "I knew I had to pass him (Lombard) in order to make up the two minutes I needed if I was going to win, but didn't want to pass him too quick as I didn't know if I could keep ahead of him. I figured I could do it later in the race, but when I finally decided to make the move, I just couldn't catch him."

GORDON FOWLER, 1974

261

BY THE TIME A MUSHER is ready to drive a dog team, be he recreational racer or world champion, be he a junior driver or in his seventh decade, many miles will have passed beneath paw and mukluk. Days and weeks of training will have yielded a ready dog team and a ready driver. The whole outfit will know each other's limitations, inclinations, qualifications. Still, the driver must know not only what his dogs can give, but how to get it out of them. Once on the runners of the sled, each driver derives his own special satisfaction from the race at hand. Preparations vary with the situations and goals of the drivers, but the rules are the same for everybody, and the object of a race is to win.

Before the Race

During the week before a race a dog driver spends a lot of time writing dogs' names on little pieces of paper. Like the baseball team manager, he must assign his athletes to the position each fills best, only with dogs the possibilities are more numerous. While pencilling in names beside the sketch of his gangline, the driver mulls over the abilities of each dog. After each day's training session the lineup may be changed slightly, with an eager, faster dog moved forward in the team, or one who is slacking off dropped back to where he can be more promptly persuaded. This switching around can occur even as the team goes to the starting line, and often circumstances of the race necessitate changes out on the trail.

Sometimes a driver plans to alter his lineup during the race. Lloyd Slocum, for example, kept a six-year-old veteran on his team, a dog who rarely pulled at the beginning of a race. By the time the race was ten miles old, this dog had just begun to warm up, so Slocum would stop and move her forward. She had retained enough energy so that as the other dogs began to flag, she picked up her pace and brought the rest home at a good rate. A dog like this is often balanced with a younger dog, a go-getter who will, in his youthful exhilaration, pull too hard at the start and have little energy left for the miles at the finish. An excellent command leader may shy at crowds, and for this reason begin a race back in the team. Once the team is out on the trail the driver can stop and bring this dog forward, depending on him to take all the commands for the rest of the race. The starting leader might be dropped back into the vacated position, or might stay and run double lead, if he can be persuaded by the expert to take the turns.

The physical condition and mental attitude of the dogs are closely watched during the week before a race. No time is left to heal a cut pad or to give a sour dog a chance to regain his enthusiasm. Training for the race must continue, but it must be done with even greater finesse. Routine is a confidence-builder for the dogs, so drivers try to schedule training sessions for midday, when the races usually begin.

Race Day

On the day of a race, the drivers like to get to the harnessing area two or three hours early. In the case of the bigger races, drivers' meetings are held during the morning, or, at important professional contests, the evening before. These meetings provide a chance for the drivers to ask questions of the officials, to go over the rules, or to swap information on trail conditions and how many dogs will be optimum for the distance and kind of snow. The Nome Kennel Club's original rule about dropping or adding dogs during a race is the pivot around which the size of each team revolves. Dogs may be dropped, but never added, and a dropped dog must be brought in on the sled. An unusual near-infraction of this rule occurred during the second running of the Iditarod Trail Race, when Alaskan driver Tom Mercer, nearly three weeks on the trail, discovered that one of his bitches was pregnant. He dropped her off at the next official station, thereby avoiding the embarrassment of reaching Nome with several more dogs than he had started out with.

A long race, 15 or more miles a day, calls for more dogs on a team, especially if the trail is slow. Deep snow on the trail, the chance of a snowstorm during the race, or a slushy trail due to warm weather, mean tough going. The more dogs on the team the easier it is for each dog. Yet the more dogs on the team the more potential trouble, and the ultimate speed is limited by the slowest dog. Especially in a three-day race a driver will run more dogs on the first day, so if he has to drop any dogs on succeeding days he will still have enough to make a strong finish. In the 1975 World Championship at Anchorage, George Attla began with 15 dogs, Doc Lombard with 12. The temperature was cold but the trail was soft, with snow flurries making it slower. By the third day, although Attla was down to 12 dogs, Lombard had dropped four, and his eight remaining dogs could not keep up the pace. He had, according to Attla, been "out-dogged."

On a well-packed trail with cold temperatures, or an old trail with icy spots, teams are kept to a minimum. Great speed under these conditions is hazardous for men and dogs, and many an expensive sled has been broken by sudden contact with a tree on a slippery curve. Yet if the trail

STAKED OUT AND WAITING FOR THE RACE. Dom Blodgett's baying coonhounds lend a strange note to the northern atmosphere of a sled dog race.

Charles L. Booth, Courtesy Cascadian Kennels

A STRONG, EAGER TEAM NEEDS A HANDLER FOR EVERY PAIR OF DOGS to get it safely to the starting line. Ray Coppinger and friends at Kingston, New Hampshire, in 1965.
Jean Baxter

A DIFFERENT APPROACH to a dog race: Emily Groves' Husky-Border Collie cross-breds are ready but calm. Pittsfield, N.H., 1973. *Barry Eton*

deteriorates to slush or gets covered by deep snow for the second day, eight or nine dogs are seldom enough to go the distance in the fastest time. Racing times will suffer, then, as most of the drivers will be running the smaller teams dictated by the first day's fast trail. Such a situation might give an edge to a driver with a bigger but slower team, a driver whose speed would ordinarily not place him near the top finishers but who could have run his big team intact on the fast trail the day before. Such is the luck of the sled dog race.

Arriving at a race well in advance of the starting signal gives the dogs time to get out of their boxes, to stretch and sniff their surroundings. Sled dogs are tethered by short neck chains to a long chain running from the rear of their truck perhaps to the front of someone else's, across the snow to a tree, or to rings spaced around their own traveling rig. Thus spread out, the calmer among them lie patiently waiting to be harnessed, trying to ignore the leaps and barks of their excited teammates. As the time for the first teams to go out approaches, the air of anticipation picks up, and soon every dog is on his feet. Already-harnessed teams pass by, the dogs straining on the tuglines, their feet scrabbling for purchase, but their would-be charge to the starting line is dampened by the several handlers who hold the gangline with two hands and try to keep their own feet under them as they thread their way past trucks and tethered dogs.

Big teams are generally started at two-minute intervals, the exact starting time for each team scheduled before the race. A team late to the starting line is still clocked from its appointed time, and if an entered team does not show, there will be a four-minute wait for the next team.

Behind the starting chute, waiting while the team at the line is counted down, the dogs in the next team scream and·yammer to be let go, and when the team in front is finally released, their eagerness fairly explodes. But the bow of their sled must hold the line for two more minutes, the straining dogs must watch the other team disappear down the trail.

A handler will hold the sled, standing on the brake, while the driver makes his way along his line of dogs, checking necklines, tuglines, harnesses, encouraging his dogs and perhaps confiding in his leader. The dogs seem to think only of catching that other team: why are we waiting! Let's GO! But their early enthusiasm must be curbed so there will be enough energy left to finish the course at a fast pace. Back on his sled, the driver and his handlers listen intently above the din of the dogs to the countdown, anticipating that exact moment when the handlers can jump aside and the driver can yell, "Hieek! Go get 'em!!"

The rush from the chute is irrepressible, but before the first half mile is passed, a good team will have settled into a ground-eating, energy-saving lope. Everybody begins to concentrate on the trail ahead.

Strategy for Winning

Since each team is running against the clock, it is not always easy for a driver to know exactly how he is doing. Not until the first day's heat is over and the times are posted will he be sure just where he stands. Drawings for starting positions in the first heat are usually random. A driver wears a number bib which shows his starting position, and by observing the numbers on the teams he passes, or which pass him, he can tell roughly how fast his team's speed is relative to the others. In the 1974 Rondy, 23 drivers left the chute before George Attla, but by the end of the first day's heat he had passed 17 of them. When he passed number 23, he knew he had already made up the two minutes that separated their starting times.

Strategy in a sled dog race is just as important as in any other race. In fact, the differences in starting times lend an even greater dimension to this sport, for a slower team can let a faster team go by and then stay with it for a while, the dogs spurred on by the chase. The front contenders, especially after the first day's heat, know whom they have to beat in order to win. By the end of the second heat in the 1974 Rondy, Doc Lombard carried a lead of two minutes and six seconds over Attla. Attla, relying on his slightly overfed dogs to deliver that extra power on the third day, promised to "try like hell" to catch the Doc. Running all out, he blistered the 26½-mile championship course a full minute and 23 seconds faster than Lombard—but fell 43 seconds short of the winner's total time.

Writing in the Anchorage *Daily Times,* sports writer Gordon Fowler captured the essence of strategy as two of the greatest sled dog drivers vied for the championship:

> "Although most had the Doc listed as a cinch going into the final leg, with Attla given only an outside shot, the race turned into a furious two-man duel through the halfway point on Sunday when former champion Gareth Wright of Fairbanks made a valiant effort to overtake both Lombard and Attla and had everyone on their toes for a while.
>
> "Although Wright trailed Lombard by 6:03 and Attla by nearly four minutes going into yesterday's final heat, he by no means gave up easily.
>
> "Pulling all stops, Wright left the chute in high gear and caught Attla just before crossing the Tudor checkpoint and by the time they hit Pole Line, was breathing fast down the Doc's back with Attla some fifty yards behind him. As they started down the back trail, Wright and his dogs, who apparently sensed the chase, kept the pressure on and passed Lombard, which at that point meant that he had gained four minutes on the Doc and was just two minutes out of first overall.
>
> "However, after completing the pass, Wright was unable to pull away from the Doc whose dogs took up the chase themselves with Attla right on his heels.

DOC LOMBARD JOKING WITH HIS DOGS while waiting for the countdown in the Anchorage World Championship in 1970. *Maxine Vehlow*

" 'He had me scared when he passed me,' Lombard said afterward, 'I decided then to just try to ride behind him and stay close and make my move later. I could see George pulling up behind me and know what a competitor he is and knew I couldn't sit behind Wright forever,' he added."

This was the spot where Attla made his decision to wait a bit before trying to pass Lombard, but Lombard was also figuring out his tactics as the finish line drew closer:

"As the three teams moved into the area of the Powerhouse in the flats, Lombard suddenly decided it was time to make his move and opened up, quickly passing Wright's team which after the earlier charge was beginning to slow. Seeing the Doc making his move, Attla hit high gear and as they hit Campbell Crossing, Attla passed Wright and from there on it was Doc looking over his shoulder at Attla to the finish line.

"Through the 15th Street and Cordova checkpoint, Attla got as close as he would get, however, as he was within 36 seconds of the Doc for overall time but could get no closer as Lombard staved him off in a furious stretch run down Fourth Avenue, beating him to the finish by almost two blocks.

"Wright's big push at the start cost him third place as he slipped back and wound up in fourth, with Leonard Kriska of Koyukuk, running his first Rondy race, finishing with a good 102:52 final leg and 320:37 overall to better Wright's total time of 322:32.

"Lombard picked up $3,300 in total prize money while second place was worth $2,300 to Attla. Kriska pocketed $1,450 and Wright $1,100."

A 43-second gap between first and second in a five-hour, eighty-mile race is as good as a photo finish. If Wright had not passed Attla and Lombard and excited their dogs the race might have been slower and Attla might have made up more of those 43 seconds. On the other hand, in a long, close race like the Rondy, both Attla and Lombard had probably decided not to chase Wright, counting on his team to "run out of gas" long before the finish. The champion dog drivers know what their dogs can do, and are careful not to ask a great deal more from them at the wrong time.

In the 1975 World Championship at Laconia, chasing a fast team brought trail-wise Dick Moulton from a long third position to a breath-taking first. With former champion Lloyd Slocum ahead of him by 25 seconds, and Harris Dunlap, winner of the first two day's heats, a full minute and 55 seconds ahead, Moulton had to plan his third day's strategy right down to the final foot. Dunlap, in first place, would start; Slocum would run out two minutes later; and Moulton would leave the chute two minutes after Slocum. Moulton knew he had to make up at least one minute and 54 seconds on the leader and finish within a minute and 34 seconds of Slocum, in order to beat either of them by one second. He also knew that Slocum is one of the fastest finishers in the sport.

Moulton's team had a number of Alaskan Husky-Walker Coonhound crosses on it, including his splendid leader, Attla. The team is known to be a fast starter but sometimes, coming home, cannot maintain the pace. By the halfway mark in the third heat, Moulton had caught and passed Slocum and was running less than a minute behind Dunlap. This meant that he had gained over three minutes on Dunlap and was now in first place. But the last miles are the longest for Moulton, and he feared that his tired dogs might slacken the pace, for Dunlap was out of sight and catching up with him was out of the question.

As reported by Dick Molburg in *Team and Trail:*

> "Moulton's forty years of experience in sled dog racing was handy in this situation and was evident when shortly after Moulton crossed the nine-mile (halfway) mark and headed home on the fastest section of the trail, he forced Slocum to re-pass him and proceeded to follow him home, letting Lloyd Slocum set the pace as he had to in order to maintain his second-place position.
>
> "It worked for Moulton by giving him a slim nine-second margin for the final win. It didn't work for Slocum who was beaten by Dunlap by 28 seconds for the day and he ended up in the third slot."

The prize money for the race, including day money: $1,975 for Moulton, $1,475 for Dunlap, $1,075 for Slocum.

The Lure of the Dog Team

Sled dog racing, intense as it is for front-running prize-money conten-ders, can also satisfy the slowest tail-ender. The lure of the dog team entices beginners into a whole new world of experiences, and simply completing the course can take as much concentration for a novice as winning does for Moulton or Dunlap.

Strategy for Jack Thaler, a lone New Jersey musher in his first big race at Rangeley, Maine, involved not much more than keeping his team progressing along the trail. The first sled dog driver in New Jersey several years ago, Thaler slowly put together a team of sled dogs and trained them on the beaches of South Jersey and the cornfields of North Jersey. Finally deciding he could not let a second year of this go by without trying his team in a real race, he entered the international competition at Rangeley. It took longer than he had allowed to harness up his team, and

CARL HUNTINGTON'S DOG WISHES HE HAD A HOOD to pull up against the snow, too. At the Anchorage World Championship, 1974.   *Maxine Vehlow*

by the time he got out on the trail he was seven minutes behind his scheduled starting time:

"To say the least I was embarrassed but at least I was now under way. The dogs were working quite well and it was such a pleasure to be gliding across the frozen lake and up through the snow-covered woods. It was cold and windy but it was heaven after two and a half years of planning, talking and thinking about dogs and racing.

"This particular race was about 18 miles long with a stop overnight in the next town and then a return the next day on the same trail.

"As the miles went by other dog teams and drivers caught up to me. Most all had larger teams than I. As each team approached and yelled 'Trail!' I quickly pulled my sled and team to one side and let them go by. This was one of the few race rules I was familiar with. It was extremely enjoyable watching teams of ten to twelve and fourteen dogs go by. A more beautiful sight in the wilderness I had never experienced.

"There were a few occasions along the trail when we encountered deer and rabbits. I was knowledgeable enough to keep my team in control but I must admit that my heart was really pounding when three deer jumped out of the bush and one of them almost landed in the sled.

"As the afternoon light was fading I approached one of the several checkpoints where race officials had been stationed. It was at mile 12—only six more miles out. The officials asked if everything was okay and gave my gear and dogs a quick look. I said I was a little cold but there were no problems.

"Out of the high bush country and onto the lake I proceeded. By this time the sun had set and every team that had left the starting line after me had long since passed by. I was the last team on the trail.

"My dogs by this time were really pooped. They were down to a walk but I didn't mind too much. The important thing was that I was finally participating in a race and I really hated to think that the trail would soon be coming to an end. The dogs plodded along and from time to time I would give them a two-minute break.

"As the trail wound around the lake in and out of coves I encountered things like half-eaten oranges and at first I wondered why. By the time I finished the last few miles I realized that one becomes very thirsty while working with the team. In many races since I've found it advantageous to take some fruit along in a little bag attached to the sled. Just one more little trick learned by experience from other, more professional, dog drivers.

"In my training runs I'd managed to get about 75 miles on my dogs. Surely, I thought, this would be adequate for most any race. As I approached the last mile or so of the trail I realized that I probably should have a lot more training on those dogs.

"It was dark now and the last mile, down the main street in town, was in sight. As I passed houses I could hear people applauding. What a great

LEAPING AGAINST THE LINES in anticipation of the World Championship race ahead: George Hood's dogs at Anchorage in 1974. *Maxine Vehlow*

Facing pages: THE CHARGE FROM THE CHUTE: New England champion Jim Tilton whirls down the trail at Pittsfield, N.H., in 1973.   *Barry Eton*

275

finish to such a wonderful afternoon on the trail. Almost all of the spectators had left by now but I could see the official race car just ahead. With one last encouraging word to my team we crossed the finish line. Those who braved the hours there laughed and clapped for me. It was great.

"Then, it was shattered. The race officials walked up, took my race number off, and told me I was disqualified for taking so long. My heart sank to some degree, but I soon realized that I had kept all these officials here, waiting for me, long after all the other teams had arrived, not to mention the fact that darkness had long since set in."

Jack Thaler has a lot more experience under his parka now, and he is ready for another crack at Rangeley. His strategy will no doubt include more sophisticated techniques than simply coming in before dark.

Who else races sled dogs nowadays, and why? What is the attraction of keeping anywhere from two to twenty or even two hundred sled dogs in the back yard? The reasons are as varied as the people. Don Smith, a race marshall for the Rocky Mountain Sled Dog Club, speaks of the variety involved. A sled dogger has to deal with the different personalities of the members of his team; some don't want to do anything, others are winners with a natural drive. Coping with all of the dogs, with his own physical fitness, and with the conditions of the trail, pushing here, lifting there, cajoling somewhere else, controlling the whole potentially explosive group, keeps Smith intensely absorbed in sled dogs.

Norman Vaughan began driving dogs as a youngster in New England; at the age of 69 he was still mushing, driving in the Iditarod Trail Race in 1975. Sam Kroneck of Oneida, New York, has mushed the New York trails every year since 1960, when at age 64 he took up the sport with a team of Samoyeds. Now 79, his fall and winter schedule fill the gap left by the end of his baseball coaching season. He may not be the fastest sled dog racer in New York, but he always finishes, and his own satisfaction transcends that of many.

Lance Peithmann of Fieldbrook, California, drives a small team of German Shepherds for fun, but a serious and useful extension of his interest has resulted. He devotes a great deal of his time to giving underprivileged and handicapped children a chance to forget their own problems, teaching them about driving a dog team. The constructive physical and mental therapy of this activity is gained by the children almost without their noticing.

The "George Attla of the East" is Brian Riley of Cherry Hill, New Jersey, an amputee musher who looks on his wooden leg as somewhat of an advantage in sled dogging—no frozen toes to worry about, and no pain either when an injudicious sled dog once lunged for Riley's leg.

A STAMPEDE FINISH at Cle Elum, Washington, in 1970. Dick Ross (#2) and Ronald Brown (#15), drive for the finish with a lot of huskies and one Irish Setter.   *Mally Hilands*

NEW ENGLAND'S VETERAN VOLUNTEER CHECKERED-FLAG WAVER, Orrin Dunn, marks the finish of Carol Rice and her pretty team of black and white Siberian Huskies. Gardner, Massachusetts, 1974.

L. Coppinger

A CHAMPION DRIVER GIVES HIS ALL IN A SLED DOG RACE.
Dick Moulton, finishing first at Laconia in 1971. *L. Coppinger*

LYDIA "GRANNY" HOKE, age 74, competing at Cle Elum, Washington, in
1970. *Kip Rutty, Courtesy Northern Dog News*

Working in amputee rehabilitation, Riley has taught skiing, diving, hiking and climbing, and finds that he has progressed to the point where he has no disability, except that he cannot run more than a hundred yards at a good clip. A loose team would be a disaster for him, so his elkhound and husky team is trained to be exceptionally obedient.

The Family Sport

A strong point that keeps many mushers engrossed in sled dogs is its appeal to whole families. Gene Gallagher of Reading, Pennsylvania, and his colleague Harvey Saltzer of Harrisburg, share experiences common to the hundreds of recreational sled doggers.

"The thing I enjoy most about this sport is that it's a family activity," Gallagher has noted. "When you go to a race you see entire families, not just individuals. Of course, the dogs are as much a part of the family as the rest of us."

Saltzer's initiation into sled dogging he shares with many. "I had my husky as a pet until a friend asked me to go watch a sled dog race in the winter of 1971. That's all it took for me to get the bug. Now I own five dogs and I hope to grow to a total of ten. Seems like this racing gets into your blood."

Wives and friends are rapidly drawn into the sport, for a dog driver needs help with his team at the races. Wives and friends then often decide that racing a team looks like more fun than freezing on the sidelines, waiting. Children are just as impressionable as adults, the appeal of the dog team is irresistible.

Children and dogs together are naturals anywhere, but on the sled dog course their relationship takes on a more sophisticated and practical scope. A young sled dogger learns not only about his dog but about himself as well. Once on the runners, a junior musher quickly learns how to control a situation; he learns that the time he spends preparing himself and his dog does make a difference in the race. Some of the youngsters are barely tall enough to see over the handlebar of their sled, but with a retired lead dog to teach them the ropes, self-confidence and a respectable racing record are not far away. Problems and triumphs, defeats and victories, all add a measure to the development of a self-assurance which lasts a lifetime.

Omer Berube, New England musher and a president of the Lakes Region Sled Dog Club, wrote in 1974 about kids and their sled dogs, equating the junior programs with baseball's little leagues. Indeed, proficiency with the family pet or dad's old leader can lead to the acquisition of another dog or two, and progression follows through the one- and two-dog classes to the three- and five-dog classes. Dedicated youngsters will train their own teams, harnessing up and taking a run before or after school. One-dog mushers in Alaska can be as young as three years old, but most junior classes begin with six-year-olds. In Murphys, California, junior drivers participated in a 4-H project on all aspects of dog driving: making equipment, training, maintaining, handling, learning the race rules and training for winter survival. Two of the youths won a 4-H gold medal for their sled dog presentation, one of only eight gold medals awarded out of 122 demonstrations. And then, putting their teams to the test, Dean Harris and Robin Smith swapped firsts and seconds in the junior races at Hobart Mills and at Tahoe.

Junior races are short, sometimes only a quarter of a mile for the one-doggers, sometimes a mile for the three-dog teams. Strategy for the littlest drivers consists of keeping the dogs going in the right direction; the bigger mushers will hop off the runners and run, pushing the sled to help the team. A victory brings a look of pleasure and pride not even matched by Lombard's or Attla's; and, usually, a rededication to daily training runs.

The extensive junior program is not the only reason sled dog racing appeals to whole families. If a parent is putting together a senior team he or she usually has an extra dog or two, or maybe more, and these dogs are available for use on a second-string team. The scorecard at any sled dog race will show entrants with the same last name in several classes: Dad may run in the senior unlimited class, Mom in the five-dog class, and one or two of their offspring appear in the junior classes. During the week they may all train together, selecting the best dogs for the unlimited team. Perhaps they take turns from race to race with the star dogs, although many clubs prohibit the use in junior races of dogs from a more advanced class.

Once on the runners each driver is on his own, one against the competition, but he has depended on the rest of his family to get him to the starting line. When he finishes, they will be there to catch the team and lead it back to the truck, while the flushed racer hangs breathlessly onto the handlebar, or drops into the basket, exhausted. Then it is his turn to help the next member of the family out to the starting line. At the end of the day's races, driving home gives time for experiences to be shared, triumphs applauded or problems analyzed. Strategies and dogs are discussed and plans made for the next race. The interdependence and outdoor action of a sled dog race lure many families from their Saturday television, and promotes a togetherness unusual in any sport.

A ONE-DOGGER IN ACTION: Holly Beth Sylvester of New Hampshire leans her sled into a curve.
Lisa Fallgren Uloth

A THREE-DOGGER STARTS OFF IN THE SNOW: Karyn Coppinger of Massachusetts with a Border Collie on lead, and an Alaskan Husky and a Husky-Shepherd hybrid.
L. Coppinger

"DON'T TOUCH ME!" yelled Randy Thomas, age 11, for he was not about to be disqualified for receiving help he did not need. Priest Lake, Idaho, circa 1968.   *Lee Remsburg*

HALF OF A FATHER-SON RACING TEAM: George Chambers (ISDRA historian) racing in the five-dog class at Cle Elum, Washington, in 1970, with four huskies and one Golden Setter (left lead).   *Mally Hilands, Courtesy Cascadian Kennels*

MATT MUNFORD IS YOUNG, but he does his share with the dogs, and receives his rewards along with his dad, Dale Munford of Michigan; 1974.

Leona Hutchings

FRECKLES AND HOPEFUL CHALLENGES ABOUND whenever the youngsters gather at the trophy display. Ft. Devens, Massachusetts, 1973.

L. Coppinger

Weight Pulls and Other Added Attractions

In recent years weight-pulling contests have been added to the activities at sled dog races. These contests, too, originated among the dog drivers in turn-of-the-century Alaska, but for a long time failed to command the interest that the races did. Exciting competitions like the one at Lake of the Woods, Oregon, in 1973, are attracting more people and their dogs to these tests of strength. The Oregon match featured the unbeaten Lobo, a huge black Malamute, pulling head to head against Traleika, a show champion Malamute. The contest had the spectators shrieking. Both dogs were driven ISDRA style, from behind, for a distance of twenty feet. Traleika, belonging to Ed and Kay Rodewald of Oregon, gave up at the 1,200-pound mark, but Howard Baron, from Big Bear Lake in California, kept adding weight to Lobo's sled for a shot at the record. The crowd roared at each pull, but the 165-pound Lobo had to quit at 1,830 pounds when his footing vanished in eight inches of slush and water covering the lake ice. It was quite an exhibition, and whetted appetites for more of the same.

Rules for weight-pulling contests vary slightly from region to region, although ISDRA has developed a standardization which clubs can adopt. Generally, a dog weighing over 65 pounds is in a different class from a lighter dog; a distance is specified (from 6 to 50 feet) and a time limit (1 to 2 minutes) for the dog to cover that distance, with increasing loads. A weight-pulling harness is wider and heavier than a racing harness, and as the dog strains forward, a spacer bar set behind his tail keeps the traces off his hind legs. No leashes are allowed, no help of any kind.

Claims of records fly back and forth, all of them impressive. Of course snow conditions affect the performances to a tremendous degree. Vic Rowell of Michigan observed that his hundred-pound Malamute, Tuffy Tim-Pat, C.D., worked just as hard to move 900 pounds under poor conditions as he did to move his best load of 2,000 pounds under good conditions. Although the feats of dogs like the 75-pound Charlie who in 1959 pulled over forty times his own weight for fifty feet cannot be discounted, without details of snow conditions, evaluations are difficult. In terms of sled dogs pulling loaded sleds on snow, modern records hover at around one ton: 2,200 pounds for a Malamute named Naki at Fairbanks in 1970; 2,205 pounds for the great Baranoff, three-quarters Samoyed and one-quarter German Shepherd, in 1973; 2,060 pounds each for Traleika and Chipanof at Sisters, Oregon, in 1974.

It seems that the dog must have at least as much pride in the pull as does his owner, for the enthusiasm and drive of a weight-pulling dog is unceasing. He will outpull himself, time and again, and pull the last,

TOM HINDMARCH AND HIS FATHER, after Tom won the
1975 Sourdough Rendezvous at Whitehorse.
Sandy Neumann, Whitehorse Star

VIC ROWELL'S FAMOUS TUFFY talks at a weight pulling contest in
Michigan. *Leona Hutchings*

heaviest load with even more determination than the first. A popular favorite at Rocky Mountain Sled Dog Club events during the late 1960's was Koppy, a 75-pound Samoyed belonging to Merle and Carolyn Mays of Arvada, Colorado. At Grand Lake in 1971, on a cold day with lots of fast snow, Koppy, at age 11, was greeted by cheers from the crowd, which sensed that there might be a new Samoyed record in the making.

Kay Rodewald described this great moment in a sled dog's life: "The load was 1,125 pounds, and nobody thought Koppy could move the sled. The dog knew better, for he got down low and began to dig in with all of his might and all of his heart. Slowly the sled started to move and the spectators held their breath. In the quiet before the cheering started, Carolyn Mays' soft voice could be heard calling, 'Koppy, Koppy,' as she sat some distance in front of the pulling area with her arms around Sam, their lead dog. It was only then that all realized that this wonderful old veteran, now breaking his own record, pulled to the sound of Carolyn's voice, to the scent of Sam and to the directions given by Merle, for Koppy was blind."

Other competitions with sled dogs include ski-joring races, like the fast, one-quarter-mile race behind three dogs at Rangeley, Maine, or the 120-mile, Scandinavian-style cross-country race which begins in Newberry, Michigan. There are lead dog contests, "scramble races" after two-dollar bills, and the favorite "stampede races," in which the musher and his partner begin the race stretched out in a sleeping bag, must get out, gather up their equipment, harness the dogs, and drive a short distance—usually a few miles—with one partner on the sled, the other driving.

Interest is also picking up for some old-fashioned freight races, with a minimum sled load of at least fifty pounds per dog. These are more than "little Iditarod" races, for even though training and conditioning is just as critical and competition is just as keen as in a big money race, these contests offer more sled doggers a chance to get involved. Not only do these events require fewer dogs, thus appealing to people unable to keep a large kennel, but the pace is slower, the scenery more visible, and the chance to travel with fellow mushers is greater.

Many dog drivers are adding skis or snowshoes to their small dog teams and finding infinite pleasure in just cruising cross-country. After a new snowfall the landscape is transformed into an elusively familiar but strange world. The sky fairly crackles with blue, the trees stand silent under great puffs of white; an occasional rabbit track or lacework left by a bird patterns the snow. The quiet is breathtaking. The spell cast over both dogs and musher is compelling, and it takes them back, far back, along the trail of the sled dog. Frantic weekend races and world championships are forgotten, images of the desperate serum run to Nome and the boisterous All-Alaska Sweepstakes evaporate in the cold, dry air. Sliding silently down the sled dog trail, the modern musher no longer needs to wonder when, or why, man first combined a dog and a sled.

STORM, THE WELL-TRAINED WEIGHT-PULLER of George Washington, "bringing home the bacon," 1800 pounds of dog food, in a contest in Whitehorse.   *Sandy Neumann, Whitehorse* Star

THE GREAT BARANOFF pulling at Priest Lake, Idaho.   *Mally Hilands*

Postface

___

I. Rules Governing Races

Nome Kennel Club Rules and Regulations, 1912
(From Article 3, Rules and Regulations of the Nome Kennel Club)

Rule 1. The race will be started at __ o'clock, April __, on Front Street opposite Barracks Square, Nome, Alaska; but the judges may, by unanimous consent, on account of stormy weather, postpone the race until a later date.

Rule 2. The route will be from Nome to Safety; thence to Dixon; thence to Topkok Hill; thence over or around Topkok Hill; thence to Timber Road House; thence to Council; thence over the head of Melsing Creek to Boston Creek, across the Fish River Valley to Telephone Creek, over the divide to Death Valley; thence across Death Valley to Camp Haven; thence to First Chance; thence over the divide into Gold Run; thence to Candle, and from Candle to Nome over the same route.

Rule 3. Teams will start one minute apart, the first team leaving at __ o'clock, and the time of each team starting be reckoned as at __ o'clock.

Rule 4. Each team must take all of the dogs with which it started to Candle and return with the same dogs, and none others, to the starting point in Nome.

Rule 5. The team accomplishing this in the least time will be declared the winner of the race, and the team accomplishing this in the second best time will be declared second, and the team accomplishing this in the third best time will be declared third.

Rule 6. When any team in the race meets another, the right of way shall belong to the homeward bound team, and it shall be the duty of the person driving the out-going team to get out of the way of the homeward-bound team and assist it in passing.

Rule 7. When one team shall overtake another team going in the same direction, the team behind shall have the right of way, and it shall be the duty of the driver in front to pull out of the trail and assist the driver of the team behind in passing; and in the event that one team shall pass another, and the team behind shall hang on to the team in front for half an hour, then the team behind shall have the right of way, and upon demand of the driver behind, the team ahead shall pull out of the trail and assist the team behind in passing; except that this rule shall not apply on the homeward stretch from Fort Davis to Nome.

Rule 8. Each team shall have the choice of its own sled, subject only to the condition that some kind of a sled must be drawn; and at the option of the drivers, sleds may be changed during the race.

Rule 9. At all Road-houses and public stopping places along the route, the first team arriving shall have the choice of public stable room, and any interference by any parties afterward arriving, is strictly prohibited.

Rule 10. During the race each team and its driver shall have all of the assistance he desires, subject, however, to the following limitations:
First—During the race no team shall be allowed at any time in any manner to use any other dogs than those started with;
Second—Pacing in any and all of its forms is strictly prohibited; nor shall any team connected in any way with any team in the race, follow any racing team until all of the racing teams shall have passed the next telephone station; nor shall any such team precede any racing team on the trail by a less distance than one telephone station; and said team or teams shall at all times be subject to the directions of the judges of the race;
Third—No team shall be allowed to secure any other team to haul any of its dogs or its driver;
Fourth—No team shall have any person other than the driver take hold of the sled while the team is in motion, which interference is in the driver's power to prevent;

Fifth—No teams shall have any person or persons to instruct the driver while his team is actually traveling.

Rule 11. The cruel and inhuman treatment of dogs by any driver is strictly prohibited under penalty of losing the race and forfeiture of the owner's team.

Rule 12. Every person entering or driving a team in the race will be required to conduct himself in a perfectly fair and honorable manner, under penalty of forfeiture of the prize and his dog team, and expulsion from the Club.

Rule 13. In awarding the cup and prize money, these rules shall be interpreted by the judges according to their spirit; it being understood that the race is to be awarded on merit, and not on technicality.

Rule 14. The driver of any team quitting the race shall report the same to the judges in Nome before he makes any movement toward returning to the starting point; and thereafter his movements shall be subject to the direction of the judges.

Rule 15. The race shall not be decided by the judges until all of the teams starting in said race have returned to Nome, or the owners thereof waive the right of protest in writing; and in no event shall such decision be rendered until twenty-four hours after three teams shall have finished the course.

Rule 16. In the event of a driver of a team in the race being behind and away from his sled and the team at the finish of the race, the finishing time of such team shall be the time the driver crosses the tape.

Rule 17. In consideration of the premises and the mutual promises herein contained, each entry agrees with the Nome Kennel Club to abide by the rules of the race as herein set forth, otherwise to forfeit his team to the Nome Kennel Club; and for such purpose agrees to make, or cause to be made, a bill of sale covering his team if so demanded by the judges of the race, and as evidence of such agreement hereto sets his hand seal.

Dated at Nome, Alaska, this _____ day of April, 19__.

II. The Champion Dog Drivers

All-Alaska Sweepstakes, Nome

1908	Albert Fink, owner; John Hegness, driver
1909	Jacob Berger, owner; Scotty Allan, driver
1910	Charles Ramsay, owner; John Johnson, driver
1911	Allan and Darling, owners; Scotty Allan, driver

	1912	Allan and Darling, owners; Scotty Allan, driver
	1913	Bowen and Delezene, owners; Fay Delezene, driver
	1914	John Johnson
	1915	Leonhard Seppala
	1916	Leonhard Seppala
	1917	Leonhard Seppala

Fur Rendezvous World *Championship, Anchorage*		*North American* *Championship, Fairbanks*
Jake Butler, Anchorage	1946	Andy Kokrine, Tanana
Earl Norris, Anchorage	1947	Andy Kokrine
Earl Norris	1948	Charles Titus, Minto
Jake Butler	1949	Dan Snyder, Noorvik
Gareth Wright, Fairbanks	1950	*Gareth Wright
Raymond Paul, Galena	1951	Horace "Holy" Smoke
Gareth Wright	1952	Horace "Holy" Smoke
Clem Tellman, Knik	1953	Horace "Holy" Smoke
Raymond Paul	1954	*Raymond Paul
Raymond Paul	1955	Wilbur Sampson, Noorvik
Jim Huntington, Huslia	1956	*Jim Huntington
Gareth Wright	1957	Bergman Sam, Huslia
George Attla, Huslia	1958	Alfred Wells, Noorvik
Jimmy Malemute, Galena	1959	Roland Lombard, Wayland, Mass.
Cue Bifelt, Huslia	1960	*Cue Bifelt
Leo Kriska, Koyukuk	1961	Beattus Moses, Allakaket
George Attla	1962	Roland Lombard
Roland Lombard	1963	*Roland Lombard
Roland Lombard	1964	*Roland Lombard
Roland Lombard	1965	Keith Bryar, Center Harbor, N.H.
Joee Redington, Knik	1966	Roland Lombard
Roland Lombard	1967	*Roland Lombard
George Attla	1968	Bill Taylor, Fairbanks
Roland Lombard	1969	George Attla
Roland Lombard	1970	George Attla
Roland Lombard	1971	Harold Greenway, Fairbanks
George Attla	1972	*George Attla
Carl Huntington, Galena	1973	Harold Greenway
Roland Lombard	1974	Alfred Attla, Hughes
George Attla	1975	*George Attla

*Dual Champions—winners of both races in one year

Fur Rendezvous Women's World Championship, Anchorage		Women's North American Championship, Fairbanks
No race	1952	Effie Kokrine, Tanana
Joyce Wells, Anchorage	1953	Effie Kokrine
Natalie Norris, Anchorage	1954	Effie Kokrine
Kit MacInnes, Anchorage	1955	Kit MacInnes
No race	1956	Kit MacInnes
Rosie Losonsky, Fairbanks	1957	Rosie Losonsky
Vera Wright, Fairbanks	1958	Vera Wright
Kit MacInnes	1959	Rosie Losonsky
Kit MacInnes	1960	Libby Wescott, Fairbanks
Kit MacInnes	1961	Kit MacInnes
Barbara Parker, Anchorage	1962	Jean Bryar, Center Harbor, N.H.
Barbara Parker	1963	Jear Bryar
Barbara Parker	1964	Jean Bryar
Shari Wright, Fairbanks	1965	Shari Wright
Shirley Gavin, Chugiak	1966	Rosie Losonsky
Shari Wright	1967	Clara Ketzler, Fairbanks
Anne Wing, Millbrook, N.Y.	1968	Rosie Losonsky
Shirley Gavin	1969	Carol Lundgren, Fairbanks
Shirley Gavin	1970	Natalie Norris
Carol Lundgren	1971	Jean Bryar
Carol Lundgren Shepherd	1972	Roxy Wright Woods, Fairbanks
Roxy Wright Woods	1973	Jean Bryar
Roxy Wright Woods	1974	Jean Bryar
Roxy Wright Woods	1975	Roxy Wright Woods

World Championship Sled Dog Derby
Laconia, New Hampshire

1956	Charles Belford, Deerfield, Mass.
1957	Emile Martel, Lorretteville, Quebec
1958	Art Allen, Cedar Rapids, Iowa
1959	Art Allen
1960	Keith Bryar, Center Harbor, N.H.
1961	Ernie Brunet, Gatineau Point, Quebec
1962	Keith Bryar
1963	Keith Bryar
1964	Charles Belford
1965	Charles Belford
1966	Charles Belford
1967	Eddie Sylvain, Lac Beauport, Quebec
1968	Dick Moulton, Center Harbor, N.H.

1969	John Piscopo, Jr., Tilton, N.H.
1970	John Piscopo, Jr.
1971	Lloyd Slocum, Gorham, Maine
1972	Lloyd Slocum
1973	Dick Moulton
1974	No race—no snow
1975	Dick Moulton

All American Championship
Ely, Minnesota

1970	Jerry Riley, Nenana, Alaska
1971	Dick Moulton, Center Harbor, N.H.
1972	Dick Moulton
1973	Dick Moulton
1974	Tom Mathias, Decatur, Michigan
1975	George Attla, Huslia, Alaska

Iditarod Trail International Championship
Anchorage To Nome, Alaska
1,049 Miles

1973	Dick Wilmarth, Red Devil, Alaska
1974	Carl Huntington, Galena, Alaska
1975	Emmitt Peters, Ruby, Alaska

International Sled Dog Racing Association
Point Champions

Unlimited Class

1972	George Attla, Huslia, Alaska
1973	Roland Lombard, Wayland, Massachusetts
1974	Roland Lombard
1975	George Attla

Limited Class
Seven-dog Maximum

| 1974 | Judy Allen, Swisher, Iowa |
| 1975 | TIE: Craig Hilpipre, Cedar Rapids, Iowa Terry Martin, Jerome, Idaho |

Five-dog Maximum

| 1975 | Art Christensen, Jefferson, Oregon |

Three-dog Maximum

| 1975 | Al Price, Medford, Oregon |

III. Sled Dog Clubs of the World

ISDRA Area I, Alaska

Alaska Dog Mushers' Association, Fairbanks
Alaskan Sled Dog and Racing Association, Anchorage
  Junior Alaskan Sled Dog and Racing Association
Allakaket Dog Mushers
Ambler Mushers' Association
Aurora Dog Mushers' Club, Wasilla
Bethel Sled Dog Committee
Chugiak Dog Mushers' Club
Iditarod Dog Mushers' Club (for Anchorage to Nome drivers only)
Koyukuk Dog Mushers' Association
Montana Creek Dog Mushers' Association
Nenana Dog Mushers' Association
Nome Kennel Club
Nondalton Sled Dog Racing Association
Noorvik Dog Mushers' Association
Norton Sound Sled Dog Club, Unalakleet
Nulato Dog Mushers' Association
Peninsula Sled Dog and Racing Association, Soldotna
Point Hope Dog Mushers' Association
Selawik Dog Mushers' Association
Tanana Dog Mushers' Association
Tok Dog Mushers' Association

ISDRA Area II, Western Canada

Arctic Sled Dog Club of Ontario
British Columbia Sled Dog Association, Vanderhoof
Fort Nelson Sled Dog Club, British Columbia
Fort Paskoyak Sled Dog Club, The Pas, Manitoba
Fort Smith Dog Mushers' Club, Northwest Territories
Interior British Columbia Sleddog Club
Northern Ontario Sled Dog Club, North Bay
Northern Professional Dog Racing Association, Fort McMurray, Alberta
Prince Albert Sled Dog Club, Saskatchewan
Rendezvous Sled Dog Club, Prince George, British Columbia
Siberian Husky Club of Canada, Ontario
Thunder Bay Kennel and Training Club, Ontario
Voyageur Sled Dog Club, Manitoba
Whitehorse Sled Dog Club, Yukon Territory
Yukon Dog Mushers, Whitehorse

Club d'Attelages de Chiens du Quebec (formerly Stadacona S.D.C.)
Gatineau Sled Dog Club, Quebec
Lower Canada Sled Dog Racing Association (formerly Laurentian S.D.C.)
Nova Scotia Sled Dog Club

ISDRA Area IV, Northeast United States

Connecticut Valley Siberian Husky Club
Down East Sled Dog Club, Maine
Green Mountain Mushers, Vermont
Lakes Region Sled Dog Club, New Hampshire (formerly Laconia S.D.C.)
Narragansett Bay Sled Dog Club, Rhode Island
New England Sled Dog Club
Northeast Overlanders
Siberian Husky Fanciers of Connecticut
Siberian Husky Fanciers of Vermont
Vermont Sled Dog Club
Yankee Siberian Husky Club

ISDRA Area V, Mid-Atlantic States

All Breed Pulling Club, New York-New Jersey
Arctic Sled Dog Club of America, New York
Canadian-American Sledders, New York
Delaware Valley Siberian Husky Club
Delaware Valley Samoyed Club
Empire Alaskan Malamute Association, New Jersey
Garden State Siberian Husky Club, New Jersey
Maryland Sled Dog Club
Mason-Dixon Sled Dog Racing Association, Virginia
Mid-Atlantic Sled Dog Racing Association (six clubs)
Mohawk Valley Sled Dog Club, New York
Northern Sled Dog Association, New York
Pennsylvania Sled Dog Club
Ramapo Valley Siberian Husky Club, New York
Seneca Siberian Husky Club, New York
Siberian Husky Club of Greater New York

ISDRA Area VI, Central States

Gateway Northern Breed Club
Great Lakes Sled Dog Association, Michigan
Midwest Sled Dog Club, Illinois
Trail Breakers Sled Dog Club, Ohio

ISDRA Area VII, Plains States

Ely Sled Dog Committee, Minnesota
Head of the Lakes Sled Dog Association, Minnesota
North Star Sled Dog Club, Minnesota
Pierce County Sled Dog Club, Wisconsin
St. Louis Sled Dog Club, Missouri
Wisconsin Trailblazers Sled Dog Club

ISDRA Area VIII, Western States

American Dog Mushers' Association, Idaho (extinct)
Big Sky Sled Dog Drivers' Association, Montana
California Sled Dog Club, Hacienda Heights
Cascade Sled Dog Club, Oregon
Central California Siberian Husky Club
Central Oregon Dog Mushers' Association.
Central Washington Dog Mushers' Association
Glacier Country Mushers, Montana
Inland Empire Sled Dog Association, Washington
Jackson Hole Sled Dog Club, Wyoming
Kanganark Mushers Dog Sledding Club, Utah
Montana Mountain Mushers (formerly Sacajawea S.D.C.)
Northern California Alaskan Malamute Association
Northwest Sled Dog Association, Washington
Rocky Mountain Sled Dog Club, Colorado
Sierra Nevada Dog Drivers, California
Sno-King Alaskan Malamute Fanciers, Washington
Southern Arizona Husky Club
Southern Idaho Dog Drivers
Southern Oregon Sled Dog Club

ISDRA Area IX, Europe

German Club for Northern Dogs
Norwegian Sled Dog Club
Siberian Husky Club of Finland
Swiss Club for Northern Dogs
Trail Club of Europe

National and International Organizations

Alaskan Husky Club
International Siberian Husky Club (formerly Seppala S.H.C.)
International Sled Dog Racing Association
Organization for Working Samoyeds
Siberian Husky Club of America
Siberian Husky Owners' Association

IV. Sources of Equipment and Information

Equipment

Hall's Alaskan Cache Kennel, Jackson, MI. 49201
Katmai Kennels, Milaca, MN. 56353
Kelson Reg., Como, P.Q., Canada
Maxima, Yardley, PA. 19067
Nordkyn Outfitters, Moses Lake, WA. 98837
Tun-Dra, Nunica, MI. 49448
Zima, Kila, MT. 59920

Periodicals

Alaska Magazine, Box 4-EEE, Anchorage, AK. 99509
The Gangline, Yankee Siberian Husky Club, Ballard Hill, Lancaster, MA. 01523
The Howler, New England Sled Dog Club, RFD 4, Box 305B, Manchester, N.H. 03102
Info, International Sled Dog Racing Association, Box 11, Bakers Mills, N.Y. 12811
Mile-Hi Musher, Rocky Mountain Sled Dog Club, 460 S. 43rd St., Boulder, CO. 80303
Northern Dog News, Box 310, Snohomish, WA. 98290
Team and Trail, Center Harbor, N.H. 03226
Trailblazer, Wisconsin Trailblazers Sled Dog Club, Oshkosh, WI. 54901
Trail Talk, Mohawk Valley Sled Dog Club, Rome, N.Y. 13440
Trail Time, Great Lakes Sled Dog Club, Twin Lake, MI. 49457
Tug Line, North Star Sled Dog Club, Bemidji, MN. 56601

Books

Attla, George. *Everything I Know About Training and Racing Sled Dogs.* Arner Publications, Rome, N.Y. 1972 (revised 1975).
Fishback, Lee. *Training Lead Dogs My Way.* Bastion Press, Snohomish, WA. 1974 (paper).
Fishback, Lee, and Mel Fishback. *Novice Sled Dog Training.* Bastion Press, Snohomish, WA. No date (paper).
Fishback, Lee, and Mel Fishback. *The Sled and Harness Book,* Bastion Press, Snohomish, WA. 1972 (paper).
Foley, Louise, and Raymond Thompson. *The Siberian Husky.* Raymond Thompson Company, Lynnwood, WA. 1962 (paper).
International Siberian Husky Club. *The Siberian Husky.* International Siberian Husky Club, Chesley, Ontario. 1969 (paper).
International Sled Dog Racing Association. *The Cremation of Sam McGee Cookbook.* Bev-Ron Publishing Co., Kansas City, KS. 1974 (paper).

Levorsen, Bella (editor). *Mush! A Beginner's Manual of Sled Dog Training*. Arner Publications, Rome, N.Y. 1975 (paper).

Montana Mountain Mushers. *Mushing–Try It, You'll Like It*. Montana Mountain Mushers, Helena, MT. 1975 (paper).

New England Sled Dog Club. *Fiftieth Anniversary: 1924–1974*. New England Sled Dog Club, Carlisle, MA. 1974 (paper).

Siberian Husky Club of Southern California. *The Siberian Husky Primer*. Siberian Husky Club of Southern California, Hacienda Heights, CA. 1975 (paper).

Thompson, Raymond. *The Sled Dog Encyclopedia*. Raymond Thompson Company, Lynnwood, WA. No date (3 volumes, paper).

Thompson, Raymond. *Cart and Sled Dog Training*. Raymond Thompson Company, Lynnwood, WA. No date (paper).

Thompson, Raymond. *Sled and Harness Styles*. Raymond Thompson Company, Lynnwood, WA. No date (paper).

ISDRA Film Library

Films and slides available for group showings. Kenneth W. Negaard, P.O. Box 400, St. Cloud, MN. 56301

V. Selected Bibliography

Allan, A.A. ("Scotty"). *Gold, Men and Dogs*. G.P. Putnam's Sons, N.Y. 1931.

Anderson, Eva Greenslit. *Dog-Team Doctor*. The Caxton Printers, Caldwell, Idaho. 1940.

Balikci, Asen. *The Netsilik Eskimo*. Natural History Press, Garden City, N.Y. 1970.

Boas, Franz. *The Central Eskimo*. University of Nebraska Press, Lincoln. 1964 (reprint).

Bruemmer, Fred. "The Northernmost People." *Natural History* 83(2): 24–33 (February) 1974.

Bruemmer, Fred. *Seasons of the Eskimo, A Vanishing Way of Life*. New York Graphic Society, Greenwich, CT. 1971.

Buchanan, William J. "Making of a Champion." *Reader's Digest,* March, 1970: 106–112.

Butler, Colonel W.F. *The Great Lone Land*. Sampson, Low, Marston, Searle and Rivington, London. 1883.

Byrd, Richard E. *Discovery*. G.P. Putnam's Sons, N.Y. 1935.

Carpenter, Frank F. *Alaska, Our Northern Wonderland*. Doubleday, Page and Co., Garden City, N.Y. 1923.

Chernetsov, V.N. and W.I. Moszyńska. *Prehistory of Western Siberia*. McGill-Queen's University Press, Montreal. 1975.

Cherry-Garrard, Apsley. *The Worst Journey in the World*. Dial Press, N.Y. 1930.

Crane, Robert Dickson. "The Siberian Chukchi Sleddog." *Northern Dog News* 14(2): 5 (March) 1972.

Darling, Esther Birdsall. *Baldy of Nome*. A.A. Knopf, N.Y. 1947.

Darling, Esther Birdsall. *The Great Dog Races of Nome*. Iditarod Trail Committee, Knik, AK. 1969 (reprint).

Darling, Esther Birdsall. *Navarre of the North*. Doubleday, Doran and Co., Garden City, N.Y. 1930.

Denison, Merrill. *Klondike Mike*. William Morrow and Co., N.Y. 1943.

de Poncins, Gontran. *Kabloona*. Reynal and Hitchcock, N.Y. 1941.

Distad, Jack, and Linda Distad. "Racing in Fairbanks, Past and Present." *Alaska Dog Mushers' Association Souvenir Magazine*: 12–15. 1965.

Elliott, Rachel Page. *Dogsteps: Illustrated Gait at a Glance*. Howell Book House, N.Y. 1973.

Fishback, Mel. "Alaskan Husky and Indian Dogs." *Northern Dog News* 5(6): 7–9 (July) 1963.

Garst, Shannon. *Scotty Allan, King of the Dog-Team Drivers*. Julian Messner, N.Y. No date.

Gubser, Nicholas J. *The Nunamiut Eskimos: Hunters of Caribou*. Yale University Press, New Haven. 1965.

Herbert, Wally. *Across the Top of the World*. G.P. Putnam's Sons, N.Y. 1971.

Hobbs, William H. "Peary, The Ace Among Dog-sledgers." *Explorers Club Tales*. Dodd, Mead and Co., N.Y. 1936.

Howarth, David. *The Sledge Patrol*. Macmillan, N.Y. 1957.

Hubbard, Bernard R. ("The Glacier Priest"). *Mush, You Malamutes!* America Press, N.Y. 1932.

Huntington, James, and Elliott Lawrence. *On the Edge of Nowhere*. Crown, N.Y. 1966.

Kraft, Virginia. "Belle of the Mushers." *Sports Illustrated*, January 23, 1967: 54–63.

Lake, Doris. "Dog Race to Nome." *Team and Trail*, June 1973: 16–18 (reprinted from *Alaska Native News*).

Levorsen, Bella. "Tuffy." *Alaska Dog Racing News*, July 1968.

London, Jack. *The Call of the Wild*. Macmillan, N.Y. 1903.

Lyon, McDowell. *The Dog in Action*. Howell Book House, N.Y. 1950.

Marks, Jiggs. "A Survey of Crossbreeding." *Alaska Dog Mushers' Association Souvenir Magazine*: 23–25. 1965.

Marston, Muktuk. *Men of the Tundra*. October House, N.Y. 1969.

Mirsky, Jeannette. *To the Artic!* University of Chicago Press, Chicago. 1970 (reprint).

Nansen, Fridtjof. *In Northern Mists*. AMS Press, N.Y. 1969 (2 volumes, reprint of 1911 edition).

National Geographic Society. *Book of Dogs*. National Geographic Society, Washington, D.C. 1958.

Nelson, Richard K. *Hunters of the Northern Ice*. University of Chicago Press, Chicago. 1969.

O'Brien, John Sherman. *By Dog Sled for Byrd*. Wilcox and Follett, Chicago. 1934.

Pettyjohn. "A Circle City Dog Puncher." *The Alaskana*, Anchorage. 1973.

Ricker, Elizabeth M. *Seppala: Alaskan Dog Driver*. Little, Brown and Co., N.Y. 1930.

Rivett-Carnac, Inspector C.E. "Northern Bush Travel." *R.C.M.P. Quarterly,* October 1938.

Shereshevskii, E.I., P.A. Petryayev and V. G. Golubev. *Yezdovoye Sobakovodstvo* (The Breeding, Training and Use of Sled Dogs). Izdat. Glavsevmorputi (Publ. House of the Bureau of Northern Sea Communications), Moscow. 1946.

Soper, J. Dewey. *Canada's Eastern Arctic*. Canadian Department of the Interior, Ottawa. 1934.

Swenson, Olaf. *Northwest of the World*. Dodd, Mead and Co., N.Y. 1944.

Tanner, John D. "Pure-bred Dogs." *American Kennel Club Gazette* 90(9): 120–121 (September) 1973.

Ungerman, Kenneth. *The Race to Nome*. Harper and Row, N.Y. 1963.

Von Wrangell, Baron Ferdinand P. *Le Nord de la Sibérie*. Librairie d'Amyot, Éditeur, Paris. (2 volumes) 1843.

Walden, Arthur Treadwell. *A Dog-puncher on the Yukon*. Houghton Mifflin, Boston. 1928.

Wescott, Bob, and Libby Wescott. "What is the Alaskan Husky?" *Alaska Dog Mushers' Association Souvenir Magazine:* 27–33. 1965.

Index

Akita, 210, 211
Alaska:
   freighting teams, 38–
   45, 68, 70, 73–74, 83
   racing (early), 82–93,
   167, (modern), 111–122,
   147, 152–56, 177–78,
   182, 187–203, 260
   serum run, 60, 62–64,
   66–67, 69
   training, 253
Alaskan Husky, 6, 151,
   177–186, 189, 193, 201,
   212–15, 222–23, 281
Alaskan Malamute
   AKC registration, 170
   origin, 42, 207
   sled dog, 201, 204,
   207–208
   weight pulling, 284–86
All-Alaska Sweepstakes,
   65, 82–89, 158, 160,
   167
Allan, Scotty, 164–67,
   243
   All-Alaska Sweepstakes,
   85–88
   California, 90, 133
   World War I, 67–68, 71
Allen, Art, 148, 237
   racing schedule, 258
Allender, Kent, 248
Allen, Johnny, 92, 194
Althaus, Tom, 143
Anchorage (Alaska):
   early races, 93

World Championship Sled
   Dog Race, 111–16, 147,
   152–56, 177, 192–94,
   200, 263, 267–69, 271,
   273
Ashton (Idaho):
   American Dog Derby, 93–
   95
Attla, George, 156, 178,
   187–191, 196, 198, 214
   Anchorage, 154, 263
   feeding dogs, 256
   race strategy, 267, 269
   racing schedule, 258,
   260
   selecting dogs, 214
   training dogs, 253
Aurora Husky, 194

Bacon, Ethel, 254
Baron, Howard, 284
Belair, Jean, 150
Belford, Dr. Charles,
   139, 177–181, 192
   feeding dogs, 256
   selecting dogs, 245,
   248
   World Championships,
   151
Berube, Omer, 279
bird dogs, 94–95, 134,
   217, 219, 220, 282
Black, Robert, 80
Blankenship, Guy, 77, 78
Blatchford, Percy, 86,
   158

Blodgett, Dom, 128, 217,
   218, 264
Bolduc, Helen, 150
Border Collie, 218, 252,
   265, 281
Bridges, Dolores, 150
Brooks, (now Woods) Roxy
   Wright, 193–195
Brown, Ronald, 277
Brown, W. R., 97, 106
Bruemmer, Fred, 59, 76
Bryar, Jean, 117, 118,
   181–85, 218
Bryar, Keith, 151, 152,
   177, 182, 188
Busby, Bob, 92
Butler, Jake, 93, 114,
   153
Byrd, Richard E., 56–58,
   186

Canada:
   freighting teams, 34–
   37, 40–41, 59, 74
   racing (early), 96,
   104–108, (modern), 136–
   142, 147–48, 151, 172–
   174, 215, 216, 257
   Royal Canadian Mounted
   Police, 48–53, 57
Carson, Johnny, 118
Celusnik, Jae, 253
Chambers, George, 282
Chilkoot Husky, 134
Chinook, 97, 168, 169,
   215

Chinook Kennels, 72, 170, 172, 185–86, 208
Christensen, Art and Dorothy, 134
Chukchi (people), 20, 32, 73, 146
Clark, Florence, 100
Coppinger, Karyn, 281
Coppinger, Ray, 79, 252, 265
Cordingly, Don, 95, 217
Corriveau, Bob, Sr., 249
Couture, Gerry, 231
coyote, 217
Crane, Dr. Robert, 20
Crosson, Joe, 162

Dalmatian, 217, 219
Deerfield (Mass.) massacre, 34
Demidoff, Lorna, 126
De Poncins, Gontran, 22
Dingo, 217
Dog Mushers' Hall of Fame, 157–59, 195
Downing, Ben, 158
Drown, Howard, 231
Dual Championship, 112, 177, 187, 194, 214
Dufresne, Frank, 81
Dunlap, Christopher, 242
Dunlap, Harris:
    race strategy, 269–270
    training dogs, 251
Dunn, Orrin, 277
Duval, Tat, 126

Europe:
    freighting teams, 59, 149
    racing, 141–46, 210–212, 257
    training, 254–55
    World War I, 67–68, 71
    World War II, 67–69, 71–72

Fairbanks (Alaska):
    racing (early), 91–93
    North American Championship, 111, 112, 177, 182, 185, 189
    Women's North American Championship, 93, 112, 117, 185, 194
Fallgren, Gus, 128
Fink, Albert, 85, 87
Fishback, Lee, 225
    training dogs, 251

Food for dogs, 25, 76, 106, 255–57
Fowler, Gordon, 261, 267
Franklin, Sir John, 32–33
Frost, Freeman "Jack," 127
Fur Rendezvous, 118, 120, 156, 173
    See also Anchorage

Gallagher, Gene, 279
Gardner, Vernon "Brud," 127
Garst, Shannon, 167
Giteles, Ray, 131
Goosak, William, 86, 88
Goyne, Walter, 105

Hall, Frank, 239–241
Harkness, Marjory Gane, 261
Harnesses:
    leather, 37, 230, 232
    racing, 227, 229–230
Hegness, John, 87
Hilpipre, Merv, 154
Hindmarch, Tom, 138, 285
Hobbs, William H., 55
Hoke, Lydia "Granny," 278
Hound:
    "Canadian" or "Quebec," 106–108, 154, 172–174, 215–16, 222
    racing, 94–95, 128, 154, 186, 216–18, 222, 264
    Targhee, 94, 203, 215
Hudson's Bay Company, 34–37
Huntington, Carl, 253, 271
Huntington, Jim, 187, 188, 214
Huot, J. Oliva, 150
"husky":
    origin of name, 23
Huslia (Alaska), 187, 188, 214

Iditarod Trail Race, 111, 117, 119–122, 197–98
Indian Dog:
    See Village Dog
Ingstad, Benedicte, 145
Innuit (people), 207
International Sled Dog Racing Association (ISDRA):
    first president, 178
    first proposed, 110

in Europe, 146
    point championships, 146, 156
    U.S. organization, 110
    weight pull rules, 284
Irish Setter, 92, 94, 95, 194, 213, 215, 217, 244–45, 277

James, Byron, 77, 244
Jean, Joe, 89, 91
Johnson, John "Iron Man," 87, 88
Junior races, 112, 191, 194, 279–283

Kasson, Gunnar, 60, 64, 67
Kent, Tud, 94, 95
Kokrine, Bergman, 92
Korgen, Reinhard, 74
Kraft, Virginia, 200, 203
Kriska, Leo, 156
Kroneck, Sam, 276

Laconia (N.H.):
    Laconia Sled Dog Club, 101
    World Champion Sled Dog Derby, 100–101, 147, 149–152, 154, 162, 180–183, 269–270
Lake Placid (N.Y.):
    Third Winter Olympics, 102–104, 172, 174
Lawrence, Kent, 126
LeCour, Bob and Katie, 209
Levorsen, Bella, 118, 135, 251
Levorsen, Bob, 135, 190, 258
Lewis, Chuck, 120
Link, Gary and Nancy, 217, 219
Livengood Sweepstakes, 92–93, 194
Lombard, Dr. Roland, 101, 115, 147, 156, 173–181, 191, 196
    Anchorage, 154, 263, 268
    feeding dogs, 256
    race strategy, 267, 269
    Siberian Huskies, 207
    The Pas, 148
    training dogs, 250
London, Jack, 42
Lyman, John, 213, 217, 244

Mace, Stuart, 80
Mackenzie River Husky, 42,
  212
Mahoney, "Klondike Mike,"
  43, 45
Mail teams, 37–39
Malamute:
  See Alaskan Malamute
Malamute (people), 42
Mäntysalo, Esa, 59, 145
Marston, Marvin R.
  "Muktuk," 71, 158
Martel, Emile, 148, 216,
  223
Masek, Grace, 259
Mathias, Tom, 130
Mays, Merle and Carolyn,
  286
McClintock, Leopold, 33,
  54
McDougall, J. Malcolm,
  110, 141
McHardy, Rick, 132
McLean, Carrie, 159
McMullin, Terry, 59
McVay, Laura, 129
Meakin, Jack, 138
Mendelsohn, Roger, 74, 80
Mercer, Tom, 263
Mitchell, Gen. William
  "Billy," 159
Molburg, Dick, 139
Moody, Ed, 241
Moody, Lester, 127
Moulton, Dick, 184–87,
  278
  Chinook Kennels, 102
  Laconia, 151, 162
  race strategy, 151,
    269–270
  training dogs, 254
Moulton, Marlee, 150
Mudgett, Donna, 116, 244
Munford, Matt and Dale,
  283
"mush":
  origin of word, 31

Nansen, Elizabeth, 110
  See also Elizabeth
  Ricker
Nansen, Fridtjof, 20, 22,
  34
  redesigned harnesses,
    229–230
New England:
  racing (early), 95–104,
    163, 168, (modern),
    123, 125–28, 151, 174–
    186, 264–65, 269–270,

272, 274–78
  Sled Dog Club, 97–100,
    123, (in Olympics), 102
Nome (Alaska):
  Gold Rush, 40, 81, 82
  racing, 82–91
  serum run, 60, 62–67
  (re-enactment), 117
Noongwook, Chester, 39
Norris, Earl, 109, 198,
  200–203
Norris, J. P., 198, 200,
  202–203
Norris, Natalie, 114,
  198, 200, 202
North American
  Championship:
  See Fairbanks
Norwegian Elkhound, 210,
  212
Nunamiut (people), 73

O'Brien, John, 58
Okleasik, Isaac, 153
Olympics, Third Winter,
  102–104, 172, 174

Parry, Edward, 54
Peary, Robert E., 54–55
Peithmann, Lance, 276
Phillips, Linda, 129
Post, Wiley, 162
Powell, Wesley, 152

Ramsay, Fox Maule, 87, 88
Redington, Joe, 119, 158,
  195–99
  feeding dogs, 256
Redington, Joe, Jr.
  (Joee), 195–99
Redington, Ramie, 196, 197
Retrievers, 94–95, 173,
  217
Rice, Carol, 277
Ricker, Elizabeth, 98, 99
  See also Elizabeth
  Nansen
Riley, Brian, 276, 279
Riley, Jerry, 154
Rivett-Carnac, C. E., 48,
  157
Rodewald, Ed and Kay,
  284, 286
Rogers, Will, 162
Romig, Dr. Joseph H., 159
Ross, Dick, 277
Rowell, Vic, 284, 285
Russia:
  freighting teams, 19–
    24, 73

racing, 146–147
  See also Siberia
Russick, Shorty, 105–106,
  108, 148
Ruud, John, 134, 245

St. Godard, Emile, 148
  Olympics, 102–104, 172–
    174
Saltzer, Harvey, 279
Samoyed, 141, 208–210,
  232, 284, 286, 287
Samoyed (people), 20, 208
Saunderson, Sandy, 52, 57
Saxton, Kenneth "Stubby,"
  100
Scott, Robert F., 55
Seeley, Eva "Short," 103,
  126, 170–72
Seppala, Leonhard, 148,
  152, 159–164, 180
  All-Alaska Sweepstakes,
    88–91
  Canada, 106, 148
  first dog team, 244
  New England, 96–98, 206
  Olympics, 102–104
  Ruby Derby, 89, 91
  serum run, 60, 64, 65,
    67
Shackleton, Ernest, 55
Shearer, Bill, 72, 127,
  253
Shields, Mary, 77
Siberia, 20–24, 27–29,
  86, 146–47, 167
  See also Russia
Siberian Husky:
  AKC registration, 98,
    206
  Alaska, 65, 87, 114,
    178, 200
  Europe, 143, 145
  New England, 78, 96–98,
    126–132, 192, 204, 245
  Nome, 86–88
  Olympics, 102–104
  original, in Siberia,
    20–22, 24, 29
  racing, 91–92, 104,
    138, 160, 163, 167,
    173, 175–182, 206–207,
    231, 277
  World War II, 69
Siwash (people), 42
Sleds:
  freighting, 21, 35, 37,
    38, 40, 41, 43, 46, 49,
    57, 61, 90, 226, 228–
    229, 240

racing, 65, 87, 226–29, 232, 238, 240–41, 249
Yukon, 40, 41
Slocum, Lloyd, 245
feeding dogs, 256
race strategy, 151, 269–270
selecting a team, 245, 262
training dogs, 253–54
Smith, Don, 276
Snowmobiles:
and dog teams, 56, 59, 65, 73, 74, 76, 198
Royal Canadian Mounted Police, 51
scientific use, 56–59
Solomon Derby, 89
Soper, J. Dewey, 23
Spalamute, 194, 222
Stefansson, Vilhjalmur, 47
Stickman, Joe and Fred, 91, 191
Sturdevant, Bill, 188, 190
Sullivan, Billy, 188
Swenson, Olaf:
importation of huskies, 88
selecting a team, 260
Swiss Club for Northern Dogs, 142–43
Sylvester, Holly Beth, 281

Targhee Hound, 94, 194, 203, 215, 222

Thaler, Jack, 270, 272, 276
The Pas (Canada):
racing (early), 104–108, (modern), 137
World Champion Sled Dog Race, 147–48, 151
Thomas, Lowell, 150
Thomas, Randy, 282
Thompson, Colin, 104
Thompson, Raymond L., 159
Tilton, Jim, 274–75
Trail Club of Europe, 144
Training rigs, 129, 132, 236, 238–39, 242, 246
Trucks, dog, 127, 236–37, 246
Tungus (people), 22

United States ("Lower Forty-eight"):
freighting teams, 70, 72, 80
racing (early), 93–104, 163, 168–170, (modern), 123–36, 147, 151–52, 154, 176–77, 180–86, 257–58, 277–79, 281–83
training, 239, 242, 253–54, 259
See also Ashton, Laconia, New England

Van Leeuwen, Els, 143–44, 254–55
Van Sickle, Lloyd, 72, 194, 210
Van Zyle, Jon, 202

Vaughan, Norman:
Byrd Expedition, 58–59
Iditarod Trail Race, 276
World War II, 71–72
Village Dog, 209, 212–15
Walden, Arthur, 42, 81, 95, 97–98, 106, 168–170, 215
Ward, Ralph, 224
Wehle, Bob, 217, 219
Weight-pulling contests, 284–87
Welch, Dr. Curtis, 62
Wheeler, Harry, 164, 180, 206
Whitney, Caspar, 37
Wickersham, Judge James, 31, 159
Williams, Clyde "Slim," 158
Wilmarth, Dick, 119, 120, 124
Wilson, Bill, 110
Wing, Anne, 115, 116
Wolf, 42, 217
Women's races:
early, 93, 112
modern, 112, 114, 115, 116, 117, 185
Woods, Roxy Wright, 193–195
Wrangell, Ferdinand von, 19, 32
Wright, Gareth, 113, 187–188, 191–95
feeding dogs, 256
race strategy, 267, 269

304